# SO ORDERED

ASPEN COURSEBOOK SERIES

# SO ORDERED

## The Writer's Guide for Aspiring Judges, Judicial Clerks, and Interns

JILL BARTON

*Professor of Legal Writing & Lecturer in Law*
*University of Miami School of Law*

Published by Wolters Kluwer in New York.

Wolters Kluwer Legal & Regulatory U.S. serves customers worldwide
with CCH, Aspen Publishers, and Kluwer Law International products.
(www.WKLegaledu.com)

To contact Customer Service, e-mail customer.service@wolterskluwer.com,
call 1-800-234-1660, fax 1-800-901-9075, or mail correspondence to:

    Wolters Kluwer Law & Business
    Attn: Order Department
    PO Box 990
    Frederick, MD 21705

Design and book composition by Keithley & Associates, Inc.

Cover art: seamartini

Printed in the United States of America.

1 2 3 4 5 6 7 8 9 0

ISBN 978-1-4548-8333-3

Library of Congress Cataloging-in-Publication Data

Names: Barton, Jill (Professor of Legal writing), author.
Title: So ordered: the writer's guide for aspiring judges, judicial clerks,
    and interns / Jill Barton, Professor of Legal Writing & Lecturer in Law,
    University of Miami School of Law.
Description: New York : Wolters Kluwer, [2017] | Includes index.
Identifiers: LCCN 2017024583 | ISBN 9781454883333
Subjects: LCSH: Legal composition. | Judicial opinions—United
    States—Language.
Classification: LCC KF250 .B379 2017 | DDC 808.06/634—dc23 LC record
    available at https://lccn.loc.gov/2017024583

## About Wolters Kluwer Legal & Regulatory U.S.

Wolters Kluwer Legal & Regulatory U.S. delivers expert content and solutions in the areas of law, corporate compliance, health compliance, reimbursement, and legal education. Its practical solutions help customers successfully navigate the demands of a changing environment to drive their daily activities, enhance decision quality and inspire confident outcomes.

Serving customers worldwide, its legal and regulatory portfolio includes products under the Aspen Publishers, CCH Incorporated, Kluwer Law International, ftwilliam.com and MediRegs names. They are regarded as exceptional and trusted resources for general legal and practice-specific knowledge, compliance and risk management, dynamic workflow solutions, and expert commentary.

*For Mom and Dad*

# Summary of Contents

# CONTENTS

# PREFACE

A judge's writing is powerful. With just nine letters at the bottom of the page—"So Ordered"—a judge can protect a person's basic rights, shift a fortune from one company to the next, or determine whether a defendant walks free. In this book, you will learn how to craft these commanding words. And you'll learn how to do so with style, by studying handpicked examples from the nation's best judicial writers.

*So Ordered* shows you step-by-step how to devise, organize, write, and edit a judicial document. With more than 100 examples from real cases, the book will teach you how to write like a judge—and how to tackle assignments as a judicial clerk or intern.

In *So Ordered*, you'll first learn how to write documents that judges use behind the scenes to help decide cases. You'll see how to write a research memo in a trial court case. Then, you'll learn how to transform it into a publishable court order. At the appellate court level, you'll discover how to write a bench memo that explains and analyzes a case to help judges understand the legal issues and prepare for oral argument. From there, you will draft an appellate opinion, carefully detailing who wins and loses, the supporting law, and the reasons why.

*So Ordered* also shows you how to craft the most creative of judicial documents: minority opinions. You'll learn how to draft a dissent when you don't agree with the majority rule and a concurrence when you want to detail different reasons for a decision. For each judicial document, *So Ordered* shows you the steps to shape each section, from the case caption and introduction to the legal analysis and conclusion.

With each lesson, you'll practice skills that will help you succeed not just in law school but in any legal career. That's because judicial documents require you to clearly and concisely present a well-reasoned and well-organized analysis of legal issues. And that skill will enrich your work as an intern or law student, as a judicial clerk or lawyer, or as a county judge or justice at the highest bench in the country. So if you've ever dreamed of being a judge, working for one, or writing like one, then these next pages are for you.

# Acknowledgments

I am indebted to the many talented writers whose inspired words appear on these pages. This book is richer because of the great number of dedicated wordsmiths sitting on the bench. I appreciate that I can always turn to a judge's writing when I want to share an example of not just great legal writing, but writing that is great in any field.

I am privileged to work at the University of Miami School of Law, where Dean Patricia D. White and Vice Dean Osamudia James offer generous support and encouragement for writing projects. I am grateful to my colleagues, especially Rachel H. Smith, for being a constant and energetic supporter. And to Christina M. Frohock, Rachel Stabler, and Annette Torres—thank you for always being willing to share advice. Special thanks go to my stellar research assistant, Elaine Kussurelis, who checked every sentence and citation. And thank you to research assistants Blayne DeGiovani and Meera Khan, who helped with early research. I also appreciate the efforts of the Miami Law librarian staff, particularly Pam Lucken, who is unfailing in her ability to dig up any obscure source.

I owe great appreciation to Florida District Court of Appeal Judge Leslie B. Rothenberg for hiring me and letting me see the judicial process behind the scenes. And thanks to all the judges at Florida's Third District Court of Appeal, especially Judges Vance E. Salter, Frank Shepherd, and Richard J. Suarez, for sharing their wisdom with me while I was a judicial clerk and in the many years since.

Credit for this book also goes to the team at Aspen Publishers, especially Donna Gridley and David Herzig, and to Sarah Hains and Kathy Langone at The Froebe Group. I also appreciate the efforts of the reviewers and my colleagues in the legal writing community—too many to name—who offered ideas and advice for this project along the way. I am grateful to be a part of a wonderfully supportive and talented community.

Finally, thank you to Lucky the Dog for sleeping quietly at my feet during the many hours of writing, rewriting, and editing—and for making me take the occasional ball-fetching break. And my greatest thanks go to my husband, Eric, who read every word and listened to me debate every page with patience. This book and my life are better for it.

# SO ORDERED

# CHAPTER

# 1

# INTRODUCTION TO JUDICIAL WRITING

The words that make up law don't come easily. Judges write and rewrite, they think and rethink, and they edit their words over and over again. They write opinions and so much more—orders, decrees, dissents, and concurrences, to name a few.

And they receive help along the way, from the judicial clerks and interns laboring anonymously in the background. This book explains how you too can research and write the documents that judges and their clerks and interns routinely draft. It will explain step by step how to start and finish each type of judicial document, from orders and jury instructions at the trial court to opinions and dissents at an appeals court. It will also explain how to write research memos and bench memos: internal documents that judicial clerks and interns prepare to help their judge and their court better understand the cases before them.

An assignment to draft a document for a judge comes with a weighty responsibility. Judges need to get cases right, and they need to explain their reasoning clearly, concisely, and objectively. The audience of a judicial order or opinion is vast. Judges not only communicate with the attorneys and parties in a case, they also communicate to the world what the law is and why and how it works.

As you work on drafting the documents described in the coming chapters, you will follow the judicial process. You'll begin in the trial court, learning how to write a research memo and trial court order. Then, you'll move on to the appellate court level, where you'll learn how to write a bench memo, opinion, concurrence, and dissent. You'll also learn how to edit your work to perfect every sentence and every citation—because that's what your judge will expect. And finally, you'll gain a glimpse of what happens behind the scenes, how judges employ different strategies and styles to decide the law. Throughout this book, you will learn how judges write, how many have created an art form with their words, and how you too can write like a judge.

# CHAPTER

# JUDICIAL ETHICS

"An independent, fair and impartial judiciary is indispensable to our system of justice. The United States legal system is based upon the principle that an independent, impartial, and competent judiciary, composed of men and women of integrity, will interpret and apply the law that governs our society."

—ABA Model Code of Judicial Conduct[1]

The words that judges write in opinions last forever. They endure in published reporters, online databases, and news and government websites. They are interpreted, scrutinized, celebrated, and lamented—sometimes for decades or generations to come. So judges have to get their words right, and they have to show their credibility, humanity, and neutrality while doing so.

When they fail to be fair, people take notice. In one egregious example from 2012, a trial court judge in Fort Lauderdale, Florida, tried to be creative in sentencing a man accused of domestic violence. The man had pushed his wife onto a couch, put his hand on her neck, and lifted a fist to hit her. Instead of the traditional sentence ordering the accused and alleged victim to live apart, Judge John "Jay" Hurley ordered the man to take his wife on a date—specifically stating that the accused should buy his wife flowers, take her to dinner at Red Lobster, and then take her bowling.[2] Not

---

1. ABA Model Code of Judicial Conduct (Feb. 2007), http://www.americanbar.org/content/dam/aba/migrated/judicialethics/ABA_MCJC_approved.authcheckdam.pdf.
2. Danielle A. Alvarez, *Judge Orders Husband in Marital Spat: Go on a Nice Date*, Sun-Sentinel, Feb. 7, 2012, at 1A.

surprisingly, international media attention and outrage from advocates for domestic violence victims followed.[3]

The embarrassment that flows from intense media scrutiny is warning enough. But a single ethical misstep could also ruin the career of a judge or a judicial clerk. Consider what happened to judicial clerk Paul Walsh. Walsh worked on a contentious case at the Massachusetts Superior Court involving a $1 billion family supermarket empire. The losing side's lawyers believed Walsh's judge was prejudiced against them, so they set up three fake job interviews with Walsh in 1997 to try to pry confidential information from him about how the judge was predisposed to rule against them.[4] When the third fake interview in Boston failed to work for the lawyers, they threatened to go public with damaging information about Walsh.[5]

Walsh then made the correct ethical choice: He went to the FBI, which organized a reverse sting operation. Lawyers Gary C. Crossen and Kevin P. Curry were disciplined and disbarred.[6] The disbarment order noted that "'confidentiality in judicial deliberations' is akin to presidential privilege, the purpose of which is to permit presidents 'to explore alternatives in the process of… making decisions and to do so in a way many would be unwilling to express except privately.'"[7]

The public expects judges—and the judicial clerks and interns who help them—to uphold the law and to show respect for the parties and the process. When a judge's actions or words disappoint, a judge not only sidesteps ethical rules and guidelines but also diminishes the credibility of the judiciary. Thus, ethics codes for judges set high expectations. The American Bar Association's Model Code of Judicial Conduct opens by stating that "judges, individually and collectively, must respect and honor the judicial office as a public trust and strive to maintain and enhance confidence in the legal system."[8] That's a challenging mandate, and it shows why a judge's every action and word can be scrutinized so carefully.

---

3. Linda Trischitta, *Judge John Hurley Moves on from Broward's Colorful Bond Court*, Sun-Sentinel, June 7, 2016, at 1A.

4. Gerard O'Neill, *The Demoulas Trap*, Boston Magazine, Dec. 2006, http://www.bostonmagazine.com/2006/12/the-demoulas-trap/.

5. Charles W. Sorenson, Jr., *Are Law Clerks Fair Game? Invading Judicial Confidentiality*, 43 Val. U. L. Rev. 1 (2008).

6. *See id.*

7. *In re Crossen*, 880 N.E.2d 352, 373 (2008) (quoting *United States v. Nixon*, 418 U.S. 683, 708 (1974)).

8. ABA Model Code of Judicial Conduct, *supra* note 1, at 1.

## A.  ETHICS RULES FOR JUDGES

All judges follow some form of ethics rules or guidelines. The Code of Conduct for United States Judges begins by describing venerable principles for judges to uphold:

> An independent and honorable judiciary is indispensable to justice in our society. A judge should maintain and enforce high standards of conduct and should personally observe those standards, so that the integrity and independence of the judiciary may be preserved. The provisions of this Code should be construed and applied to further that objective.[9]

The judges bound by the code include nearly all federal judges: U.S. circuit judges, district judges, Court of International Trade judges, Court of Federal Claims judges, bankruptcy judges, and magistrate judges. U.S. Supreme Court justices are noticeably absent from this list. They are not bound by any formal ethics code.

Some Court observers criticize the omission of Supreme Court justices from an official ethics code.[10] But U.S. Supreme Court Chief Justice John G. Roberts has explained that all justices "do in fact consult the Code of Conduct in assessing their ethical obligations," and that the code then "plays the same role for the Justices as it does for other federal judges."[11]

Chief Justice Roberts also emphasized that every federal judge since 1789 has taken an oath and solemnly pledged to "administer justice without respect to persons," "do equal right to the poor and to the rich," and "faithfully and impartially discharge and perform" their judicial duties.[12]

At state courts, judges take similar oaths. Each state supreme court also adopts a judicial code of conduct. State ethics committees investigate violations. For example, in Texas, an independent State Commission on Judicial Conduct is charged with investigating allegations of judicial misconduct or judicial disability and disciplining judges.

---

9. Code of Conduct for United States Judges (2016), http://www.uscourts.gov/judges-judgeships/code-conduct-united-states-judges.

10. Lincoln Caplan, *Does the Supreme Court Need a Code of Conduct?*, New Yorker, July 27, 2015, http://www.newyorker.com/news/news-desk/does-the-supreme-court-need-a-code-of-conduct.

11. Chief Justice's Year-End Rep. on the Fed. Judiciary, at 4 (2011).

12. *Id.*

## B. ETHICS RULES FOR JUDICIAL CLERKS AND INTERNS

Judicial clerks and interns must uphold the same values as their judges. From the moment you begin as an intern or clerk, you will have access to confidential and sensitive information. The inner workings of the court are exciting, but case files, discussions, and deliberations must stay inside the courthouse walls. The *Law Clerk Handbook*, published by the Federal Judicial Center, explains how the same standards apply to judges and their clerks:

> Law clerks play important roles in the judicial process and must maintain its integrity. Because of the close association between the judge and law clerks, your professional and personal actions reflect on your judge and ultimately on the judiciary as a whole. You are held to the very highest standards of conduct. Like judges, you hold a position of public trust and must comply with the demanding requisites of that position.[13]

Holding a position of public trust means that judicial clerks and interns must avoid even an appearance of impropriety in any action they take—both in their professional and personal lives. For instance, while many professionals may comment on social media or a personal blog about things that happen at work or in the news, judicial clerks cannot. One judicial clerk resigned from the New Jersey Superior Court after she commented on Facebook about a news story involving a state trooper who died after colliding with a deer.[14] Leslie Anderson wrote, "I agree that it is sad and heart-wrenching for the family members left to suffer the consequences of the trooper's recklessness—especially for the deer family who lost a mommy or daddy or baby deer." Although she quickly took down her post, screenshots preserved it. The troopers' union president said the comment showed Anderson couldn't be impartial, which her job required.[15]

The *Law Clerk Handbook* advises using common sense to deal with many ethical questions, but it cautions that restrictions in some areas are "not intuitively obvious."[16] Those areas include rules on confidentiality; conflicts of interest; outside legal activities; dealings with prospective employers; outside professional, social, and community activities; receipt of gifts and honoraria; and political activity.[17]

---

13. Fed. Judicial Ctr., *Law Clerk Handbook* 2 (2007), https://public.resource.org/scribd/8763855.pdf.

14. Martha Neil, *Judicial Law Clerk Quits After Taking Heat for Web Posts Criticizing State Trooper Who Died in Crash*, A.B.A. J., June 4, 2015, http://www.abajournal.com/news/article/judicial_law_clerk_quits_after_taking_fire_for_facebook_posts_criticizing/.

15. *See id.*

16. *Law Clerk Handbook*, *supra* note 13.

17. *Id.*

Most judicial clerks and interns, for example, are not allowed to talk with attorneys involved in cases before their courts. The *Handbook* advises that "clerks must be firm in resisting any effort by attorneys to gain improper advantage, to win favor, or to enlist sympathy." This guideline suggests that judicial clerks should not only avoid small talk with attorneys in the courtroom but also that they should avoid any conversation if they happen to see an attorney on an active case at the supermarket or a bar. Check the links available at the end of this chapter to review the specifics of these rules—for both federal and state judiciary employees—before ethical questions arise.

The requirements of loyalty and confidentiality for judicial clerks run deep. Former U.S. Circuit Judge Ruggero J. Aldisert said that the relationship between a judge and a clerk is as "sacred as that of priest-penitent."[18] He outlined the ethical rules for his new clerks in stern terms:

> I have retained you as researchers and editors, but you are also my lawyers. As lawyers, you are absolutely forbidden to disclose the intimate details of this lawyer-client relationship, of the decisionmaking and decision-justifying processes that take place in these chambers. This court is a family, and there will be times that I will make remarks about my family members. They will be uttered sometimes in the heat of passion or despair. They will not be repeated beyond the chambers door. Even if I occasionally blow off steam, remember that these judges are my colleagues and will be my friends long after you are gone from here.

This advice suggests that judges' deliberations may become heated, but they cannot be discussed with anyone outside of the judge's chambers. The ethics rules specifically forbid talking with journalists—and this prohibition extends to sharing information on social media platforms.

## C. ETHICS AND SOCIAL MEDIA

The proliferation of social media poses thorny questions that most judicial codes have not yet addressed.[19] For instance, can a judge endorse an attorney on LinkedIn? Can a judicial clerk "like" the site of a political candidate? If a judge is Facebook friends with an attorney in a case, does "unfriending"

---

18. Ruggero J. Aldisert, *Super Chief: Earl Warren and His Supreme Court—A Judicial Biography; by Bernard Schwartz*, 72 Cal. L. Rev. 275, 282 (1984) (book review).

19. Pennsylvania's code, one of few recently updated to address social media, references electronic platforms only once, stating generically that judges who participate in social media "shall avoid comments and interactions that may be interpreted as *ex parte* communications concerning pending matters or matters that may appear before the court." Judicial Conduct Bd. of Pa., Code of Judicial Conduct (2014), http://judicialconductboardofpa.org/code-of-judicial-conduct/.

the attorney fix any disqualification issue? An Arizona advisory opinion said the answer to all of those questions is no. The opinion noted that the "ethics switch is not so easily turned on and off." [20]

Still, questions about social media are not always answered so uniformly. A California advisory opinion reached a slightly different conclusion on the "unfriending" question, urging judges to "unfriend" an attorney if they learn the attorney is part of the judge's online social networking community and has a case pending before the judge. [21] The opinion added that all online interaction with that attorney must stop and that the "unfriending" must be disclosed to the parties. [22]

Several states—Florida, Massachusetts, and Oklahoma among them—have advised their judges to avoid the "unfriending" question altogether by not "friending" any attorney who may appear before them. [23] Oklahoma takes it one step further by prohibiting judges from "friending" their judicial clerks, other staff, social workers, and those who may appear before the court. Both the Florida and Massachusetts opinions note that "friending" attorneys violates states ethics rules because it "conveys the impression to the public that the lawyer so recognized is in a special position to influence the judge." [24]

The warnings that can be read into these advisory opinions imply that judges, their judicial clerks, and their interns should approach social media carefully. Whether you are aspiring to be a judge or working as a clerk or intern, one of the many unspoken requirements of working in the judiciary is knowing what kinds of ethical pitfalls you may face—and how to avoid them.

## D.  CONSEQUENCES

Just as lawyers can be disbarred, fired, and sanctioned, so too can judges. The reasons are too colorful to make up. Thomas Porteous, a federal judge in Louisiana, served 14 years before the Senate impeached him for receiving cash and favors from lawyers, using a false name to elude creditors, and intentionally misleading the Senate during his confirmation hearings. [25]

A judicial committee removed Chicago Judge Valarie Turner from office in 2016 after she allegedly let a lawyer wear her robe and rule in two

---

20. Ariz. S. Ct. Judicial Ethics Advisory Comm., Advisory Op. 14-01 (2014).
21. Cal. Judges Assoc. Judicial Ethics Comm. Op. 66 at 10-11 (2010).
22. *Id.*
23. Okla. Judicial Ethics Op. 2011-3 (2011); Mass. Comm. on Judicial Ethics Op. 2011-6 (2011); Fla. Judicial Ethics Advisory Comm. Ops. 2010-06 (2010), 2009-20 (2009).
24. *See, e.g.,* Fla. Judicial Ethics Advisory Comm. Op. 2010-06 (2010).
25. Jennifer Steinhauer, *Senate, for Just the 8th Time, Votes to Oust a Federal Judge,* N.Y. Times, Dec. 9, 2010, at 27.

of her cases.[26] The Florida Supreme Court suspended Miami Judge Jacqueline Schwartz in 2015 after she allegedly appeared drunk on the bench and yelled an expletive at a store owner.[27] And the Indiana Supreme Court permanently removed Judge Kimberly J. Brown from the bench in 2014 after she delayed the release of ten defendants from jail and put off ruling in other cases—by days, weeks, and months in some cases.[28]

The public expects judges to be ethical "on and off the bench," writes acting New York City Supreme Court Justice Gerald Lebovits.[29] "Judges resolve disputes. They create, apply, and enforce rights and obligations. Judges affect lives."[30] Judges are responsible for their own ethical behavior, of course, but also that of the judges who serve with them and the lawyers who appear before them. More specifically, judges have a duty to take action when other judges and lawyers violate ethics rules.[31] Some states go so far as to specify what types of corrective or investigative actions a judge must follow.[32]

Judicial clerks and interns, working behind the scenes, witness the good and the bad, and they can learn from both. U.S. Supreme Court Justice Sonia Sotomayor described the value of that insider knowledge when she expressed regret for not working for a judge after law school: "I did one thing really wrong—I didn't clerk after I left law school," she said. "In a year of clerking, you see more about the practice of law than you'll see in 10 years of practice."[33] That valuable experience is worth the small cost of following rules that require you to avoid involvement in politics, community affairs, and social media.

## E. CHART OF ETHICS GUIDELINES AND RULES

The following chart lists various ethics guidelines and rules for judges and their judicial clerks. While these titles may not sound like fun vacation reading, knowing the rules contained within them is crucial for new clerks and interns.

---

26. Special Order 2016-42 (Cook County Cir. Ct. 2016).
27. *Inquiry Concerning a Judge v. Jacqueline Schwartz*, No. SC16-135 (Fla. Apr. 19, 2016).
28. *In re Hon. Kimberly J. Brown, Judge of the Marion Superior Court*, No. 49S00-1308-JD-560, at 7-9 (Ind. Mar. 4, 2014).
29. Gerald Lebovits, *Ethical Judicial Writing — Part I*, 78 N.Y. St. B.J. 64 (2006).
30. *Id.*
31. *See, e.g.*, ABA Model Code of Judicial Conduct Rule 2.15 (2007).
32. Leslie W. Abramson, *The Judge's Ethical Duty to Report Misconduct by Other Judges and Lawyers and Its Effect on Judicial Independence*, 25 Hofstra L. Rev. 751, 756 (1997).
33. Justice Frank Sullivan, Jr., *Judicial Clerkship Program Celebrates Its 10th Anniversary*, 48 Judges' J. 4 (2009).

### Ethics Guidelines for Judges

- **ABA Model Code of Judicial Conduct, (February 2007):** Like the ABA's Model Code of Professional Responsibility for lawyers, this code for judges is a professional code aimed at establishing a minimum standard for ethics and professionalism among the judiciary. http://www.americanbar.org/content/dam/aba/migrated/judicialethics/ABA_MCJC_approved.authcheckdam.pdf

### Federal Code of Judicial Conduct

- **Code of Conduct for United States Judges:** This code applies to all federal judges, except for U.S. Supreme Court justices. http://www.uscourts.gov/judges-judgeships/code-conduct-united-states-judges

### State Codes of Judicial Conduct

These codes apply to state judges and their employees, including judicial clerks, externs, interns, research attorneys, and other employees. Most codes are online. Here is a sample:

- **California Code of Judicial Ethics:** http://www.courts.ca.gov/documents/ca_code_judicial_ethics.pdf
- **Florida Code of Judicial Conduct:** http://www.floridasupremecourt.org/decisions/ethics/index.shtml
- **Michigan Code of Judicial Conduct:** http://courts.mi.gov/courts/michigansupremecourt/rules/documents/michigan%20code%20of%20judicial%20conduct.pdf
- **Ohio Code of Judicial Conduct:** http://www.supremecourt.ohio.gov/LegalResources/Rules/conduct/judcond0309.pdf
- **Pennsylvania Code of Judicial Conduct:** http://judicialconductboardofpa.org/code-of-judicial-conduct/
- **Texas Code of Judicial Conduct:** http://www.txcourts.gov/media/514728/TXCodeOfJudicialConduct_20020822.pdf

### Ethics Guidelines for Judicial Clerks and Interns

- **Federal Judicial Center,** *Law Clerk Handbook*: http://public.resource.org/scribd/8763855.pdf
- **Code of Conduct for Judicial Employees:** http://www.uscourts.gov/sites/default/files/vol02a-ch03_0.pdf
- **Maintaining the Public Trust: Ethics for Federal Judicial Law Clerks:** http://www.lawschool.cornell.edu/publicservice/upload/Federal-Judicial-Center-Ethics-Brochure.pdf

# CHAPTER

3

# THE JUDGE'S PURPOSE
# AND AUDIENCE

Judges write opinions to educate. They write to educate the litigants and lawyers involved in the case or those who will be involved in similar cases in the future. They write to educate citizens, who in some states vote on whether to retain or remove judges from the bench. They write to educate law students poring over casebooks, politicians pushing legal boundaries, professors assessing changes, and their colleagues on the court, especially those with a dissenting voice.

And yet movies and television shows often have the judge in "a bit part, sitting passively amidst the soaring rhetoric of the attorneys, the heroism or villainy of their clients, and the moral compass of the jurors"—as U.S. Supreme Court Chief Justice John G. Roberts has noted.[1] In reality, the judge holds the central role in the judicial process—to decide "matters of the greatest magnitude"[2] and "ensure fair process and justice for the litigants."[3]

Judges explain their role and educate their vast audience with two main purposes in mind: to explain the court's rationale and to provide consistency in the law by following and setting precedent. This practice of abiding by precedent or "standing by things decided" translates from the Latin "stare decisis."[4] The doctrine means that once a court decides a point or

---

1. Chief Justice's Year-End Rep. on the Fed. Judiciary, at 3-4 (2016).
2. *Id.* at 1 (quoting *The Papers of George Washington* 322 (Dorothy Twohig ed. 1987)).
3. *Id.* at 4.
4. See Chapter 10, pages 175-79, for a further discussion on *stare decisis*.

legal principle, it's no longer open for examination except "for urgent reasons and in exceptional cases."[5]

Following well-settled law helps the judiciary create consistency, which helps it maintain credibility. But simply writing, "the law makes it so," is not enough. As U.S. Supreme Court Justice Elena Kagan explains, "[y]ou don't want to just announce a judgment. Part of what we do here is reason about cases. And part of what we should show the American public is how we reason about cases. So it's not just like 'here's the question, here's the answer, end of the matter, we're done.'"[6]

Readers deserve a deeper rationale, and that's why judges detail their reasoning so extensively in written opinions. Patricia M. Wald, a former chief judge for the D.C. Circuit Court of Appeals, explains that she wants "the reader to come away with some overriding feel for the judging process" and an understanding that she was fair to both sides, not predisposed to one result.[7] In her written opinions, she aims to explain many aspects of her decision:

- The issues and why they are important;
- What the law has previously stated about the issues and whether it provides consensus or conflict;
- Her understanding of the arguments on both sides; and
- Her rationale for why one side prevails.[8]

By explaining how the law works in each case, judges help readers understand how courts will decide future cases. By giving a fair voice to the winning and losing sides, they avoid looking careless or agenda-driven.[9] And by spelling out their understanding of the facts and the law in each particular case, they enlighten and inform—and in some cases, they inspire.[10]

> **WRITING TIP: Write for your audience.**
> Justice Elena Kagan says she writes with a particular audience in mind. "What I try to do is to write so that a non-lawyer can understand it. But not any non-lawyer," she explains. "I don't want to explain things that really don't need to be explained. So I guess I have in mind the reader of the *New Yorker* or something like that."[11]

---

5. *Black's Law Dictionary* (10th ed. 2014) (quoting William M. Lile et al., *Brief Making and the Use of Law Books* 321 (3d ed. 1914)).

6. Interview by Bryan A. Garner with Justice Elena Kagan, United States Supreme Court Building, West Conference Room, in Washington, D.C. (July 16, 2015).

7. Patricia M. Wald, *"How I Write" Essays*, 4 Scribes J. Legal Writing 55 (1993).

8. *Id.*

9. *See* Gerald Lebovits, *Ethical Judicial Writing—Part II*, 79 N.Y. St. B.J. 50 (2007).

10. *See* Wald, *supra* note 6, at 60.

11. Interview by Garner, *supra* note 5.

CHAPTER

# WRITING RESEARCH
# AND BENCH MEMOS

On November 22, 2000, George W. Bush asked the U.S. Supreme Court to stop the recount in Florida and declare him president over his rival Al Gore. Soon, memos flew among the justices at a pace never before seen.[1] The first memos came from Justices Sandra Day O'Connor and Anthony Kennedy, jurists well known for their valuable swing votes and their reliance on their judicial clerks.[2] The two joined the conservative justices to decide the case in favor of Bush.

Behind the memos and the momentous decision in *Bush v. Gore*—and behind most cases in U.S. courts—are the judicial clerks and their memos. These research and bench memoranda regularly serve as the first drafts of published opinions,[3] so they not only apply the law, they can create it.

In federal courts, trial judges hear nearly 400 cases each year. That's nearly 30 percent more than 20 years ago.[4] On many days, the only way to propel the wheels of justice through the backlog is to divvy up the work. The research memo helps resolve cases swiftly because it can address one

---

1. *See* David Margolick, *The Path to Florida*, Vanity Fair, Oct. 2004.

2. Jeffrey S. Rosenthal & Albert H. Yoon, *Judicial Ghostwriting: Authorship on the Supreme Court*, 96 Cornell L. Rev. 1307, 1337 (2011).

3. *See, e.g.*, Gerald Lebovits, *Judges' Clerks Play Varied Roles in the Opinion Drafting Process*, 76 N.Y. St. B.J. 34, 35 (2004); John Bilyeu Oakley & Robert S. Thompson, *Law Clerks in Judges' Eyes: Tradition and Innovation in the Use of Legal Staff by American Judges*, 67 Cal. L. Rev. 1301 (1979).

4. Transactional Records Access Clearinghouse at Syracuse University, *Some Federal Judges More Overburdened than Others, Study Finds*, Oct. 14, 2014, trac.syr.edu/whatsnew/email.141013.html.

issue in a pending case, allowing the judge to break up a case into more wieldy parts, instead of tackling the whole thing at once.

Research and bench memoranda are comparable to the office memoranda that most first year law students write. The only difference is that research and bench memos analyze part of a pending case, with real legal questions that may involve a party's livelihood or freedom—or in the *Bush v. Gore* example, determine the leader of the free world. With this divide-and-conquer approach, multiple judicial externs, interns, and clerks can figure out cases simultaneously. This chapter will show you how to develop and draft a research memo for a trial court and a more complex bench memo for an appellate court. The chapter begins by describing each of the six common parts of a research memo, using a 2012 California case involving a *pro se* prisoner who alleged that a prison employee retaliated against him and violated his First Amendment rights.

---

### Common Parts of a Research Memo

1. Memo Heading
2. Question Presented
3. Brief Answer
4. Facts
5. Discussion with Legal Analysis
6. Conclusion and Recommendation

---

## A. COMMON PARTS OF A TRIAL COURT RESEARCH MEMO

### 1. Memo Heading

The heading lays out four basic facts about the research memo. The "to" and "from" lines are simple enough. The subject line should reference the specific case and issue that the memo is analyzing. The date should reflect the date that the memo is completed—not the date it was started—although the two might be the same in the fast-paced world of trial courts. The following example shows what the top of a research memo may look like.

> **RESEARCH MEMORANDUM**
>
> TO:       JUDGE ILLSTON
> FROM:   ELODIE MORELLI
> SUBJECT: WHETHER DEFENDANT IN GEIER V. STREUTKER, NO. 10-1965, IS
>          ENTITLED TO QUALIFIED IMMUNITY
> DATE:     APRIL 9, 2012

## 2.  Question Presented

Consider this the headline of the memo. The question presented describes the memo's big issue, elaborating on the basic issue outlined in the heading and setting the stage for the rest of the document. It states the specific legal question and adds a few legally significant facts for context.

The question can begin as a phrase with "whether," or it can begin with a question word, like "is" or "does" or "did." The following examples show how to construct a question presented using either format. Both begin with the specific legal question, then list a few key facts. They focus on one of the research questions from the civil rights lawsuit in *Geier v. Streutker*, which is used as an example throughout this chapter and the next.

### Question Presented

Whether the Defendant is entitled to the qualified immunity defense for allegedly violating the Plaintiff's First Amendment rights when the Defendant said she was merely informing the Plaintiff of the proper way to make appointments for medical treatment.

—This version includes the procedural background and a key fact that supports the defendant's case.

### Question Presented

Is Streutker entitled to the qualified immunity defense when she stated that she was explaining how to request appointments to Geier, who had submitted at least ten duplicate requests, and not silence him in violation of his First Amendment right to seek dental care?

—This question provides more specific facts, giving context to the legal question.

Each of these questions frame the issue effectively. The exact style and level of detail depends on the preferences of the writer and the judge. Keep in mind that there's no single magic formula for writing well. Different formats and styles—as long as they convey the proper substance clearly—can achieve success.

**WRITING TIP:**
Aim to convey the proper substance with a clear style. The format and level of detail can vary based on the preferences of the writer and recipient.

### 3. Brief Answer

While the question presented serves as the headline, the brief answer is a summary of the memo's grand finale. The brief answer responds directly to the question presented, describing the memo's analysis and conclusion and the law that supports it.

The answer should begin with a definitive "yes" or "no" to answer the question, followed by a sentence or two summarizing the law and at least a sentence or two summarizing the analysis and conclusion. The following examples show two possible brief answers for the previous question presented examples. The second provides more detail and citations. The level of detail you provide will depend on the complexity of the case and the preferences of the judge.

Brief Answer

This version condenses the rule into one short sentence and the analysis and conclusion into a second sentence.

— Yes. An officer is entitled to qualified immunity when the officer's conduct does not violate a constitutional right or when it would be seen as reasonable in the circumstances. Here, the Defendant shared information that the Plaintiff apparently needed; therefore, she is entitled to the qualified immunity defense.

Brief Answer

This answer begins with a definitive answer, then a summary of the major rule with a citation to a leading case.

The last two sentences summarize the analysis and conclusion, building on the facts provided in the second question presented example.

— Yes. The qualified immunity defense requires the court first to determine whether the alleged facts show the defendant's conduct violated a constitutional right, and second, whether it would be clear to a reasonable person that the conduct was unlawful. *Saucier v. Katz*,
— 533 U.S. 194 (2001). Here, because Streutker believed she was assisting a patient who misunderstood the way to make appointments, her conduct was reasonable. Thus, she is entitled to the qualified immunity defense.

### 4. Facts

This section tells the story of the case and details what led to the dispute. It should include all the facts that are legally significant to your precise legal question. It may also include helpful background facts or details that are particularly compelling—like the fact in the next example that the plaintiff faces threats from other inmates. The facts section typically follows a chronological organization. It begins by describing the parties and the background needed to provide context for the dispute. Then, it details the legally significant facts in narrative form and ends with the procedural history.

This section might need only a few paragraphs to describe what happened. Try to narrow the narrative to the facts essential to the legal question. Use paragraph breaks, topic sentences, and transitions to help your reader move through the story of the case and understand what's at stake. The next example is adapted from the facts section in *Yellowbear v. Lampert.*[5]

Facts

Andrew Yellowbear has been sentenced to life in prison for murdering his daughter. In January 2011, he was transferred to the Wyoming Medium Correctional Institution and placed in the segregation unit (not because of any disciplinary infraction he has committed, but because of threats against him).

— At the start, the section introduces the plaintiff with helpful background details.

Mr. Yellowbear is an enrolled member of the Northern Arapaho Tribe and has deeply held religious beliefs. For that reason, he seeks access to his prison's sweat lodge—a house of prayer and meditation that the prison has supplied for those who share his Native American religious tradition.

— Then, the section describes the background of the dispute.

Because of Mr. Yellowbear's segregation, the prison has denied his repeated requests to use the sweat lodge. Prison officials insist that the cost of providing the necessary security to take Mr. Yellowbear from the special protective unit to the sweat lodge and back is "unduly burdensome."

— Next, the section details the prison's position.

Mr. Yellowbear disagrees. He has sued under 42 U.S.C. § 1983 and 42 U.S.C. §§ 2000cc, the Religious Land Use and Institutionalized Persons Act, in a further attempt to access the sweat lodge and practice his faith.

— The procedural background ends the section and sets up the analysis of the legal issue.

## 5. Discussion with Legal Analysis

The discussion section is the heart of the memo. It addresses the legal question in detail, describing the relevant law and analysis. The structure is simple, following an organization known by the acronyms IRAC or CREAC.

The structures work in about the same way. IRAC begins with an issue statement, rather than a conclusion. And CREAC includes an E for explanation of the law, though both structures explain the law.[6] Either organization makes for an effective discussion section in a memo.

---

5. 741 F.3d 48, 51-53 (10th Cir. 2014); No. 11-CV-346-J, 2012 WL 12846894, at *2 (D. Wyo. June 12, 2012).

6. This organizational framework for legal analysis is sometimes also abbreviated as BaRAC (Bold assertion-Rule-Analysis-Conclusion), CRAC (Conclusion-Rule-Analysis-Conclusion), CREXAC (Conclusion-Rule-Explanation-Analysis-Conclusion), and TREAT (Thesis-Rule-Explanation-Analysis-Thesis). These organizations are essentially the same.

> ### How to Organize the Discussion Section
>
> | | |
> |---|---|
> | I = Issue | C = Conclusion |
> | R = Rule and Explanation of Law | R = Rule |
> | | E = Explantion of Law |
> | A = Analysis, Application, Argument | A = Analysis, Application, Argument |
> | C = Conclusion | C = Conclusion |

### a. Issue Statement or Conclusion

Some writers, including U.S. Supreme Court Chief Justice John G. Roberts, sometimes prefer to begin with an issue statement and save the conclusion for the end. An issue statement can help readers keep an open mind about the analysis because they don't know the answer up front. Using the issue statement as the starting point also reflects the fact that the writer has not yet written—or possibly not fully thought through—the legal analysis and reached a conclusion. For this reason, law school exams and essays on the bar exam usually begin by stating the issue.

To start the discussion section of a research memo with an issue statement, first consider the assignment. The instructions probably detailed a clearly defined legal question. For instance, for an assignment relating to *Geier v. Streutker*, the civil rights case, a judge might ask for a memo analyzing whether the defendant would prevail on the qualified immunity defense.

But suppose the assignment comes with a more generic question, one that's not clearly defined in legal terms. The question might not reference the potential qualified immunity defense. Instead, it might be posed more generally as, find out if prison employees are immune from lawsuits filed by inmates. Or, even more generally as, does the defendant have any potential defenses? From these general questions, you can better define your specific legal question by identifying the rule from a constitution, statute, or case. The parties' filings in the case should reference the controlling rule, but if they don't, secondary sources are always a good place to start

**RESEARCH TIP:**
Use key words to search secondary sources, which can lead you to primary legal authorities for your rule.

One way to find the controlling rule is to search key words in a database, like Westlaw or LexisNexis. The basics in *Geier v. Streutker* are that an inmate is suing a prison employee for a civil rights violation. Searching under "secondary sources" for the key words "civil rights action government employee defenses" in Westlaw brings you to a number of helpful secondary sources, including an entry in American Law Reports called "Immunity of public officials from personal liability in civil rights actions brought by public employees under 42 U.S.C.A. § 1983."[7] This entry in the secondary source defines the qualified immunity defense, providing the rule and citations to relevant cases. From here, you can describe the issue in specific legal terms and draft the issue statement to begin the discussion.

Once the legal question is identified, the issue statement should add some context by adding a key fact or two or by identifying the parties. This context makes the issue similar to the question presented—but without the question mark at the end. The following issue statement demonstrates one effective way to begin a research memo.

### Discussion

> This memo analyzes whether the Defendant, an employee of San Quentin State Prison, is entitled to the qualified immunity defense when the Plaintiff, an inmate, alleges that the Defendant violated his First Amendment right to seek dental care.

## b. Rule Statement

Next up in the memo is the rule statement, which defines the broadest controlling rule. The rule statement is typically a sentence or two, immediately following the issue statement, and may complete the first paragraph of the discussion section.

---

### Finding the Rule and Explaining the Law

1. Check the parties' filings for the rule.
2. Double check their research, starting with secondary sources.
3. Search key words in secondary sources.
4. Scan the table of contents of relevant secondary sources for helpful entries, starting with general information and moving toward more specific.
5. Identify primary authorities—constitutions, statutes, and cases—as the source for the rule.
6. Expand your list of relevant cases to study how courts explain the law.

---

7. 63 A.L.R. Fed. 744.

To find the controlling rule, start with your assignment materials. The parties likely identified the controlling rule in their motions. Even so, you should double check their work by doing your own research. For instance, in *Geier*, the defendant detailed the controlling rule for the qualified immunity defense in a motion for summary judgment. To confirm this rule, review the secondary source entry we found in our research for the issue statement: "Immunity of public officials from personal liability in civil rights actions brought by public employees under 42 U.S.C.A. § 1983."

Scanning the table of contents of this entry in the secondary source leads to Section I, "Preliminary Matters" and Section II, "General Considerations," which includes the following helpful explanation of the relevant qualified immunity rule:

> The official immunity afforded legislators, judges, and prosecutors is an absolute immunity defeating liability at the outset. Virtually all courts have recognized, either implicitly or explicitly, that, unlike the absolute immunity enjoyed by public officials acting in a judicial capacity, state officials sued in employment situations under 42 U.S.C.A. § 1983 are entitled only to a qualified immunity, a defense dependent upon good-faith action. The decisions in the following cases, involving actions brought by public employees, exemplify the rationales taken by the courts in support of this rule.[8]

From here, the entry lists some helpful cases that state the rule and describe its two parts. The following rule statement comes from a U.S. Supreme Court case, *Ashcroft v. al-Kidd*:

> Qualified immunity shields federal and state officials from money damages unless a plaintiff pleads facts showing (1) that the official violated a statutory or constitutional right, and (2) that the right was "clearly established" at the time of the challenged conduct.[9]

Once identified, you can rework the rule statement to fit with the specific case. The following rule statement narrows the *Ashcroft* rule by referencing only state (not federal) employees and only constitutional (not statutory) rights to reflect the specific nature of the state constitutional case in *Geier*.

### Discussion

> This memo analyzes whether the Defendant, an employee of San Quentin State Prison, is entitled to the qualified immunity defense when the Plaintiff, an inmate, alleges that the Defendant violated his First Amendment right to seek dental care. Qualified immunity shields state employees from money damages in civil rights lawsuits unless

---

8. *Id.* (footnote omitted).
9. 131 S. Ct. 2074, 2080 (2011).

the plaintiff demonstrates that the employee violated a constitutional right and the right was "clearly established" at the time. *Ashcroft v. al-Kidd*, 131 S. Ct. 2074, 2080 (2011).

—The rule statement follows the issue statement in IRAC and describes the two parts of the qualified immunity analysis.

From here, the memo should explain the two parts of the rule, with illustrations from relevant cases that explain how courts apply each part.

The rule for every memo will be different, depending on the legal question. A memo's rule might have key terms that need to be defined, or it could be a legal test with a set number of elements that need to be explained. Or the rule might include a set of factors or a list of exceptions that courts should consider. Another type of rule is a balancing test, where each part of the test needs to be described. Whatever the type, a research memo should clearly and objectively state the governing rule, followed by a detailed explanation of each part of the rule.

### c. Explanation of the Law

The explanation of the law will describe how to apply the rule, by detailing examples of how courts have interpreted, applied, and analyzed the same law in other cases. To figure out how to organize the explanation, read relevant cases to see how courts structure and detail their explanation. The case that you cited for the rule statement should be a useful starting point. It should not only explain how to apply the rule but also cite additional helpful cases.

The *Ashcroft* case, cited for the rule in the *Geier* memo, does just that. First, it provides a broad explanation of the two-part rule, and then it explains which of the two parts courts should apply first. Finally, it describes how to apply each part. The case also cites additional helpful cases—all of which guided the development of the following explanation section example (highlighted in gray):

#### Discussion

This memo analyzes whether the Defendant, an employee of San Quentin State Prison, is entitled to the qualified immunity defense when the Plaintiff, an inmate, alleges that the Defendant violated his First Amendment right to seek dental care. Qualified immunity shields state employees from money damages in civil rights lawsuits unless the plaintiff demonstrates that the employee violated a constitutional right and the right was "clearly established" at the time. *Ashcroft v. al-Kidd*, 131 S. Ct. 2074, 2080 (2011). Courts have discretion to decide which of the two parts of the qualified-immunity analysis they analyze first. *Id.*

—The memo follows the IRAC structure: It begins with an issue statement, then states the rule.

—A single, broad explanation statement ends the memo's first paragraph, setting up the more detailed explanation that follows.

Under the first part of the analysis, courts must first analyze the constitutional question. *See id.* With an alleged First Amendment violation, the plaintiff has the burden of showing that retaliation for the exercise of his First Amendment right motivated the employee's

The first explanation paragraph describes how to analyze the first part of the rule, citing two cases in support.

— actions. *Mt. Healthy City Sch. Dist. Bd. of Educ. v. Doyle*, 429 U.S. 274, 287 (1977). Further, the plaintiff must assert that the retaliation chilled the plaintiff's exercise of his right and that "the action did not reasonably advance a legitimate correctional goal." *Rhodes v. Robinson*, 408 F.3d 559, 567-68 (9th Cir. 2009). The plaintiff does not need to show that he was silenced, just that his First Amendment rights were chilled.

A helpful quote from a key case fleshes out the explanation.

— *Id.* at 569. "The proper analysis is whether a person of ordinary firmness would be chilled or silenced from exercising future First Amendment rights." *Id.*

The opening clause helps orient the reader to the fact that this paragraph focuses on the second part of the rule.

— Under the second part of the analysis, a government employee's conduct violates clearly established law when, at the time of the challenged conduct, the contours of the right are "sufficiently clear that a reasonable official would understand that what he is doing

The rest of the paragraph explains the practical application of this part of the rule.

— violates that right." *Anderson v. Creighton*, 483 U.S. 635, 635 (1987). Even if the violated right was clearly established, qualified immunity shields an officer when he makes a decision that, even if constitutionally deficient, reasonably misapprehends the law governing the circumstances he confronted. *Brosseau v. Haugen*, 543 U.S. 194, 198 (2004). If "the officer's mistake as to what the law requires is reasonable . . . the officer is entitled to the immunity defense." *Id.* at 205.

### d. Analysis

The analysis section of a research memo offers the chance to act as a judge, possibly for the first time in your legal career. Here, you not only predict how the case should come out, but you also detail how the analysis supports the conclusion. The tone should be authoritative and definitive, just like the tone a judge would have when writing an order or opinion.

Another key feature of the analysis section is that it should be objective. The section should fairly analyze the specific facts of the case according to the relevant law. The parties' pleadings in the case are a helpful starting point for identifying key arguments, but they focus on arguing only one side. The research memo should tackle the legal question from the beginning and approach it from a middle ground, looking at the arguments on both sides, determining which side should prevail and why some arguments win and others lose.

The analysis is the most complex part of any legal document. It should fully develop and detail every major lawful argument. One way to effectively detail arguments is to compare and contrast the facts in your case with the facts, reasoning, and holdings from cases described in the explanation. You can draw analogies to cases with holdings that agree with your conclusion and distinctions to cases that find for the other party.

The most effective analogies and distinctions are substantive, parallel, and specific.[10] Analogies that are substantive show why your facts are legally significant and connected to the relevant law, rather than being superfluous. For example, because Geier was seeking dental care, another case involving an inmate seeking dental care might seem analogous. But that fact is not connected to the relevant law. What's important is how the inmates might have been discouraged from seeking any kind of care. A substantive analogy or distinction focuses on what's important under the relevant law.

Additionally, analogies should be parallel and specific. It's not enough to write, "Like *Ashcroft*, the Defendant here is protected by qualified immunity." First, this sentence compares the *Ashcroft* case to a person, which is not parallel or grammatically correct. Second, the sentence is conclusory and fails to use specifics to show why the cases are similar. Analogies that compare your facts to specific details from supporting cases will most effectively show your reader why your conclusion is correct. The following is one example of how to construct a substantive, parallel, and specific analogy:

> Just as the defendant in *Ashcroft* reasonably interpreted the Fourth Amendment and committed no constitutional violation by arresting and detaining a material witness, the Defendant here acted reasonably by following standard practice, and his conduct did not chill the Plaintiff's First Amendment rights. Thus, the Defendant here is protected by qualified immunity, like the defendant in *Ashcroft*.

Another way to build the analysis is to describe how the law should apply under your interpretation of it. For instance, if the governing rule from the case involves a legal test, you can describe how the test operates with the specific facts of your case. Finally, the analysis may describe counterarguments—arguments from the losing side that do not support your conclusion—but it should do so in a way that dismisses them, explaining definitively why they are unsuccessful.

Because the analysis section is complex, keep in mind basic organizational principles to help the reader understand the progression of the arguments. Begin with a thesis statement that summarizes the major argument or arguments that support the conclusion. Then, use topic sentences at the start of each paragraph to set up each distinct point of analysis. The following excerpt of an analysis section from the *Geier* memo shows how to structure an effective analysis paragraph, beginning with a topic sentence summarizing a key point and then providing support. It also addresses a

---

10. Jill Barton & Rachel H. Smith, *The Handbook for the New Legal Writer* 58-60 (2014).

counterargument with a sentence that begins, "even if." This construction easily allows the writer to dismiss the losing argument.

A topic sentence indicates that this paragraph analyzes one part of the rule and helpfully summarizes the paragraph's main argument.

A counterargument is addressed and dismissed with the common "even if" construction.

Citations indicate specific legal support.

A conclusion focuses specifically on qualified immunity.

— Because Streutker was following standard practice, Geier's case fails under the second part of the qualified-immunity analysis. Streutker explained to Geier that his duplicate requests for dental care would delay his treatment, which is a reasonable action that no reasonable official would understand to violate a right. *See Anderson*, 483 U.S. at 635. Even if Geier had shown that Streutker violated a constitutional right, she has presented evidence that she reasonably believed that she was not impinging on Geier's rights. A reasonable mistake on her part would still entitle her to the immunity defense. *See Brosseau*, 543 U.S. at 198. But here, the record shows that Streutker was simply informing Geier how to use the notification system properly and that abuse of the system would create unnecessary work and delays. Her actions were reasonable and did not violate Geier's rights, thus she is entitled to qualified immunity.

### e. Conclusion

The discussion section ends with a conclusion. This statement keeps the reader focused on the overall legal question and follows the specific analysis. It can be brief, especially because the memo ends with a more formal conclusion and recommendation section.

## 6. Conclusion and Recommendation

This final section is the most exciting part of the research memo. The conclusion and recommendation detail exactly who should prevail, how the court should rule, and what the holding should be. If the analysis raised any questions or results in a close call, the recommendation should explain those concerns too. For a simple, single-issue memo, this section typically is one to four sentences. The following example provides a conclusion on the qualified immunity question and a recommendation on how to rule on the defendant's summary judgment motion in the case.

Conclusion and Recommendation

The first sentence summarizes key facts. The second sentence describes the analysis and conclusion. The third sentence recommends how the judge should rule.

— Streutker was following standard practice and believed she was assisting a patient who misunderstood the way to make appointments. Her conduct was reasonable, thus entitling her to the qualified immunity defense. Streutker's request for summary judgment should be granted.

## Checklist for Writing a Research Memo

&#10148;&#10148;

- ☐ Use a formal memo heading with an appropriate description of the subject and the proper date.
- ☐ Use headings for the main sections: the question presented, brief answer, facts, discussion, and conclusion and recommendation.
- ☐ Identify the precise question and key facts in the question presented.
- ☐ Concisely explain the most relevant law and most pertinent analysis in the brief answer.
- ☐ Follow a logical IRAC or CREAC organization for the discussion.
- ☐ If beginning with an issue statement, precisely state the legal question; if beginning with a conclusion, precisely state the legal question and provide a specific reason in support.
- ☐ State the rule objectively and with a citation in proper *Bluebook* form.
- ☐ Explain the relevant law using key cases to show how courts interpret, apply, and analyze the law in similar cases. Cite every sentence in proper *Bluebook* form.
- ☐ Approach the analysis objectively, detailing substantive, parallel, and specific analogies and distinctions that support your conclusion.
- ☐ State your final conclusion and a supporting reason with precision.
- ☐ For the final conclusion and recommendation, explain your level of certainty.
- ☐ Revise the memo for large-scale organizational issues, checking to make sure that topic sentences reflect each paragraph's substance.
- ☐ Proofread to ensure correct grammar, punctuation, style, and citations.

## B. MODEL RESEARCH MEMORANDUM WITH ANNOTATIONS

In *Geier v. Streutker*, the U.S. district court in California addressed two issues: First, did a dentist at a state prison retaliate against an inmate in violation of his First Amendment rights? And second, is the dentist as a state employee entitled to the qualified immunity defense?

Most of the examples in the first part of this chapter focused on the second question. The following research memo tackles the first. These examples closely track the judge's order, included on pages 66-69 of Chapter 5. These similarities reflect that a research memo often serves as the basis for the order or opinion that's published in the case. The work on a research memo regularly serves as a first draft of the law.

Use this model research memo as a guide for developing your own first draft of the law, from the heading and question presented to the conclusion and recommendation.

## RESEARCH MEMORANDUM [11]

TO:     JUDGE ILLSTON
FROM:   ASHLEY SAWYER SMITH
SUBJECT: WHETHER DEFENDANT RETALIATED AGAINST PLAINTIFF IN
            GEIER V. STREUTKER, NO. 10-1965
DATE:    APRIL 10, 2012

---

### QUESTION PRESENTED

The **question presented** fleshes out the more generic issue statement from the subject line above and adds facts for context.

Did the Defendant, a dentist, retaliate against the Plaintiff, an inmate, in violation of his First Amendment right to seek dental care when she told him not to file duplicate requests for appointments?

### BRIEF ANSWER

The **answer** provides a summary of the rule, a summary of the analysis, and a definitive conclusion.

No. A First Amendment retaliation claim requires a plaintiff to establish that a state actor was motivated to retaliate and that the state actor's conduct chilled the plaintiff's exercise of his First Amendment rights. *Rhodes v. Robinson*, 408 F.3d 559, 567–68 (9th Cir. 2009). Here, the Defendant's goal was for the Plaintiff to use the appointment system properly, which should not chill the Plaintiff's exercise of rights. Thus, the claim fails.

### FACTS

This section chronologically tells the **story of the case** and details what led to the dispute.

Plaintiff Christopher A. Geier, an inmate at San Quentin State Prison, had many dental treatments in 2009. On June 18, 2009, the Defendant, Dr. Streutker, examined the Plaintiff and determined that he needed a tooth extracted. At the appointment, a dental assistant gave the Plaintiff a stack of at least ten dental request forms that he had submitted over the previous few weeks. The Defendant told the Plaintiff that each time he submitted a duplicate request, the evaluation process had to start over.

These **facts** are crucial to the analysis of the first part of the rule: whether the Defendant took an adverse action against the Plaintiff.

The Plaintiff acknowledges in his deposition that the Defendant was expressing concern about wasting dental resources, but at the time, he questioned the Defendant's authority. The Defendant explained that she was second in authority in the dental staff and that if he abused the request slip process in the future, he would face administrative action.

The Plaintiff then filed a grievance against the Defendant. A dentist who reviewed the grievance responded with the following conclusion:

A block quote from a letter supporting the Defendant's position provides necessary context.

> The Defendant properly informed you regarding manipulation of the Health Care Request System. After you were triaged and assigned a [dental priority code] which determined your appointment time frame,

---

11. This research memorandum is adapted from *Geier v. Streutker*, 2012 WL 1835440, No. C 10-1965 (N.D. Cal. May 19, 2012), which is included with annotations in Chapter 5.

you continued to place requests. We determined you did not have an urgent need and we provided your care well within the *Perez* timelines. You will not be disciplined for submitting a legitimate request, but you can for circumventing or manipulating the Health Care Services Request . . . System.

The Plaintiff then sued, alleging a violation of his First Amendment right to seek dental care without retaliation. Specifically, he alleges that the Defendant "threatened to have him 'dealt with' via administrative disciplinary action," which had a chilling effect on him, because he had exercised his right to "refile unanswered requests for emergency care."

> The section ends by describing the lawsuit and focusing on facts essential to analyzing the second part of the rule: whether the Defendant's conduct chilled the Plaintiff's exercise of rights.

## DISCUSSION

This memo analyzes whether the Defendant, a dentist, retaliated against the Plaintiff, an inmate, in violation of his First Amendment right to seek dental care. The Defendant seeks summary judgment on this claim, which is proper when the pleadings, discovery, and affidavits raise "no genuine dispute as to any material fact," entitling the Defendant to judgment as a matter of law." *See* Fed. R. Civ. P. 56(a). Material facts are those that may affect the outcome of the case. *Anderson v. Liberty Lobby, Inc.*, 477 U.S. 242, 248 (1986).

> The discussion begins with an **issue statement** to follow the **IRAC** structure. A description of the pending motion follows, along with a summary of the **legal standard**. Another option, illustrated in the trial court order in Chapter 5, is to break up the legal standard in its own section.

To establish a First Amendment violation, the plaintiff must first assert that a state actor took some adverse action against him because of his protected conduct. *Rhodes v. Robinson*, 408 F.3d 559, 567–68 (9th Cir. 2009). On this point, the plaintiff has the burden of showing that retaliation for the exercise of protected conduct was the "substantial" or "motivating" factor behind the defendant's actions. *Mt. Healthy City Sch. Dist. Bd. of Educ. v. Doyle*, 429 U.S. 274, 287 (1977).

> The next paragraph states the first part of the governing **rule**, then an **explanation** of how to apply it.

Secondly, the plaintiff also has the burden of showing that the defendant's action chilled his exercise of rights and did not reasonably advance a legitimate correctional goal. *Id.* That a plaintiff's First Amendment rights were chilled, though not necessarily silenced, is enough. *Id.* at 569. "The proper inquiry asks 'whether an official's acts would chill or silence a person of ordinary firmness from future First Amendment activities.'" *Mendocino Envtl. Ctr. v. Mendocino Cnty.*, 192 F.3d 1283, 1300 (9th Cir. 1999).

> This **explanation** paragraph explains the second part of the rule and adds a helpful quote from a new case to show how to apply it.

Here, the Plaintiff has not raised a genuine dispute of fact that the Defendant took an adverse action against him. The Defendant did not take, or threaten to take, an adverse action against the Plaintiff. Instead, the Defendant made clear to the Plaintiff that he could continue to file request slips for legitimate purposes, but an abuse of that system would result in discipline. The Defendant's motivation was for the Plaintiff to understand how to use, rather than misuse, the appointment request system. Therefore, the Plaintiff has not shown a triable issue of fact that retaliation for the exercise of protected conduct was the "substantial" or "motivating" factor behind the Defendant's actions. *See Mt. Healthy City Sch. Dist. Bd. of Educ.*, 429 U.S. at 287.

> The **analysis** follows the organization established by the explanation, analyzing the first part of the rule at the start. A thesis statement guides the reader.

A topic sentence sets up this paragraph's analysis of the rule's second part.

Additionally, the Plaintiff has not raised a genuine dispute of fact that the Defendant's conduct amounted to retaliation or that it failed to advance a legitimate correctional goal. The Defendant informed the Plaintiff that misusing the appointment request system creates a delay in treatment and unnecessary work for staff. Plaintiff acknowledged that he understood this

The analysis uses authoritative language, incorporating a key legal phrase, "legitimate correctional goal," to advance support for the conclusion.

legitimate correctional goal as the Defendant's meaning. Also, the Defendant made clear to the Plaintiff that he could continue to file slip notifications for legitimate grievances. In this way, the Defendant's conduct encouraged legitimate communication by the Plaintiff, which would not chill or silence "a person of ordinary firmness" from exercising future First Amendment rights. *See Mendocino Envtl. Ctr.*, 192 F.3d at 1300. Thus, the Defendant did not

The analysis ends with a clear **conclusion**, focused on the precise issue.

retaliate against the Plaintiff in violation of his First Amendment right to seek dental care.

### CONCLUSION AND RECOMMENDATION

The final section summarizes the conclusions to the analysis of each part of the rule. It also notes that the Defendant's motion can be granted based on any — not all — of these conclusions, lending decisive support to the **recommendation**.

The Plaintiff has not met his burden of establishing a First Amendment retaliation claim, and his case should not survive summary judgment. First, the Plaintiff has not raised a genuine dispute of fact that the Defendant took an adverse action against him. Even if he did, his claim would still fail because he also has not raised a genuine dispute of fact that the Defendant's conduct amounted to retaliation or that it failed to advance a legitimate correctional goal. Therefore, the Defendant's Motion for Summary Judgment should be granted.

## C. COMMON PARTS OF AN APPELLATE COURT BENCH MEMO

A research memo for a trial court catches a case near its inception, while writing a bench memo at an appeals court means analyzing a case closer to its end. Imagine being a new judicial clerk, just weeks after law school graduation, and having the power to help shape a final decision that declares a law unconstitutional, decides an election, punishes the guilty, or frees the innocent. These efforts begin with the bench memo, a judicial document that often serves as the first draft of an appellate opinion.

At every level of court, even the U.S. Supreme Court, judges and justices regularly follow the advice that their law clerks detail in bench memos.[12] Chief Justice William H. Rehnquist said that clerks' bench memos influence the judiciary because "sheer pressure of time often prevents a Justice from personally investigating every point involved."[13] His comments centered on what's known as a pool memo, which recommends whether the Court should grant certiorari and review a case. By helping justices decide which cases the Court will hear, clerks help set the agenda for the nation's highest court. But clerks do far more than that.

Through their bench memos, clerks also sway how cases are ultimately decided and how the reasoning will unfold in published opinions. This influence may be heightened in history-making cases like *Bush v. Gore*[14] and *United States v. Nixon*,[15] because of the political pressure to resolve newsworthy disputes quickly.

The *Nixon* case, which ultimately limited the powers of the president and led to Richard Nixon's resignation, demanded quick action by the U.S. Supreme Court. The parties filed briefs in the case on June 21, 1974, with oral argument scheduled just days later on July 8. Justice Harry Blackmun, a recent Nixon appointee, assigned a law clerk to write a bench memo to help him prepare. The memo detailed questions for Justice Blackmun to ask, and Justice Blackmun, having covered the bench memo with notes, asked three of his clerk's questions in open court.[16] The answers helped shape the Court's unanimous opinion.[17]

---

12. *See, e.g.*, Johnson et al., *Advice from the Bench (Memo): Clerk Influence on Supreme Court Oral Arguments*, 98 Marq. L. Rev. 21 (2014); Todd C. Peppers & Christopher Zorn, *Law Clerk Influence on Supreme Court Decision Making*, 58 DePaul L. Rev. 51 (2008); Corey Ditslear & Lawrence Baum, *Selection of Law Clerks and Polarization in the U.S. Supreme Court*, 63 J. Pol. 869 (2001).

13. William H. Rehnquist, *Who Writes Decisions of the Supreme Court?*, U.S. News & World Report, Dec. 13, 1957.

14. David Margolick, *The Path to Florida*, Vanity Fair, Oct. 2004.

15. Johnson et al., *supra* note 12, at 22.

16. *Id.* at 25.

17. *United States v. Nixon*, 418 U.S. 683 (1974).

The bench memo can be the first thing a judge reads about a case. Also known as a bench brief, it helps the bench understand the parties' positions and develop questions for oral argument. Bench memos summarize the parties' arguments and the relevant law in a pending case, but they also independently analyze the issues and recommend how to proceed. Judicial clerks typically write these memos for the bench using the parties' briefs, the record, and their own research and analysis.

This section of the chapter details how to write each part of a bench memo and how to use the stack of papers from the case as your starting point. Although the style and format might vary depending on the judge's preferences and the court's practices, most bench memos contain the following seven parts, from the opening caption to the closing recommendation.

---

### Common Parts of a Bench Memo

1. Case Caption
2. Introduction
3. Statement of the Issue and Short Answer
4. Facts and Procedural History
5. Standard of Review
6. Discussion
7. Recommendation

---

The structure here is similar to that of a trial court research memo, and both serve the same purpose: to help the judge decide how to answer a legal question. But the tone and substance of a bench memo differ in some ways—just as the tone and substance of an opinion in a trial court and an appellate court differ. Acting New York City Supreme Court Justice Gerald Lebovits explains the difference like this: "[A] trial-court opinion should offer a logical, disinterested explanation of the case for the litigants that allows appellate review," while appellate opinions "review trial-court opinions for correctness and sharpen the issues for further appellate consideration."[18]

Appellate courts don't review everything a trial court does. Instead, appellate courts address only those issues that are preserved—meaning that the litigants presented the issue to the trial court, the judge ruled on the issue, and the harm or objection to the ruling was made part of the appellate

---

18. Gerald Lebovits, *Ethical Judicial Writing — Part I*, 78 N.Y. St. B.J. 64 (2006).

record. This preservation rule is a basic first step for any appeal. If a party does not preserve an issue for appeal, it waives the issue, and the appeals court cannot review the decision on the matter.[19]

## 1. Caption

This section is straightforward. It lists six basic facts about a case: the names of the judges, author, case, and attorneys, as well as the date completed and the date for oral argument. As with everything in judicial writing, getting each fact right is essential. The judge will check the caption to make sure the bench has no conflicts with the parties or the attorneys. If a conflict exists and the judge needs to be recused, the bench memo will have a new audience in another chambers. The format follows the style of a heading for a memo, and while it will vary depending on the preferences of the judge and court, it could look something like this:

---

**BENCH MEMORANDUM**

| | |
|---|---|
| TO: | JUDGE DOSS |
| FROM: | JOY DITTEBRANDT |
| CASE NAME AND NO.: | *SHARAMITARO*, APPELLANT, *V. MARCELANO*, APPELLEE, 14–56784 |
| ATTORNEYS: | SARA TAYLOR, FOR THE APPELLANT; QUINCY SHIELDS FOR THE APPELLEE |
| DATE: | JUNE 9, 2015 |
| ORAL ARGUMENT DATE: | SEPTEMBER 14, 2015 |

---

## 2. Introduction

This opening section maps out the basics of the case before you. It should describe the issues and give some context to help the judge understand what's at stake. That usually means providing key facts and a rudimentary description of the law. Except for especially complex cases, the introduction needs only a paragraph or two to familiarize the judge with what's to come. The short introduction in the next example frames the legal issue by describing the most important facts. It then describes the legal question the court confronts in deciding the case.

---

19. *See* Fed. R. Civ. P. 51 Instructions to the Jury; Objections; Preserving a Claim of Error; Fed. R. Crim. P. 56 Preserving Claimed Error.

## Introduction

<table>
<tr>
<td>

The first two sentences describe the key, legally significant facts, providing context for the dispute.

</td>
<td>

— Two California Highway Patrol officers stopped Lorenzo and Jose Navarette to conduct an investigatory stop based solely on an anonymous 911 caller who reported that a reckless driver ran her off the road. About 15 minutes later, the officers stopped the Navarettes' vehicle, which matched the caller's description, without corroborating anything

</td>
</tr>
<tr>
<td>

Next, the introduction concisely summarizes the petitioners' argument.

</td>
<td>

— other than the innocent details of the anonymous tip. The Navarettes contend that the police lacked reasonable suspicion to stop their vehicle, thus violating the Fourth Amendment. The issue here is whether the police needed to corroborate more than the innocent details of the

</td>
</tr>
<tr>
<td>

Finally, the introduction summarizes the legal issue.

</td>
<td>

— anonymous tip for the traffic stop, or if the report of a reckless driver was enough for the traffic stop under the totality of the circumstances.

</td>
</tr>
</table>

## 3. Statement of the Issue and Short Answer

This section builds on the introduction, first describing the issue, along with some key facts. If you have already written the introduction, then you probably have the information needed to write the issue statement. The issue statement can frame the legal question as a phrase beginning with "whether" or "if," or as a question, typically beginning with "does" or "when" or "is." The issue statement also should incorporate key facts to provide context.

 Next comes the short answer. As the title implies, it should be concise. Typically, a short answer contains one to three sentences summarizing the law and one to three sentences summarizing the analysis and conclusion. The answer is your first chance to tell the judge whether the appellant or appellee should win the case. It should be definitive and begin with a yes or no—without any hedging. It should also be backed up with the relevant law and citations.

 You probably won't be ready to write the short answer at the outset of drafting a bench memo. Consider that if you are just starting the review of a case, you might not understand the facts and the legal issue well enough to draft the issue statement. Coming up with an answer that you feel confident about will require research and a deeper understanding of the relevant law and your analysis. Either hold off on writing the short answer until you have completed a draft of the discussion section or draft a placeholder representing your best guess at an answer at the outset.

 For a bench memo addressing more than one distinct legal issue, title this section "Statement of the Issues and Short Answers." Then list the first issue and answer, followed by the second, and so on. This organization will give the judge an outline of the analysis in the bench memo.

 The next example—from *Navarette v. California*—picks up from the previous example of an introduction.

### Statement of the Issue and Short Answer

**Issue:** When an anonymous tipster reports that a reckless driver ran her off the road, does an officer need to corroborate the dangerous driving before stopping the suspected vehicle about 15 minutes later?

**Answer:** No. Under the totality of the circumstances, the anonymous tip asserting that a reckless driver almost ran another driver off the road served as a reasonable basis for officers to stop the car for reckless or suspected drunk driving. The Fourth Amendment allows an officer to stop a vehicle when he has "a particularized and objective basis for suspecting the person stopped of criminal activity." *United States v. Cortez*, 449 U.S. 411, 418 (1981). Also, the eyewitness account and the short time between the tip and the stop made the tip sufficiently reliable. *See Alabama v. White*, 496 U.S. 325, 328-32 (1990). Finally, states have a significant interest in stopping drunk or reckless drivers. *Michigan Dept. of State Police v. Sitz*, 496 U.S. 444, 453 (1990).

— This issue statement begins by providing key facts, then asks what the law requires for this type of traffic stop.

— The answer begins with a definitive "no," followed by a concise conclusion.

— A statement of the major rule supporting the conclusion follows.

— The final two sentences apply the facts to other rules, providing two more arguments in support.

## 4. Facts and Procedural History

This section tells the story behind your case. It typically begins by explaining the legally relevant facts that started the dispute and ends by describing the lower court ruling that led to the appeal.

Begin with the appellate record: the official account of what happened at the hearing or trial that's being appealed. The record includes filings, motions, orders, and transcripts, and the parties are limited to using only the information in the record in their arguments.

An appeal usually has gone through several rounds of he-said, she-said, so the appellate record can contain factual discrepancies. Scour the record to resolve the discrepancies or identify the inconsistencies for the judge. For instance, in family law cases, an appellate court might need to review whether an award of child support or alimony was reasonable. Evidence in the record might show conflicting evidence of the parties' incomes and assets. The parties' briefs might further inflate or deflate these numbers with arguments supporting their side and diminishing their opponent's side. Your role is to try to verify one account of the facts over the other—or to figure out if the truth lies somewhere in between.

If the record leaves so many holes that the facts remain foggy, make a note of the discrepancies. For example, in one bench brief, Justice Blackmun's clerk noted two questions, which the justice later asked in oral argument: "Could the Idaho court have appointed both mother and father as joint administrators?" and "Is it correct that the estate amounted to less than $1,000?"[20]

---

20. Johnson et al., *supra* note 12, at 39.

Resolving discrepancies can be tricky and time consuming. For some appeals, it might require a review of boxes of records. But that doesn't mean that the facts section needs to span dozens of pages. Consider this section to be an overview of the case—highlighting only the legally significant facts and the key rulings in the lower courts.

This section also should be objective, and it might include citations to the record, depending on the judge's preference. For organization, a chronological narrative works best. Keep in mind other organizational principles too, including paragraph breaks, topic sentences, and headings. Here's a breakdown of what judges expect in a facts section:

1. The legally relevant facts, with any discrepancies resolved;
2. An explanation of any unresolved factual inconsistencies;
3. The procedural history, including a summary of the order being appealed; and
4. Any background facts needed to provide context or to tie the story together.

The following example of a facts and procedural history section describes what happened in *Navarette v. California* up until the U.S. Supreme Court granted certiorari, meaning it agreed to hear the appeal. The section uses a chronological organization and sets up the analysis by highlighting the legally significant facts and recounting the lower court rulings being appealed.

### Facts and Procedural History

The section begins chronologically, with the initial 911 call.

A 911 caller reported that a pickup truck had run her off the road about five minutes before. The caller identified the location, and truck's make, model, color, and license plate. The 911 dispatcher relayed the tip to the California Highway Patrol. About 15 minutes later, two officers on patrol spotted the truck traveling down the highway. They made a U-turn,

This sentence describes the absence of a fact and evidence of corroboration.

and about five minutes later, they pulled over the truck. The officers did not witness erratic or reckless driving prior to the traffic stop.

This sentence describes the absence of a fact and evidence of corroboration.

The officers smelled marijuana when they approached the truck and found four bags containing over thirty pounds of marijuana when they searched the truck. They arrested the petitioners: Lorenzo Prado Navarette, the driver, and José Navarette, the passenger. Petitioners were charged with transporting marijuana and possession of marijuana for sale pursuant to California Health & Safety Code §§ 1135, 11360(a).

The final paragraph contains the procedural history, beginning with what happened at the trial court and concluding with the U.S. Supreme Court granting cert.

Petitioners moved to suppress the evidence, alleging that the officers lacked reasonable suspicion to stop them because the anonymous tip was not sufficiently reliable and because the officers did not corroborate the tip by witnessing reckless driving before the stop. The magistrate denied the petitioners' motion at a suppression hearing and the Superior Court agreed, finding that the officers had reason-able suspicion of unlawful activity, which justified the traffic stop. *People v. Navarette*, 2012 WL 4842651, *9 (Cal. Ct. App. Oct. 12, 2012). Petitioners pleaded guilty and were sentenced to 90 days in jail plus three years of probation. The California Supreme Court denied review. This Court granted certiorari, *Navarette v. California*, 134 S. Ct. 50 (2013).

> **WRITING TIP:**
> To make the procedural history its own section, break out this last paragraph with a separate heading.

## 5. Standard of Review

The standard of review might raise another point of disagreement in the parties' briefs. Most briefs will describe the standard of review under a separate heading, which provides a helpful starting point for drafting this section. If the parties agree on the standard, you will still need to do some research to make sure they are correct, but the job will be much easier.

For instance, in a case appealing a motion for summary judgment, the parties probably won't get too creative in describing the well-known standard of *de novo* review. This standard means that the court will review the case anew, showing no discretion to the lower court decision. The opposite standard of review is the abuse of discretion standard, meaning the court will show great deference to the lower court ruling and reverse only if the lower court judge unreasonably departed from the law.

Consider the following sections for the standards of review in the appellant's brief, the appellee's brief, and the opinion in *Halperin v. Abacus Technology Corporation*.[21] The opinion's standard of review could mirror the section from the bench brief, considering that the bench memo often serves as the first draft of an opinion. Here, the opinion draws on seminal cases to rewrite and augment the information contained in the appellant's brief.

### Standard of Review [Appellant's Brief]

The general standard that an appellate court applies in reviewing the grant or denial of a summary judgment motion is the same as that employed by the trial court under Rule 56(c)—summary judgment is proper when it appears "that there is no genuine issue as to any material fact and that the moving party is entitled to a judgment as a matter of law." 10 C. Wright, A. Miller & M. Kane, Federal Practice and Procedure § 2716 at 643 (2d ed. 1983). *See also Helm v. W. Md. Ry. Co.*, 838 F.2d 729, 734 (4th Cir. 1985). This Court reviews the decision *de novo*. *E.E.O.C. v. Clay Printing Co.*, 955 F.2d 936, 937 (4th Cir. 1992).[22]

---

21. 128 F.3d 191, 196 (4th Cir. 1997).
22. Brief of Appellant at 2, *Halperin v. Abacus Tech. Corp.*, 128 F.3d 191 (4th Cir. 1997) (No. 96-2349), 1997 WL 33539450.

### Standard of Review [Appellee's Brief]

The appellant has properly stated the standard of review and it is incorporated herein.[23]

### Standard of Review [Opinion]

We review *de novo* the district court's decision to grant Abacus summary judgment. *See Higgins v. E.I. DuPont de Nemours & Co.*, 863 F.2d 1162, 1167 (4th Cir. 1988). Summary judgment is appropriate only "if the pleadings, depositions, answers to interrogatories, and admissions on file, together with the affidavits, if any, show that there is no genuine issue as to any material fact." *See* Fed. R. Civ. P. 56; *Celotex Corp. v. Catrett*, 477 U.S. 317, 322 (1986). In deciding whether there is a genuine issue of material fact, the evidence of the non-moving party is to be believed and all justifiable inferences must be drawn in his favor. *See Anderson v. Liberty Lobby, Inc.*, 477 U.S. 242, 255 (1986).[24]

Parties are not always going to agree on the standard of review. And some might not even include the section in their brief, which means you'll need to figure it out on your own. The standard of review dictates how to review the facts and law in an appeal, so getting it wrong means the rest of the bench memo will be off too.

**RESEARCH TIP:**
Start with these secondary sources to identify the correct standard of review for your case.

In *Navarette v. California*, the parties did not include a section on the standard of review in their briefs to the state appellate court or the U.S. Supreme Court. When that happens, start your research at the beginning with secondary sources, like the *Standards of Review Primer: Federal Civil Appeals*, 229 F.R.D. 267 (2005). Or for criminal cases, choose a secondary source like *Federal Criminal Appeals*, which offers the following in Section 5:28 for a motion to suppress:

> The court of appeals applies a mixed standard of review to a district court's suppression order: it reviews the court's findings of fact for clear error and the application of the law to those facts *de novo*. *See U.S. v. Siciliano*, 578 F.3d 61 (1st Cir. 2009); *U.S. v. Stults*, 575 F.3d 834 (8th Cir. 2009) (The Court of Appeals reviews the district court's factual determinations in support of its denial of a motion to suppress for clear error and its legal conclusions *de novo*. The Court of Appeals must affirm an order denying a motion to suppress unless the decision is unsupported by substantial evidence, is based on an erroneous view of the applicable law, or in light of the entire record, it is left with a firm and definite conviction that a mistake has been made.)[25]

---

23. Brief of Appellee at 1, *Halperin*, 128 F.3d 191 (No. 96-2349), 1997 WL 33539404.
24. *Halperin*, 128 F.3d at 196.
25. Lissa Griffin, Federal Criminal Appeals § 5:28.

Use helpful entries like this from secondary sources as your starting point. Then, verify the case citations, find authorities in the appropriate jurisdiction, and complete your own standard of review section. For the *Navarette* case, that meant finding similar Ninth Circuit cases and reviewing whether they apply the same standard. Then, because the case was pending in the U.S. Supreme Court, the standard of review section cited cases from both the Ninth Circuit and the U.S. Supreme Court. The following example from the bench memo in *Navarette* shows just how it was done:

### Standard of Review

On appeal, this Court reviews lower court rulings on suppression orders under a mixed standard, reviewing conclusions of law under a *de novo* standard and findings of fact for clear error. *United States v. Enslin*, 327 F.3d 788, 792 (9th Cir. 2003). This case concerns Fourth Amendment rights against unreasonable search and seizure on the basis of reasonable suspicion: a question of law. Therefore, this Court reviews the lower court's conclusions of law using a *de novo* analysis. *Ornelas v. United States*, 517 U.S. 690, 699 (1996).

— Citing a Ninth Circuit case, the section begins by describing the mixed standard.

— Citing the U.S. Supreme Court — where the case is now pending — ends the section authoritatively.

— Then, the section explains why only one standard applies here.

## 6. Discussion

This section gets to the core of the dispute. Here, you will summarize the parties' briefs, the relevant law, and your own analysis. This summary should be concise. Even when the parties' briefs are each 50-plus pages long, the bench memo might need to summarize and analyze them in a compact 15 to 20 pages. That might mean reducing pages of arguments to a paragraph or two. But as you become the authority on the case, you will begin to feel more comfortable choosing which issues to touch on and which issues to highlight.

The discussion should be authoritative, demonstrating that you have weighed the parties' arguments against your own analysis and that you are confident in your conclusion. You'll need to judge whether the parties are trying to outsmart each other, the court, or both, or whether they have fairly and completely crafted their arguments.

The organization of this section typically follows a CREAC or IRAC framework. That's short for Conclusion-Rule-Explanation-Analysis-Conclusion or Issue-Rule (and explanation)-Analysis-Conclusion.

This organization is similar to that in a trial court order or opinion, except that the Analysis is broken down into three parts. First, summarize the appellant's arguments, then the appellee's. Finally, describe your own analysis. Thus, the basic organization would break down like one of the following structures, which looks like IRA$^3$C or CREA$^3$C:

### Organization of Bench Memo Addressing One Legal Issue

1. Issue statement or conclusion
2. Rule statement and explanation of relevant law
3. Analysis section
   i. Summary of appellant's argument
   ii. Summary of appellee's argument
   iii. Your analysis
4. Conclusion

### Organization of Bench Memo Addressing Multiple Legal Issues

1. Roadmap paragraph with summary of multiple issues or overall conclusion
2. Heading on Issue 1
   - Issue 1 statement or conclusion
   - Rule statement and explanation of relevant law
   - Analysis of Issue 1
     i. Summary of appellant's argument
     ii. Summary of appellee's argument
     iii. Your analysis
   - Conclusion on Issue 1
3. Heading on Issue 2
   - Issue 2 statement or conclusion
   - Rule statement and explanation of relevant law
   - Analysis of Issue 2
     i. Summary of appellant's argument
     ii. Summary of appellee's argument
     iii. Your analysis
   - Conclusion on Issue 2
4. [Continue with headings and IRA³C or CREA³C for each issue as needed.]
5. Overall conclusion

The following excerpt from a bench memo shows one way to structure the three-part analysis. The bench memo for *Navarette v. California* included three separate CREA³Cs, each with a reason supporting the conclusion that the traffic stop was reasonable under the totality of the circumstances: First, the Fourth Amendment allows brief investigative stops. Second, the tip was sufficiently reliable. And third, states have a significant interest in stopping drunk or reckless drivers. This excerpt addresses the third issue.

This A paragraph begins with an objective summary of the petitioners' best argument on this issue.

The petitioners argue that the public safety exception should not be applicable in this case because reckless driving does not create the type of exigency that would justify the stop. The petitioners contend that the Court in *J.L.* refused to create a firearm exception that would have allowed police to stop and frisk an individual alleged to have a weapon. Pet'rs Br. 27, citing *J.L.*, 529 U.S. at 273. The Court should similarly find no exception applicable here. This case involved a single incident of reckless driving, never connected to drunk driving in the tip. Thus, no imminent danger to public safety existed. And no heightened governmental interest justifies the State making the stop without reasonable suspicion.[26]

— It then cites to the Navarettes' brief and a leading case that they use to support their argument.

The State, however, asserts that the heightened governmental interest of protecting the public from drunk drivers tips the reasonableness balance in support of finding reasonable suspicion. The State's argument relies heavily on the *J.L.* exception and points to the numerous lower court cases that distinguish drunken driving situations from the situation in *J.L.* The State refutes the petitioners' reading of *J.L.* because it fails to acknowledge that *J.L.* recognized the importance of a heightened governmental interest in preventing imminent threats to public safety when evaluating the totality of the circumstances.

— The topic sentence here summarizes the State's case. This summary explains how the State responded to the Navarettes' argument.

Furthermore, the State suggests that requiring corroboration of reckless or drunk driving is too restrictive on officers, given the public danger that drunk driving presents. And requiring corroboration of anonymous tips for traffic violations would do away with reasonable suspicion because once officers see a traffic violation, they then have probable cause to make the stop. The State contends that, "the entire point of an investigative detention is to allow officer to assess the situation and determine whether further action is warranted." Rep'ts. Br. 38. Instead, the reasonableness of the stop and the government's interest in protecting the public from drunk or reckless drivers should be the overriding factor.

— A second paragraph summarizes the policy arguments, which the writer ultimately found convincing.

The Court should accept the State's argument because "[n]o one can seriously dispute the magnitude of the drunken driving problem or the States' interest in eradicating it." *See Mich. Dept. of State Police v. Sitz*, 496 U.S. 444 (1990). The activity alleged in the tip, "viewed from the standpoint of an objectively reasonable police officer, amount[s] to reasonable suspicion" of drunk driving. *See Ornelas v. United States*, 517 U.S. 690, 696 (1996).

— This final A paragraph convincingly summarizes the arguments in favor of the writer's conclusion that the State should prevail.

Certain driving behaviors are sound indicia of drunk driving. *See, e.g.*, *People v. Wells*, 136 P.3d 810, 811 (2006) ("'weaving all over the roadway'"); *State v. Prendergast*, 83 P.3d 714, 715-716 (2004) (crossing "over the center line" on a highway and nearly causing "several head-on collisions"). The tipster reported a specific and dangerous driving behavior—running another car off the highway—another sound indication of reckless or drunk driving. The stop was therefore proper.

— The analysis adds depth by applying cases that are not cited in the summary of the parties' briefs.

---

26. Thanks to Lauren Doyle, Andrea Martinez, Megan Pearl, Brianna Silva, and Rachael Williams for helping to create these bench memo examples.

The parties' briefs will be a helpful starting point for the discussion section, but you'll need to verify every case they cite and every argument they make. It's possible that both parties have missed issues or relevant cases, and it will be your job to find them. This double checking is all part of making sure that you apply the correct law to the correct facts and reach the correct conclusion.

The last step in building the discussion section is to consider what questions the judge should ask during oral argument. To highlight questions, drop a footnote describing each question and issue within the summary of the parties' arguments. These questions often highlight issues that will be decisive in a case. Consider this an opportunity to resolve any discrepancies and figure out exactly how the case should come out in the end.

The clerk's bench memo for Justice Harry Blackmun in *United States v. Nixon* not only outlined potential questions for oral argument but also described the purpose behind the question and the possible answer.[27] Justice Blackmun made notes on the memo while preparing for oral arguments. He asked three of his clerk's questions in open court, thus helping to decide that President Richard Nixon must hand over the tapes that ultimately showed the White House was involved in the Watergate scandal.

## 7. Recommendation

This final section spells out in detail the recommendation for how the court should rule. While the judge will want a definitive answer in this section, the recommendation may explain any reservations or outstanding questions you have. This section serves as your recommendation for how to proceed in the case, and at this point before oral argument, it's not always possible to have a clear resolution on the issues.

This section should represent your best advice and include a conclusion that defines the issue and summarizes the strongest reasoning. It should also describe whether this conclusion means that the court should affirm or reverse. The following example first states that the Court should affirm the lower court in *Navarette*. Then, it details the specific conclusion and the reasons supporting it.

Recommendation

I respectfully recommend that the Court affirm the lower court decision and hold that the Fourth Amendment does not require a police officer to corroborate an anonymous tip alleging reckless or drunk driving. The tip contained sufficient detail to make it reliable, and the vehicle represented an ongoing danger to public safety. In balancing the competing interests of protecting public safety and allowing drivers to be free from

27. *See, e.g.*, Johnson et al., *supra* note 12, at 21.

overly intrusive stops, the totality of the circumstances dictate that the anonymous tip created reasonable suspicion.

### Checklist for Writing a Bench Memo

———✦———

☐ Use a formal memo caption with (1) the names of the case and attorneys, and (2) the dates for oral argument and the memo's completion.

☐ Use headings for the main sections: introduction, statement of the issue and short answer, facts and procedural history, standard of review, discussion, and recommendation.

☐ Provide a succinct and helpful introduction to the facts and issue in the case.

☐ Identify the precise question and key facts in the statement of the issue.

☐ Concisely explain the answer, the most relevant law, and the supporting analysis in the short answer.

☐ Detail the legally significant facts and procedural history in narrative form for the facts section, resolving (or noting) any discrepancies and adding any background facts necessary to tie the story of the case together.

☐ Describe the standard of review concisely, using relevant rules and case law.

☐ Follow a logical organization for the discussion—addressing each question with an IRAC and CREAC structure and using introductory roadmap paragraphs and headings where appropriate.

☐ Describe the parties' arguments and approach your own analysis objectively, detailing substantive, parallel, and specific analogies and distinctions that support your conclusion.

☐ State your final conclusion and level of certainty, detailing specific reasons for both.

☐ Revise the memo for large-scale organizational issues, checking to make sure that topic sentences reflect each paragraph's substance.

☐ Proofread to ensure correct grammar, punctuation, style, and citations.

## D. MODEL BENCH MEMO WITH ANNOTATIONS

Judges use their clerks not just to write bench memos but also to debate and discuss their cases and to decide how they should be resolved. U.S. Supreme Court Justice Antonin Scalia famously employed one liberal clerk, who was urged to challenge Scalia's more conservative positions.[28]

---

28. Adam Liptak, *A Sign of the Court's Polarization*, N.Y. Times, Sept. 6, 2010.

With the increasing caseloads at courts across the country, judges rely on their clerks more than ever, expanding the clerks' role and deepening their ability to affect the law. This influence is so great that judicial clerks have been called the judge's ghostwriters and earned the nicknames of junior judge and junior justice.

The following bench memo example shows how a judicial clerk could influence a judge in an important constitutional case. The memo from *Florida v. Jardines* is addressed to Justice Scalia and analyzed whether conducting drug dog sniff of a home from a homeowner's porch violates the Fourth Amendment. In the 2013 case, Justice Scalia wrote the majority opinion and was joined by Justice Clarence Thomas as well as three of the Court's liberal-leaning justices—Ruth Bader Ginsburg, Sonia Sotomayor, and Elena Kagan—to hold that a search occurred.

## BENCH MEMO

To:                      Justice Scalia
From:               Tecumseh Kirby, Judicial Clerk
Case Name and No.:  Florida, Petitioner, v. Joelis Jardines, Respondent,
                      No. 11-564
Attorneys:          Gregory G. Garre (for the petitioner); Nicole A. Saharsky
                      (Assistant to the Solicitor General, supporting the
                      petitioner); and Howard K. Blumberg (for the respondent)
Date:               October 3, 2012
Hearing Date:      October 31, 2012

### Introduction

This Fourth Amendment case concerns the use of a well-trained, drug-detection dog on the front porch of a home. Police officers conducted a dog sniff for drugs at the front door of Joelis Jardines' house. After the dog alerted to the presence of drugs, the police obtained a search warrant, discovering that Jardines was growing marijuana in the house. The Florida Supreme Court held that the dog sniff violated the Fourth Amendment; the State of Florida asks this Court to reverse.

> This **opening** describes the basic facts and procedural history of the case.

Fourth Amendment jurisprudence provides two distinct frameworks to analyze whether this dog sniff amounts to a Fourth Amendment search: whether police physically intruded on a protected area without invitation and whether police violated the homeowner's reasonable expectation of privacy.

> This paragraph takes the larger question—did a search occur—and breaks it down into two issues, reflecting the memo's organization.

### Statement of the Issue and Short Answer

**Issue:** Is a dog sniff a Fourth Amendment search when police take a trained narcotics-detection dog to sniff at the front door of a suspected grow house?

> This broad **issue statement** includes key facts to provide context.

**Answer:** Yes. A dog sniff for drugs conducted at the front door of a house is a Fourth Amendment search requiring probable cause. Under the Fourth Amendment, a search occurs if the police violate the defendant's reasonable expectation of privacy, *Katz v. United States*, 389 U.S. 347, 361 (1967) (Harlan, J., concurring), or "physically occup[y] private property for the purpose of obtaining information," *United States v. Jones*, 132 S. Ct. 945, 949 (2012). Here, police physically intruded into Jardines' home; therefore, a search occurred.

> The **answer** is definitive and cites the rules from two leading cases in support. It ends with a conclusion specifying the strongest reason.

### Facts and Procedural History

Detective Pedraja of the Miami-Dade Police Department received an anonymous tip that Joelis Jardines was growing marijuana in his home. A month after receiving the tip, the Miami-Dade Police Department, Narcotics Bureau, and Drug Enforcement Administration agents set up surveillance outside Jardines'

> The **facts** section begins chronologically. It describes objectively and concisely what led to the dog sniff. It also introduces all the players in the case.

home. Among them was Detective Pedraja, who watched Jardines' home for approximately fifteen minutes. In that time, Detective Pedraja observed that the window blinds were closed and no vehicles were in the driveway. Detective Pedraja then approached Jardines' home with Detective Bartelt, who had just arrived at the scene with his drug-detection dog, Franky.

Here, in the most specific part of this fact section, the author details how, when, and where the dog's alert happened.

The entrance to Jardines' home is enclosed with an archway leading to the porch, which is six to eight feet from the front door. Detective Bartelt stepped onto Jardines' property with Franky on a six-foot leash. They walked up Jardines' driveway toward the front door of the home. When the drug-detection dog approached the porch, the dog circled around, sniffed, and sat down at the base of the front door—a signal that alerts his handler to the presence of drugs. Detective Bartelt then returned to the vehicle and informed Detective Pedraja of the dog's alert.

The particulars of the warrant, arrest, and motion to suppress are described next.

Based on this information, Detective Pedraja obtained a search warrant and conducted a search, revealing that Jardines was growing marijuana inside the home. Jardines was arrested and charged with trafficking in marijuana. Jardines moved to suppress the evidence seized at his home, arguing that the drug-detection dog's sniff was an impermissible search under the Fourth Amendment.

The last paragraph describes the procedural history, from the trial court ruling to this Court agreeing to hear the case.

The trial court granted Jardines' motion to suppress, ruling that the dog sniff was an illegal search. The State of Florida appealed the suppression order to the Florida Third District Court of Appeal, which reversed the order granting the motion to suppress. On petition for discretionary review, the Florida Supreme Court quashed the Third District Court of Appeal's decision and held that the dog sniff is a search violating the Fourth Amendment. This Court granted the State's petition for certiorari on January 6, 2012. 132 S. Ct. 995 (2012).

## Standard of Review

This section cites cases from the Eleventh Circuit and U.S. Supreme Court to analyze and describe that a *de novo* review applies.

On appeal, this Court reviews lower court rulings on suppression orders under a mixed standard, reviewing conclusions of law under a *de novo* standard and findings of fact for clear error. *United States v. King*, 509 F.3d 1338, 1341 (11th Cir. 2007). This case concerns Fourth Amendment rights against unreasonable search and seizure on the basis of reasonable suspicion: a question of law. Therefore, this Court reviews the lower court's conclusions of law *de novo*. *Ornelas v. United States*, 517 U.S. 690, 699 (1996).

## Analysis

The introductory **roadmap** begins with an **issue statement** and then details the broadest constitutional **rule**.

The Court must decide whether a dog sniff at the front door of a home is a Fourth Amendment search. The Fourth Amendment explicitly provides that "the right of the people to be secure in their persons, houses, papers, and effects, against unreasonable searches and seizures, shall not be violated." U.S. Const. amend. IV. At the forefront of Fourth Amendment protection is "the right of a man to retreat into his own home and there be free from unreasonable governmental intrusion." *Silverman v. United States*, 365 U.S. 505, 511 (1961). \

A Fourth Amendment search occurs when "the Government obtains information by physically intruding" on persons, houses, papers, or effects. *Jones*, 132 S. Ct. at 950-51. Until at least the latter half of the 20th century, this Court interpreted Fourth Amendment searches in terms of common-law trespass—a property-based approach. *Id.* at 950. This is a two-step analysis. First, this Court must conclude that the investigation occurred in a constitutionally protected area, one that harbors the "intimate activity associated with the 'sanctity of a man's home and the privacies of life.'" *Oliver v. United States*, 466 U.S. 170, 180 (1984). Next, this Court must determine whether the Government conducted the investigation by an unlicensed physical intrusion. *California v. Ciraolo*, 476 U.S. 207, 210 (1986).

*This paragraph begins to set up two Fourth Amendment analyses: one based on property rights and one based on privacy rights. The transition words of "First" and "Next" indicate the two-part property analysis.*

Later cases in Fourth Amendment jurisprudence deviated from the exclusively property-based approach and applied a "reasonable expectation of privacy" analysis to determine whether a search occurred. *Katz*, 389 U.S. at 361 (Harlan, J., concurring). As this Court has stated: property rights "are not the sole measure of Fourth Amendment violations." *Soldal v. Cook Cnty.*, 506 U.S. 56, 64 (1992). Under the privacy analysis, this Court must determine whether police officers' use of a trained drug-detection dog invaded Jardines' reasonable expectation of privacy. *Katz*, 389 U.S. at 361.

*This paragraph describes the memo's second analysis on privacy.*

The issues in this case are first, whether a dog sniff at the front door of a home constitutes a physical intrusion of a constitutionally protected area, and second, whether the dog sniff violates one's reasonable expectation of privacy.

*This final statement explicitly sets up the organization that follows, with the property analysis first, followed by the privacy analysis. This organization is reflected in the headings.*

### 1. Violation of Property Rights

### A. Curtilage

[Omitted]

### B. Unlicensed Physical Intrusion

Given that the investigation took place in a constitutionally protected area, the Court must then determine whether the investigation was accomplished through an unlicensed physical intrusion. Here, the officers' purpose was to conduct a search for drugs; their conduct was implicitly and explicitly unlicensed and therefore violated the Fourth Amendment.

*The **discussion** section begins by referencing the previous section for context. It then states the **conclusion** to start the **CREAC** on the next issue.*

Not all police intrusions onto the curtilage of the home equal a Fourth Amendment search, and a police officer not armed with a warrant may approach a home and knock, precisely because that is "no more than any private citizen might do." *Kentucky v. King*, 131 S. Ct. 1849, 1862, (2011). Also, consent can be implied from custom, usage, or conduct. 2 Cooley on Torts, 4th ed., § 248, p. 238. However, the implied invitation by custom to approach the front door is

*The **rule** and **explanation** sections describe the relevant law—as represented in the parties' briefs and independently researched by the judicial clerk. These sections begin with the broadest rule, followed by more specific rules and an example from Jones.*

not unlimited. *Prior v. White*, 180 So. 347, 355 (Fla. 1938). While officers are not required to close their eyes when passing by someone's home in a public area, an officer's attempts to gather information is severely constrained when he enters the Fourth Amendment's protected areas. *Ciraolo*, 476 U.S. at 213.

Courts, thus, have distinguished between a situation where a police officer approaches the front door of a house with the intent to question the occupant and a situation where the officer intends to search. *See Davis v. United States*, 327 F.2d 301, 303 (9th Cir. 1964). Moreover, as this Court stated in *Jones*, a trespass alone does not qualify as a search under the Fourth Amendment, but rather, the government must trespass with the intent to find something or to obtain information. 132 S. Ct. at 951. In *Jones*, the government's installation of a GPS device on a car and its use of the device to keep track of the car's whereabouts, equaled a Fourth Amendment search because the government physically invaded private property to obtain information. *Id.* at 949.

The three-part **analysis** section begins with a concise summary of the State's most compelling arguments, with citations to the parties' briefs and relevant cases.

The State argues that the dog sniff is not a substantial government intrusion into the sanctity of the home because neither the drug-detection dog nor the officer physically entered Jardines' home. Reply Br. at 14-15. Further, the State contends that the pathway leading up to the front door is a public place that is impliedly open to delivery persons, Girl Scout cookie sellers, and other visitors *Id.* at 10. Moreover, the State argues that the subjective intent of the officer is irrelevant. *See Ciraolo*, 476 U.S. 207, 212 (1986) (rejecting a challenge to "the authority of government to observe his activity from any vantage point or place if the viewing is motivated by a law enforcement purpose, and not the result of a casual, accidental observation"); Reply Br. 12.

Moreover, the State contends that where police may lawfully approach, knock, and interview residents at their front door, this Court has never restricted them from using traditional sense-enhancing tools. Reply Br. at 10. The use of a common detector dog on the front porch of a house does not trigger Fourth Amendment problems akin to invading the "inside" of a house with an uncommon high-tech device. *See, e.g., Jones*, 123 S. Ct. at 945; *Kyllo v. United States*, 533 U.S. 27 (2001); *United States v. Karo*, 468 U.S. 705 (1984); Reply Br. at 2. Even Jardines agrees that officers may employ field glasses and flashlights. Reply Br. 43. Therefore, the drug-detection dog and the officer never physically intruded onto a constitutionally protected area.

The second part of the analysis section summarizes the respondent's best points and strongest case.

Jardines, though, argues that the government physically trespassed onto a constitutionally protected area to obtain information without consent. He contends that consent cannot be implied, because unlike a young girl selling Girl Scout cookies, the officer here approached the front door with a drug-detection dog after receiving a tip that marijuana was being grown there. The presence of the drug-detection dog confirms that the officer was attempting to obtain information about what was going on inside the home, and this Court's Fourth Amendment jurisprudence states that government activity that reveals any intimate detail within the home is a search. *Kyllo*, 533 U.S. at 32-33; Resp. Br. 10.

A dog sniff by a drug-detection dog within the curtilage of Jardines' home is a Fourth Amendment search because the government physically trespassed onto a constitutionally protected area to obtain evidence of illegal activity. While the trespass alone would not be a search, the officers here trespassed with a drug-detection dog, which changed the nature of their presence from a visit to a search. The scope of a license, either express or implied, is limited to a particular area and a specific purpose. *See, e.g., New York v. Burger*, 482 U.S. 691, 698 (1987). Because the purpose of the officer's visit with the drug-detection dog was to find evidence of illegal activity inside the home, a search occurred.

> In the third part of the analysis section, the author provides an independent analysis that supports the conclusion. It begins with a thesis statement.

> The **conclusion** for this section focuses on only the second-step of the two-part property analysis.

### 2. Privacy Rights

[Omitted]

### Recommendation

I recommend that the Court affirm the Supreme Court of Florida and hold that the officers' investigation of Jardines' home—with the use of a trained drug-detection dog—was a Fourth Amendment search. The officers trespassed onto a constitutionally protected area without explicit or implicit invitation and searched for incriminating evidence inside the home that they would not otherwise have found. Alternatively, the use of the trained drug-detection dog on Jardines' front porch violated Jardines' reasonable expectation of privacy under *Katz*. Therefore, the officer's use of the drug-detection dog on Jardines' front porch is a Fourth Amendment search.

> The **recommendation** details the conclusion, which can be supported by either Fourth Amendment analysis.

CHAPTER

# WRITING TRIAL COURT DOCUMENTS

Good writing shapes the law. The writing by a trial court judge can be among the most powerful. With a declaration of "So Ordered," a judge can decide whether an individual goes free or to prison, whether votes will be counted in a presidential election, or whether the Constitution affords all married couples the same rights.[1]

The trial court often serves as merely the starting line for civil and criminal cases. But before a case is appealed, trial court judges draft various documents, including jury instructions and orders. This chapter explains how to write these two common types of judicial documents—and hopefully make them reversal proof.

Writing trial court documents ranges from routine to challenging. Some judges ask their judicial clerks—and even their judicial interns—to complete drafts of jury instructions and trial court orders. If the work is exceptional, the judge might not make a single revision before reading the instructions aloud at the end of a trial or before signing an order and publishing it for the world to see. But typically, writing trial court documents takes time and involves back-and-forth revisions between the judge and clerk.

Trial court orders are often appealed, and errors in jury instructions are a common basis for appeal, which can propel a case through years of

---

1. *See, e.g., Windsor v. United States*, 833 F. Supp. 2d 394 (S.D.N.Y.) *aff'd*, 699 F.3d 169 (2d Cir. 2012), *aff'd*, 133 S. Ct. 2675 (2013); *Gore v. Harris*, No. 00-2808, 2000 WL 1770257, at *1 (Fla. Cir. Ct. Dec. 4, 2000) *rev'd*, 772 So. 2d 1243 (Fla. 2000) *rev'd sub nom. Bush v. Gore*, 531 U.S. 98 (2000).

litigation in higher courts. So the goal in writing trial court documents is to make your work clear, concise, and correct. Judges, like everyone else, don't like to get it wrong.

## A. COMMON PARTS OF A TRIAL COURT ORDER

Trial court orders represent a judge's written decision and can be as short as a single sentence or span 100 pages or more. They might direct a party to act or memorialize a decision that a judge handed down in open court. The order that started the vote recount battle between rivals George W. Bush and Al Gore in 2000 contained just 59 words.[2] But many trial court orders need to detail a lengthy legal analysis. This approach allows the judge to explain the reasoning behind the decision to the parties, the public, and the appeals court.

To write a trial court order, you'll typically begin by reviewing the case file, conducting independent legal research, and drafting a research memo, like the one you learned to write in Chapter 4. Then, you can tackle writing a draft of the order one part at a time, beginning with the case caption and ending with the conclusion and judge's signature. The process requires a careful analysis of the issues and a meticulous attention to detail so that not a single comma, citation, or word is misplaced. The credibility of the writer and the court is at stake.

Trial court orders vary in style and substance, depending on the legal issues involved, the complexity of the case, and the judge's preferences. If you are writing your first trial court order, take a look at some examples from the judge who assigned the order. These orders will give you an idea of the style and format to follow and provide you with a template to create your own document. Depending on the issues at stake and the court's style, orders may contain a lengthy analysis or the judge may issue a "Memorandum," "Statement of Reasons," or "Opinion" along with the order to detail the reasoning behind a decision. To avoid confusion, this chapter will refer to all of these styles in the trial court as "orders," while the next chapter will refer to the comparable documents in the appellate court as "opinions."

Many orders will include a lengthy analysis that might seem overwhelming to emulate, but consider that you can break most down into the seven parts listed on the next page. This section of the book will guide you step by step through constructing each of these common parts of a trial court order. Then, it provides an exemplary trial court order for you to use as a model for your own work.

---

2. *Gore*, 2000 WL 1770257, at *1.

---

**Common Parts of a Trial Court Order**

1. Case Caption
2. Introduction
3. Background
4. Legal Standard
5. Discussion with Legal Analysis
6. Conclusion and Order
7. Judge's Signature and Date

---

## 1. Case Caption

Trial court orders begin with a formal caption that is straightforward. It typically identifies the court, parties, and judge for the record. The caption also provides a specific title for the order. The following example comes from the order appealed in *Florida v. Jardines*, which concerned whether police violated the Fourth Amendment by taking a drug-detection dog to the door of a suspected marijuana grow house.[3]

This example follows a standard style: The proper name for the court is at the top in all capital letters, the parties are on the left, and the case number and judge's name are on the right. It also bears a file stamp for the date that Judge William Thomas signed the order. Finally, the order has a precise title, which describes three essential parts:

1. The ruling—the judge granting the defendant's motion;
2. The type of motion being decided—a motion to suppress; and
3. The type of evidence at issue—items seized from the defendant's home.

---

IN THE CIRCUIT COURT OF THE ELEVENTH JUDICIAL
CIRCUIT IN AND FOR MIAMI-DADE COUNTY, FLORIDA

STATE OF FLORIDA          Case No. F06–40839
       Plaintiff,

vs.                   JUDGE THOMAS

JOELIS ALEX JARDINES,
      Defendant

**ORDER GRANTING DEFENDANT'S
MOTION TO SUPPRESS ITEMS SEIZED FROM HIS HOUSE**

---

3. *Florida v. Jardines*, 133 S. Ct. 1409 (2013).

## 2. Introduction

The sentences immediately following the caption introduce the order, concisely summing up the kind of dispute before the court and the judge's decision. The introduction often consists of just a few sentences and typically begins with an "Introduction" heading. The introduction acts as a thesis for the order and typically accomplishes three things:

1. It states the judge's decision.
2. It describes the motion or matter before the court.
3. It identifies the parties.

The introduction also might provide a reason for the ruling. The key is to provide the conclusion and the context for the analysis that follows—without unnecessary repetition. The following example introduces an order dismissing a defamation case. In two short paragraphs, the introduction details the chronology and procedural history of the case, names the relevant parties, and states the decision on two separate motions:

Memorandum and Order on Defendant's Motion to Dismiss

SAYLOR, District Judge.

This action arises out of an allegedly defamatory tweet. In November 2010, plaintiff Mara Feld arranged for her thoroughbred gelding, Munition, to be shipped to a horse farm. He was instead sent to a horse auction and may have eventually been slaughtered in Canada. Munition's fate became a topic of great debate on Internet sites dealing with horses. As part of that debate, defendant Crystal Conway posted the following message on her Twitter account: "Mara Feld aka Gina Holt—you are [omitted] crazy!"

Feld commenced this action against Conway on December 10, 2013, alleging defamation. Jurisdiction is based on diversity of citizenship. Conway has moved to dismiss under Federal Rule of Civil Procedure 12(b)(6), contending that the complaint fails to state a claim upon which relief can be granted. For the following reasons, the motion will be granted.[4]

Cases that involve more complicated disputes may require more context or explanation. The next opening sets up an order on a dispute that began eight years earlier. The first paragraph describes the drawn-out legal proceedings, while the second lists the court's decision on six separate claims by the plaintiff. For each, the judge provides a specific reason, which prepares the reader for the deeper analysis to come.

---

4. *Feld v. Conway*, 16 F. Supp. 3d 1, 2 (D. Mass. 2014) (footnotes omitted).

Order Re: Cross-Motions for Summary Judgment

Introduction

This lawsuit is the latest in a series of legal proceedings involving the parties. The saga began in 2007 when plaintiffs entered into a contract with a company called Corsair Marine, Inc. for the construction of a custom-built sailboat. For reasons disputed by the parties, plaintiffs' sailboat was never completed, and over the years the parties have been involved in litigation and arbitration in Vietnam, Singapore, and this Court. Plaintiffs have obtained default judgments in Singapore, and both sides have initiated proceedings in Singapore that are currently stayed due, in part, to this litigation. At different times the parties have attempted to settle their disputes by entering into agreements such as the *"Mareva* agreement" and an August 2012 settlement agreement, but unfortunately those efforts subsequently fell apart and became the subject of further litigation, including this lawsuit.

As set forth in this order, the Court grants summary judgment in favor of defendants on all claims alleged in the first amended complaint. The Court finds that plaintiffs' claim for promissory fraud in executing the *Mareva* agreement is precluded by plaintiffs' failure to rescind that agreement. The Court also concludes that plaintiffs' claims for breach of the 2007 sales contract and breach of the implied covenant of good faith and fair dealing are precluded by the *Mareva* agreement, while plaintiffs' claims arising out of an alleged breach of the *Mareva* agreement must, pursuant to that agreement, proceed in Singapore. In addition, based upon the undisputed evidence, the Court concludes that defendants did not breach the parties' August 21, 2012, settlement agreement, and the Court finds that plaintiffs have not raised a triable issue of fact on their conversion claim.[5]

## 3. Background

The background section contains the facts relevant to the order. At the trial court level, this section is typically titled "Background" or "Factual Background." At the appellate court level, it is generally titled "Statement of Facts." That's because trial courts are the triers of fact, and the facts are often in dispute.

This section should provide the story of the case, typically following a narrative, chronological organization. It should contain the following:

---

5. *Goldman v. Seawind Grp. Holdings Pty Ltd*, No. 13-CV-01759-SI, 2015 WL 433507, at *1 (N.D. Cal. Feb. 2, 2015).

1. The legally relevant facts;
2. The procedural background; and
3. Any other facts that are essential to telling the story, including those that are particularly emotional or needed for context.

WRITING TIP:
Use a balanced approach to selecting which facts to use and which to omit. Using too many means readers might have to sift through irrelevant background material. Using too few could imply to the losing side that some facts were not considered.[6]

Consider that you are telling a story. Try to include all the facts and background necessary for the reader to understand the dispute and for you to tie the story together. Keep this section concise and straightforward. Even for lengthy litigation, the background section doesn't need to overwhelm the reader with the entire history of a case. Instead, stick to the story of this particular dispute.

Cast the facts according to the legal standard in the case. For instance, an order on a motion to dismiss should accept the allegations in the complaint as true,[7] while an order on a motion for summary judgment will consider the parties' statements of "undisputed facts" and draw all reasonable inferences in the non-moving party's favor.[8]

For a relatively new case with a single cause of action, the background section might comprise a single paragraph, or the writer might weave the facts into the introduction or analysis without creating a separate section with a separate heading. In more complicated cases, like those deciding motions for summary judgment, where the outcome depends on the facts, the background section requires a more in-depth story.

To draft a background section of two or more paragraphs, follow the same organizational principles you would for a facts section in other legal documents. Break the story into short paragraphs. Use a topic sentence at the start of each of paragraph, and consider headings for any section that is more than a couple pages long. The following excerpt of a background section provides the necessary context for the court's decision to dismiss one of the plaintiff's claims—in three concise paragraphs. The lawsuit alleged that the school district discriminated against a 15-year-old based on a disability.[9]

**Order Granting Defendant's
Motion to Dismiss Second Cause of Action**

**Background**

Plaintiff Sarah Z. is a fifteen year old student at Sequoia Union High School District. Plaintiff has a speech and language impairment and is therefore eligible for special education services. Plaintiff alleges that she

---

6. Gerald Lebovits, *Ethical Judicial Writing—Part II*, 79 N.Y. St. B.J. 50, 64 (2007).

7. *Ashcroft v. Iqbal*, 556 U.S. 662, 678 (2009).

8. *Anderson v. Liberty Lobby, Inc.*, 477 U.S. 242, 255 (1986).

9. *Sarah Z. v. Sequoia Union High Sch. Dist.*, No. C 07-2389 SI, 2008 WL 410253, at *1 (N.D. Cal. Feb. 12, 2008).

has been receiving low and failing grades ever since starting school at the District because the District has failed to provide her with special educational services. Plaintiff brought this action against the District, the Office of Administrative Hearings ("OAH"), and District officials, namely Superintendent Patrick Gemma, Chief Administrator for Special Education Nikki Washington, Vice Principal Cliff Alire, speech therapist Karen McGee, and school psychologist Marian Welch.

— This first paragraph describes the parties and the plaintiff's general claim that the district failed to provide the services she needed for a disability.

Plaintiff asserts two causes of action. First, plaintiff alleges that the District violated her rights under the Individuals with Disabilities Education Act ("IDEA") by failing to provide her with a free appropriate public education ("FAPE"). Plaintiff alleges that the District did not provide her with a FAPE because it failed to, *inter alia*: (1) provide her with individual tutoring, (2) adopt and follow a behavior intervention plan, (3) offer a transition plan, (4) state dates, frequency and duration of offered services in the Individual Education Plan ("IEP"), (5) comply with the stay-put requirement while drafting the new IEP, (6) provide all services mentioned in the IEP, and (7) include plaintiff's parents' statements in the IEP.

— This paragraph begins with a topic sentence that provides a roadmap for the rest of the section.

— The paragraph then details the first claim in plaintiff's lawsuit. The defendant has not moved to dismiss this first claim; nonetheless, it is relevant to the dispute as a whole.

Plaintiff's second cause of action is against the individual defendants and the OAH for "deprivation of rights under color of authority" pursuant to 42 U.S.C. § 1983. Plaintiff alleges that the "right to sue is consistent with the statutory purpose of IDEA" and that "defendants' policies, practices and customs" were discriminatory and deliberately indifferent to the rights of disabled Americans. Defendants' present motion seeks to dismiss only plaintiff's second cause of action.[10]

— The final paragraph details the plaintiff's second claim, which is at issue in this order.

— The last sentence sets up the analysis required by the defendant's motion.

## 4. Legal Standard

The legal standard describes how a trial court views the facts and law and decides the case before it. This section corresponds to the standard of review section in an appellate opinion—and is often confused with it. While the standard of review describes the level of deference an appellate court affords a lower court decision, the legal standard describes how a court decides the dispute from the start.

In cases deciding whether to grant a motion, the court's decision depends on the legal or procedural rules governing the particular type of motion. A motion to dismiss will be granted if the plaintiff has failed "to state a claim upon which relief can be granted" per Federal Rule of Civil Procedure 12(b)(6). A motion for summary judgment will be granted if "no genuine dispute as to any material fact" exists, as Federal Rule of Civil Procedure 56 states.

---

10. *Id.* (citations, internal references omitted).

As a starting point, review the legal standard sections in the judge's recent orders on similar motions. Then, do a research check to make sure the rules and case law are up to date. Some orders copy the legal standard section verbatim from prior orders, but this replication can make a new document seem boilerplate or even lazy. Instead, try to cast the standard according to the particular facts and issues in the case. Acting New York City Supreme Court Justice Gerald Lebovits advises that judges "should consider each case anew, even if the issues seem familiar" because "a boilerplate opinion can ignore issues" and "amount to nothing more than an ill-advised judicial shortcut."[11]

The legal standard section generally includes a statement of the governing procedural rule, plus key language from opinions interpreting the rule. Procedural rules often involve burdens or presumptions that affect the analysis and ultimate decision in a case. For instance, when deciding a motion to dismiss, a court accepts the factual allegations in the complaint as true and views them in the light most favorable to the non-moving party.[12] In the next example, the judge details the 12(b)(6) procedural standard, which overlays the substantive legal issue in the case: whether a tax provision in a sales contract violates federal law.

### Legal Standard

A motion to dismiss is appropriate when a complaint fails "to state a claim upon which relief can be granted." Fed. R. Civ. P. 12(b)(6). To overcome this hurdle, a complaint must contain "a short and plain statement of the claim showing that the pleader is entitled to relief, in order to give the defendant fair notice of what the . . . claim is and the grounds upon which it rests." *Bell Atl. Corp. v. Twombly*, 550 U.S. 544, 555 (2007) (internal quotations omitted). The Court must "accept as true all of the factual allegations contained in the complaint," *Atherton v. District of Columbia*, 567 F.3d 672, 681 (D.C. Cir. 2009), and grant a plaintiff "the benefit of all inferences that can be derived from the facts alleged," *Kowal v. MCI Commc'ns Corp.*, 16 F.3d 1271, 1276 (D.C. Cir. 1994). However, the Court may not "accept inferences drawn by plaintiffs if such inferences are unsupported by the facts set out in the complaint." *Id.* In other words, "only a complaint that states a plausible claim for relief survives a motion to dismiss." *Ashcroft v. Iqbal*, 556 U.S. 662 (2009); *see also Atherton*, 567 F.3d at 681 (holding that a complaint must plead "factual content that allows the court to draw the reasonable inference that the defendant is liable for the misconduct alleged").[13]

---

11. Gerald Lebovits, *Ethical Judicial Writing—Part III*, 79 N.Y. St. B.J. 64 (2007).
12. *See, e.g., Atherton v. District of Columbia*, 567 F.3d 672, 681 (D.C. Cir. 2009).
13. *Pass v. Capital City Real Estate LLC*, 842 F. Supp. 2d 36, 38 (D.D.C. 2012).

Note how this example begins with a statement of the relevant federal rule of civil procedure and then provides interpretation of the rule from leading cases. The next excerpt from an order granting summary judgment follows the same format.

Legal Standard

> The Court will grant a motion for summary judgment where a party shows "that there is no genuine issue as to any material fact and that the movant is entitled to judgment as a matter of law." Fed. R. Civ. P. 56(c)(2). There is a genuine issue as to a material fact if "reasonable minds could differ" as to that fact. *Anderson v. Liberty Lobby, Inc.*, 477 U.S. 242, 250 (1986), *cited in Celotex Corp. v. Catrett*, 477 U.S. 317, 323, (1986). The burden is on the moving party to demonstrate that there is an "absence of a genuine issue of material fact" in dispute. *Celotex*, 477 U.S. at 323. The Court will believe the evidence of the non-moving party and will draw all reasonable inferences from the record in the non-moving party's favor. *Anderson*, 477 U.S. at 255. It is not enough, however, for the non-moving party to show that there is merely "*some* alleged factual dispute": the fact must be "material." *Id*. at 247 (emphasis in original). "Only disputes over facts that might affect the outcome of the suit under the governing law will properly preclude the entry of summary judgment." *Id*. at 248. Thus, summary judgment is appropriate if the non-movant fails to offer "evidence on which the jury could reasonably find for the [non-movant]." *Id*. at 252. "In determining a motion for summary judgment, the court may assume that facts identified by the moving party in its statement of material facts are admitted, unless such a fact is controverted in the statement of genuine issues filed in opposition to the motion." D.D.C. LCvR 7(h)(1).[14]

The legal standard section comes before the legal analysis in an order because it affects how a judge views the facts and law in a case. When drafting a trial court order, check your work by reviewing the background and legal standard sections together. Consider whether the standard requires the court to view the facts or draw inferences in a certain way. For example, an order on a motion for summary judgment requires the court to view all evidence and draw all factual inferences in a light most favorable to the non-moving party.[15] In this way, you can check your work as you move through drafting each part of your trial court order.

---

14. *Simmons v. District of Columbia*, 750 F. Supp. 2d 36, 38 (D.D.C. 2010).
15. *See, e.g., Crawford v. Carroll*, 529 F.3d 961, 964 (11th Cir. 2008).

## 5. Discussion with Legal Analysis

The legal analysis in a trial court order is much like the legal analysis in any other legal document. Judges tend to follow a common organizational structure, like those known by the acronyms "IRAC" and "CREAC." IRAC stands for Issue-Rule-Analysis-Conclusion. CREAC adds an E for the explanation of the law and begins with a conclusion instead: Conclusion-Rule-Explanation-Analysis-Conclusion.[16] To draft the discussion section, first consider whether you need to analyze one, two, or more legal issues. You will need an IRAC or CREAC for each legal issue.

You can start to identify the issues you need to analyze by reviewing the point headings from the parties' motions. A good point heading should explicitly state the legal issue. For example, a defendant's motion to dismiss in a California adverse possession case could have the following two point headings:

> I. The Motion to Dismiss Should Be Granted Because Plaintiff Has Failed to Allege That She Occupied Defendant's Land in an Open and Notorious Manner.

> II. Plaintiff States That She Rarely Trespassed on Defendant's Land and Therefore Has Failed to Allege That She Continuously Possessed the Land as California Law Requires.

After reviewing the point headings and independently researching and reviewing the law, you would discover that California law requires five elements for an adverse possession claim, including continuity of possession and open and notorious possession. After fully reviewing the record to make sure no other issues need to be analyzed, you would conclude that your opinion needs to address these two elements in a discussion with two separate CREACs.

But suppose the point headings above were vague regarding the issues to be analyzed. Your task might be more challenging, but you would reach the same result. After reviewing the facts in the record and the applicable law, you would discover that an adverse possession claim has five elements. After ruling out three elements that are not in dispute following a thorough review of the record and applicable law, you would identify the two elements that are at issue.

Depending on your research and analysis, you could then decide whether to address one or two issues in a lengthy analysis. Some cases will turn on

---

16. This same organizational framework for legal analysis is sometimes also abbreviated as BaRAC (Bold assertion-Rule-Analysis-Conclusion), CRAC (Conclusion-Rule-Analysis-Conclusion), CREXAC (Conclusion-Rule-Explanation-Analysis-Conclusion), and TREAT (Thesis-Rule-Explanation-Analysis-Thesis).

a single issue—even when multiple issues are in dispute. Because a plaintiff needs to establish each of the five elements in an adverse possession claim, for example, a court could decide the case solely on the continuity of possession element and decline to address the open and notorious question.

## a. Single-Issue Analysis

### i. *Conclusion or Issue Statement*

To draft an order analyzing a single issue, begin by outlining the legal analysis according to IRAC or CREAC—depending on your preference or the preference of the trial court or judge that assigned the order. Judges usually begin the discussion section with a conclusion or issue statement. Alternatively, they might skip to the rule if they just stated the conclusion in the introduction. The specific organization of your document will depend on the complexity of the case, the length of your order, and the judge's preferences. The goal is to make the outcome and underlying analysis clear to the reader from the start.

A conclusion in judicial writing should be authoritative and definitive. Some form of the conclusion could appear three times or more in an order. These conclusions should build on one another, rather than repeat statements word for word. Ideally, a conclusion states the following:

1. The legal issue;
2. The outcome in the case; and
3. One or more reasons in support.

Consider the following three conclusions from a trial court order that held that crew members were entitled to unpaid tips from a vessel that had filed for bankruptcy.[17]

#### 1. Introduction

Admiral has filed a motion for summary judgment on the crew members' claims for unpaid tips. For the reasons stated below, Admiral's motion is DENIED and summary judgment is entered in favor of the crew members on liability.

#### 2. Opening Conclusion in Discussion Section

Admiralty's main argument is that the crew members' claims for wages lie against the bankruptcy estate and not against the vessel—or the proceeds from the vessel's sale. I disagree.

---

17. *Admiral Cruise Servs., Inc. v. M/V ST. TROPEZ*, 524 F. Supp. 2d 1378, 1379-82 (S.D. Fla. 2007).

### 3. Closing Conclusion

The crew members have a valid lien on the proceeds from the sale of the St. Tropez. Accordingly, summary judgment is entered on liability in favor of the crew members and against Admiralty.

In the following example, U.S. District Chief Judge Royce C. Lamberth includes two conclusions—one in the Introduction and one at the end. The discussion section begins with a statement of the issue. The case concerns whether an individual who wishes to remain anonymous may quash a grand jury subpoena issued against a social networking site for records relating to his identity.[18]

### 1. Introduction

Before the Court is a Motion to Intervene and to Quash filed by the individual who utilizes the Twitter.com username [redacted] and the pseudonym [redacted] (hereinafter "Mr. X"). Mr. X seeks to quash a subpoena issued against Twitter by a federal grand jury in the District of Columbia for records pertaining to his identity. Upon consideration of the motion, the government's opposition, and the individual's reply, the Court will grant the motion to intervene and deny the motion to quash.

### 2. Discussion (Issue Statement)

Mr. X seeks to quash the subpoena directed at Twitter pursuant to Fed. R. Crim. P. 17(c), which permits a court to quash a subpoena *duces tecum* if "compliance would be unreasonable or oppressive."

### 3. Closing Conclusion

The government is investigating Mr. X for having made a *prima facie* threat of violence addressed to a major presidential candidate. The government has a compelling interest in pursuing that investigation, and Mr. X's identity must be known for the grand jury to make an informed probable cause determination.

### *ii. Rule and Explanation of Relevant Law*

The rule and explanation of the law come next. Judges describe the law authoritatively and objectively. Show confidence that you know the law and how to describe it by using forceful language here.

When outlining this section, keep in mind the hierarchy of legal authority. State constitutional provisions before statutes, and statutes before cases. Organize your rule and explanation with broad, general rules first, followed by more specific examples and quotations. This section does not

---

18. *In re Grand Jury Subpoena No. 11116275*, 846 F. Supp. 2d 1, 2-3, 4, 10 (D.D.C. 2012) (footnote omitted).

need to contain a treatise on the relevant law—just the parts of the law that are essential to justifying the decision. Cite relevant cases, but avoid lengthy string cites that bog down your document. And compare your work to examples from experts. The following rule and explanation excerpt comes from Chief Judge Lamberth's order in the case involving Mr. X and Twitter. Here, the discussion section begins with an issue statement, seen in the last example.

Discussion

Mr. X seeks to quash the subpoena directed at Twitter pursuant to Fed. R. Crim. P. 17(c), which permits a court to quash a subpoena *duces tecum* if "compliance would be unreasonable or oppressive. The public, acting through the grand jury, "has a right to every man's evidence." *United States v. Nixon*, 418 U.S. 683, 709 (1974) (quotations omitted). Although this right provides the grand jury with the concomitant power to subpoena witnesses, this power is not absolute. In particular, a grand jury may not compel testimony from an individual who holds a valid "constitutional, common-law, or statutory privilege," *id.*, because compliance in such a scenario would be "unreasonable or oppressive" for the purposes of Rule 17(c). *See, e.g., In re Grand Jury, John Doe No. G.J.2005-2*, 478 F.3d 581, 585 (4th Cir. 2007). Mr. X has a right under the First Amendment to post on the Internet, and to do so anonymously. *See McIntyre v. Ohio Elections Comm'n*, 514 U.S. 334, 357 (1995) ("Anonymity is a shield from the tyranny of the majority."); *Reno v. ACLU*, 521 U.S. 844, 870, 117 S. Ct. 2329, 138 L. Ed. 2d 874 (1997) (applying the First Amendment fully to the Internet); *see also Sinclair v. TubeSockTedD*, 596 F. Supp. 2d 128, 131 (D.D.C. 2009).

— The broad rule comes from a leading U.S. Supreme Court case.

— The explanation then narrows the reader's focus to the limitations on the rule and explains why the limitation is necessary.

— Here, Chief Judge Lamberth applies the law to advance the explanation. The first part of the holding in this order is that Mr. X has a First Amendment right to post online anonymously.

In practice, the "compelling interest" and "sufficient nexus" requirements involve a straightforward inquiry into whether the information sought is truly necessary to the grand jury's investigation. *See, e.g., In re Grand Jury Subpoenas Duces Tecum*, 78 F.3d 1307, 1312-13 (8th Cir. 1996); *In re Grand Jury Proceeding*, 842 F.2d 1229, 1236 (11th Cir. 1988) ("A good-faith criminal investigation...is a compelling interest"); *but cf., e.g., In re Grand Jury Subpoena*, 246 F.R.D. 570 (W.D. Wisc. 2007) (noting that the court was satisfied that "the government has a bona fide investigative need" to interview individuals who bought books from a target company, but requiring grand jury to solicit volunteers for interviews).[19]

— This paragraph begins by detailing the requirements of applying the rule.

— A parenthetical adds a specific example to further explain the law.

### *iii. Analysis*

Following the explanation of the law, a trial court order should analyze the relevant facts according to the law. When drafting this section, maintain

---

19. *Id.* at 4-5.

an authoritative tone. The analysis should contain no hedging or second guessing, unlike the analysis section in an internal research memorandum covered in Chapter 4, which might use qualifying language, such as "probably" and "likely."

Another difference between an objective memo and a trial court order is that an order should contain no counter-analysis. The order can describe the losing party's arguments if it is helpful to the analysis, but it must detail why those arguments are unsuccessful. The following excerpt from the analysis in the Mr. X case continues from the previous explanation example. Note how Chief Judge Lamberth supports his conclusion by first detailing Mr. X's arguments, then describing why they fail.

The analysis begins by explaining Mr. X's arguments, along with a citation to supporting authority. —

That approach [of asking for volunteers for grand jury interviews] has the benefit of easy application in many cases. Here, however, Mr. X argues that the government lacks a real investigative need for his identity. The First Amendment limits the authority of the federal government to criminalize speech, and in this context would only allow prosecution of Mr. X if his tweet constituted a "true threat." In order for a threat to be "true," its speaker must mean "to communicate a serious expression of an intent to commit an act of unlawful violence to a particular individual...." *Virginia v. Black*, 538 U.S. 343, 359 (2003). Mr. X argues that this is a purely objective test: Would a reasonable person view the statement as expressing a serious intent to cause harm? Since reasonable people viewing Mr. X's tweets do not know his identity, he posits that the grand jury need not know his identity to determine whether there exists probable cause to indict.

The analysis continues by authoritatively dismissing Mr. X's arguments, using transitions to guide the reader: "First" and "Further." —

There are many problems with this line of reasoning. First, although many circuits apply an objective test to determine whether a statement is a "true threat," *see, e.g.*, *United States v. Armel*, 585 F.3d 182, 185 (4th Cir. 2009), the D.C. Circuit has not ruled on the issue. Further, a close reading of *Black* raises doubts about an objectivity requirement. There, the Supreme Court held that the First Amendment permits criminalization of the act of burning a cross with intent to intimidate. The Court noted that, "while a burning cross does not inevitably convey a message

Short quotations and citations throughout to supporting authorities add credibility to the analysis. —

of intimidation, often the cross burner intends that the recipients of the message fear for their lives." *Black*, 538 U.S. at 357. Regardless of whether any individual act of cross-burning was objectively intimidating, the First Amendment permitted criminalization of the act when done with intent to intimidate. If that is the case, it seems odd that in other "true threat" cases the First Amendment would require *proof* of the threat's objective effect. More to the point, the Court spoke more generally of a true threat as the manifestation of a speaker's "intent of placing the victim in fear of bodily harm or death." *Id*. at 360.

Again, the focus was not on the objective effect of the threat, but on the speaker's state of mind. This Court therefore doubts the propriety of grafting an additional requirement of objective effectiveness on the crime of uttering a statement subjectively intended to cause fear. *Cf. United States v. Bagdasarian*, 652 F.3d 1113, 1117 (9th Cir. 2011) ("[W]ith respect to some threat statutes, we require that the purported threat meet an objective standard *in addition* [to a subjective standard], and for some we do not." (emphasis in original)); *id*. n. 14.

— Here, Chief Judge Lamberth provides his own interpretation of the law and describes how it affects his decision.

— The analysis here provides one reason why Mr. X's reasoning fails.

Although an objectivity requirement may seem prudent in some cases, an objective inquiry is uniquely problematic for anonymous threats—particularly those made on the Internet. *Cf. id*. at 1120 n. 20 (discussing how anonymity of threat can make threat appear more or less salient). The anonymity of a threatening communication introduces an element of ambiguity that renders an assessment of the threat's legitimacy difficult. A reasonable recipient of such a threat simply may not know whether she ought to take it seriously. Although the recipient of a threat may always have some doubt about the likelihood of the threatened act materializing—such as when the recipient is ignorant of basic details regarding the identified speaker—the recipient of a truly anonymous threat will rarely be able to assess its validity.[20]

— This part of the analysis then concludes by invoking policy considerations in convincing, plain language.

### b. Multi-Issue Discussion Sections

Many trial court orders address more than one issue. To guide the reader through the analyses of each issue, consider using headings, an introductory roadmap paragraph, or both. The trial court order at the end of this section addresses two distinct issues in a civil rights action: the plaintiff's retaliation claim and the defendants' claim that they are entitled to qualified immunity. To clearly delineate the distinct analyses within the discussion section, U.S. District Judge Susan Illston uses headings to mark the two sections.

In addition to headings, a multi-issue discussion section commonly begins with an introductory roadmap paragraph. A roadmap paragraph typically provides the broad conclusion and rules that give the necessary context for the more specific analyses that follow. A roadmap in a Fourth Amendment case involving both a search and seizure claim, for example, could begin with a broad conclusion or issue statement, followed by the broadest rule—the constitutional provision. Then, the roadmap could set up the analysis on each issue by summarizing the decision on the search and seizure issues. This summary serves as a thesis for the rest of the order and foreshadows the ultimate decision and its justification.

---

20. *Id.* at 5-6.

## 6. Conclusion and Order

Trial court orders typically end with a conclusion and language that formalizes the decision. The conclusion often restates the judge's decision concisely, providing an easy reference for readers who want to skip to the end of the document for the answer. The following conclusion and order from Sarah Z.'s case details the decision and the specific claim that it dismisses.

### Conclusion

For the foregoing reasons, the Court GRANTS defendants' motion to dismiss plaintiff's second cause of action in the First Amended Complaint.

IT IS SO ORDERED.[21]

All orders end with formal language. Typical closings include "SO ORDERED," "IT IS SO ORDERED," and "DONE AND ORDERED." If an order decides multiple motions or issues, a judge might list her decision on each motion separately under the heading, "IT IS HEREBY ORDERED." The goal of this brief section is to provide the reader a quick reference point that clearly states the judge's decision on each point in dispute.

## 7. Judge's Signature and Date

The final lines of a trial court order consist of a signature block and date. Listing the correct date on a trial court order is especially important because appellate rules define a deadline for appeals, and the countdown is calculated based on the date listed at the end of an order. These last lines include a blank line for a handwritten or electronic signature, with the judge's typed name and title below.

_____

A trial court order should be perfect—substantively and stylistically—before a judge issues it. Getting the substantive analysis correct is crucial to avoid reversal. Perfecting the style is also important for the judge's credibility. Typos, formatting problems, citation errors, unclear wording, and stilted language all affect a writer's reputation.

Once the substance of your order is completed and carefully revised, try to put it aside for a day—or even an hour—before you proofread it. Consider reading through the order once to review grammar and style and a second time to review citations. As a final step, check the formatting. Taking the revision one step at a time—just like you tackle the separate parts of your document one at a time—will help ensure that your trial court order reflects your best work. Use this checklist to guide your revisions.

_____

21. *Sarah Z.*, 2008 WL 410253, at *2-3.

## Checklist for a Trial Court Order

- ☐ In the caption, check the party names, case number, judge name, court name, and title for accuracy.
- ☐ Use headings for the main sections: introduction, background, legal standard, discussion, and conclusion and order.
- ☐ Provide a succinct and helpful introduction describing the conclusion and necessary context.
- ☐ In the background section, detail the legally significant facts in narrative form, and cast them according to the legal standard.
- ☐ In the legal standard section, describe the relevant rules and case law according to the facts and issue in the case.
- ☐ Follow a logical organization for the discussion—addressing each question with an IRAC and CREAC structure and using introductory roadmap paragraphs and headings for more complex orders.
- ☐ Approach the analysis objectively, detailing why one party's arguments prevail and why the other party's arguments lose.
- ☐ State the conclusion and order authoritatively.
- ☐ Revise the memo for large-scale organizational issues, checking to make sure that topic sentences reflect each paragraph's substance.
- ☐ Proofread to ensure correct grammar, punctuation, style, and citations.

## B. MODEL TRIAL COURT ORDER WITH ANNOTATIONS

As you construct your trial court order, try comparing your work to other examples. Orders from your jurisdiction will be most helpful for formatting and style. In addition, the following order is an excellent model to follow for writing style and organization. The order grants summary judgment in favor of a *pro se* prisoner who alleged that a prison employee retaliated against him in violation of the First Amendment. Judge Illston of the Northern District of California, who was recognized for exemplary legal writing by the Green Bag in 2013,[22] wrote the order in concise fashion, precisely following a defined IRAC structure. Consider how she put each section of the order together to best figure out how to draft an order on your own. The comments to the right of the order describe how she did it.

---

22. The Green Bag Almanac & Reader, Exemplary Legal Writing, www.greenbag.org/green_bag_press/almanacs/almanacs.html.

*Geier v. Streutker*

United States District Court, N.D. California

2012 WL 1835440, No. C 10–1965 SI (PR)

May 19, 2012

**ORDER GRANTING MOTION FOR SUMMARY JUDGMENT**

Susan Illston, District Judge.

### INTRODUCTION

This is a federal civil rights action in which a *pro se* state prisoner alleges that defendant Dr. Streutker, an employee of San Quentin State Prison, retaliated against him in violation of his First Amendment rights. Defendant moves for summary judgment. For the reasons set forth below, defendant's motion is GRANTED.

### BACKGROUND

The undisputed facts are as follows. Plaintiff underwent many dental treatments in January 2009. On June 18, 2009, plaintiff went to a dental appointment where he was seen by defendant Dr. Streutker, who looked at his tooth and determined that it should be extracted. During the appointment, a dental assistant handed Dr. Streutker a stack of at least 10 dental request forms submitted by plaintiff in the last few weeks. Streutker, as per usual practice, informed plaintiff that each time he submitted a duplicate request, the evaluation process had to start over. In his deposition, plaintiff acknowledges that Streutker, by saying this, was expressing concern about wasting dental resources. He told Streutker that other staff had advised him to submit the slips, and then questioned Streutker's level of authority. Streutker told plaintiff that she was second in authority in the dental staff. She also explained that if he abused the request slip process in the future, he would face administrative action. (Mot. for Summ. J. ("MSJ"), Grigg Decl., Ex. B (Deposition of Christopher A. Geier) at 12–15.)

Plaintiff filed a grievance regarding Streutker's statement and behavior. A dentist who reviewed his grievance wrote the following response:

> Dr. Streutker properly informed you regarding manipulation of the Health Care Request System. After you were triaged and assigned a [dental priority code] which determined your appointment time frame, you continued to place requests. We determined you did not have an urgent need and we provided your care well within the *Perez* timelines. You will not be disciplined for submitting a legitimate request, but you can for circumventing or manipulating the Health Care Services Request and Ducating [*sic*] System.

---

*Margin notes:*

The order begins with the **case caption** and a specific title for the document that states the type of motion and the decision.

The **introduction** (1) describes the dispute before the court, (2) identifies the parties, and (3) states the judge's decision. It acts as a broad conclusion or thesis statement for the order.

An introductory statement like this might seem superfluous, but identifying the "undisputed" **facts** when deciding a motion for summary judgment is key.

The second sentence sets up the chronological telling of the story.

This block quote details the plaintiff's initial grievance and quotes the defendant's response—a fact crucial to the analysis.

In the operative complaint, plaintiff alleges that Dr. Streutker violated his First Amendment right to seek dental care without retaliation. He alleges that, on June 18, 2009, Dr. Streutker "threatened to have him 'dealt with' via administrative disciplinary action" because Geier had, over a period of weeks, exercised his right to "refile unanswered requests for emergency care" and this had a chilling effect on him.

### [LEGAL STANDARD]

Summary judgment is proper when the pleadings, discovery, and affidavits demonstrate there is "no genuine dispute as to any material fact and the movant is entitled to judgment as a matter of law." Fed. R. Civ. P. 56(a). Material facts are those that may affect the outcome of the case. *Anderson v. Liberty Lobby, Inc.,* 477 U.S. 242, 248 (1986). A dispute as to a material fact is genuine if there is sufficient evidence for a reasonable jury to return a verdict for the nonmoving party. *Id.*

The party moving for summary judgment bears the initial burden of identifying those portions of the pleadings, discovery, and affidavits which demonstrate the absence of a genuine dispute of material fact. *Celotex Corp. v. Catrett,* 477 U.S. 317, 323 (1986). Where the moving party will have the burden of proof on an issue at trial, it must affirmatively demonstrate that no reasonable trier of fact could find other than for the moving party. But on an issue for which the nonmoving party will have the burden of proof at trial, the moving party need only point out "that there is an absence of evidence to support the nonmoving party's case." *Id. at* 325.

Once the moving party meets its initial burden, the nonmoving party must go beyond the pleadings to demonstrate the existence of a genuine dispute of material fact by "citing to particular parts of materials in the record" or "showing that the materials cited do not establish the absence or presence of a genuine dispute." Fed. R. Civ. P. 56(c). "This burden is not a light one. The non-moving party must show more than the mere existence of a scintilla of evidence." *In re Oracle Corp. Sec. Litig.,* 627 F.3d 376, 387 (9th Cir. 2010) (citing *Anderson,* 477 U.S. at 252). A "genuine issue for trial" exists only if there is sufficient evidence favoring the nonmoving party to allow a jury to return a verdict for that party. *Anderson,* 477 U.S. at 249. If the nonmoving party fails to make this showing, "the moving party is entitled to a judgment as a matter of law." *Celotex,* 477 U.S. at 323 n. 4.

At summary judgment, the judge must view the evidence in the light most favorable to the nonmoving party: If evidence produced by the moving party conflicts with evidence produced by the nonmoving party, the judge must assume the truth of the evidence set forth by the nonmoving party with respect to that fact. *Leslie v. Grupo ICA,* 198 F.3d 1152, 1158 (9th Cir. 1999). A court may not disregard direct evidence on the ground that no reasonable jury would believe it. *Id.*

---

*Annotations (right margin):*

A new paragraph describes the lawsuit, continuing with the chronological telling of the story of the case.

By ending with a description of the "chilling effect," Judge Illston explains the underlying reason for the dispute. She also focuses the reader on the determinative issue.

Orders deciding a motion, like one for summary judgment, often begin with a statement of the governing civil procedure rule and then include interpretation of the rule from leading cases.

The last three paragraphs of this section describe the burdens on the parties and the way the judge views the facts.

## DISCUSSION

### I. Retaliation

A simple heading shows that the following analysis addresses the plaintiff's retaliation claim.

"Within the prison context, a viable claim of First Amendment retaliation entails five basic elements: (1) An assertion that a state actor took some adverse action against an inmate (2) because of (3) that prisoner's protected conduct, and that such action (4) chilled the inmate's exercise of his First Amendment rights, and (5) the action did not reasonably advance a legitimate correctional goal." *Rhodes v. Robinson*, 408 F.3d 559, 567-68 (9th Cir. 2009) (footnote omitted). Plaintiff has the burden of showing that retaliation for the exercise of protected conduct was the "substantial" or "motivating" factor behind the defendant's actions. *Mt. Healthy City Sch. Dist. Bd. of Educ. v. Doyle*, 429 U.S. 274, 287 (1977); *Hines v. Gomez*, 108 F.3d 265, 267-68 (9th Cir. 1997). As to the fourth element, i.e., whether the inmate was chilled from exercising his First Amendment rights, a prisoner-plaintiff may allege that he suffered more than minimal harm—since such harm almost always have a chilling effect. *Rhodes*, 408 F.3d at 567-68 n. 11. That a prisoner's First Amendment rights were chilled, though not necessarily silenced, is enough. *Id.* at 569. The proper analysis is whether a person of ordinary firmness would be chilled or silenced from exercising future First Amendment rights. *Id.*

Because the conclusion and issue are stated in the introduction, Judge Illston chooses to state the **rule** to start this **IRAC**-style analysis.

Here, Judge Illston chooses to **explain** only the fourth of five elements. By narrowing the reader's focus, she concisely addresses the determinative issue.

Reading the facts in the light most favorable to plaintiff, the Court concludes that plaintiff has not pointed to evidence precluding summary judgment. *See Keenan v. Allen*, 91 F.3d 1275, 1279 (9th Cir. 1996). Specifically, plaintiff has not shown a triable issue of fact that Streutker's statements and behavior constituted retaliation. As to the first three elements of a retaliation claim, the undisputed facts show that defendant was not taking, or threatening to take, an adverse action against plaintiff. Rather, she was informing him, as she would inform any inmate in a similar position, that misuse of the slip notification system creates a delay in treatment and unnecessary work for staff. Plaintiff admitted at his deposition that he took this as Streutker's meaning. Plaintiff has not shown that her statements would chill a person of ordinary firmness or that the statement did not have a legitimate correctional goal. Specifically, it was made clear to plaintiff he could continue to file slip notifications for legitimate grievances. Only an abuse of that system would result in discipline of some sort. Having been informed by a person in authority such as defendant, he would now be able to understand how to use, rather than misuse the system. On such undisputed facts, plaintiff has not shown that a triable issue of fact exists that show that retaliation for the exercise of protected conduct was the "substantial" or "motivating" factor behind the defendant's actions. The evidence shows that plaintiff was encouraged, rather than dissuaded from, filing legitimate slip notifications, and was only dissuaded from abusing the process. On such a record, defendant's motion for summary judgment is GRANTED.

The **analysis** begins with a strong thesis statement, summarizing the conclusion and providing a broad reason for the decision.

The analysis continues by quickly addressing the first three elements.

The analysis then describes the fourth and fifth elements of the rule and further details why the plaintiff's claim fails.

The analysis of the first issue ends with a succinct **conclusion**.

## II. Qualified Immunity

Defendants contend that they are entitled to qualified immunity from plaintiff's claims. The defense of qualified immunity protects "government officials . . . from liability for civil damages insofar as their conduct does not violate clearly established statutory or constitutional rights of which a reasonable person would have known." *Harlow v. Fitzgerald*, 457 U.S. 800, 818 (1982). Under *Saucier v. Katz*, 533 U.S. 194 (2001), the court must undertake a two-step analysis when a defendant asserts qualified immunity in a motion for summary judgment. The court first faces "this threshold question: Taken in the light most favorable to the party asserting the injury, do the facts alleged show the officer's conduct violated a constitutional right?" *Saucier*, 533 U.S. at 201. If the court determines that the conduct did not violate a constitutional right, the inquiry is over and the officer is entitled to qualified immunity.

> This **IRAC**-style analysis begins with a simple heading and an **issue statement**, followed by the **rule** and a description of the two-step analysis that is required.

If the court determines that the conduct did violate a constitutional right, it then moves to the second step and asks "whether the right was clearly established" such that "it would be clear to a reasonable officer that his conduct was unlawful in the situation he confronted." *Id.* at 201-02. Even if the violated right was clearly established, qualified immunity shields an officer from suit when he makes a decision that, even if constitutionally deficient, reasonably misapprehends the law governing the circumstances he confronted. *Brosseau v. Haugen*, 543 U.S. 194, 198 (2004); *Saucier*, 533 U.S. at 205-06. If "the officer's mistake as to what the law requires is reasonable . . . the officer is entitled to the immunity defense." *Id.* at 205. Although the *Saucier* sequence is often appropriate and beneficial, it is not mandatory. A court may exercise its discretion in deciding which prong to address first, in light of the particular circumstances of each case. *See Pearson v. Callahan*, 555 U.S. 223, 236 (2008).

> This paragraph continues the **explanation** of the two-step analysis, noting that the court may exercise discretion.

As to the first prong, for the reasons discussed above, plaintiff has not shown that defendant violated a constitutional right. As to the second prong, even if plaintiff had shown that defendant had violated a constitutional right, defendant has presented evidence that she reasonably believed that she was not impinging on plaintiff's rights. Rather, the record shows that defendant was simply informing plaintiff how to use the notification system properly, and that abuse of the system creates unnecessary work and delays. Accordingly, defendant is entitled to qualified immunity.

> The **analysis** begins with a thesis that sets up the court's two-prong analysis. First, it addresses the threshold question by referencing the analysis in the first IRAC. Then, the analysis addresses the second step and describes why the defendant is entitled to immunity. This second IRAC then ends with a **conclusion**.

### CONCLUSION

For the reasons stated above, defendant's motion for summary judgment (Docket No. 50) is GRANTED. The Clerk shall enter judgment in favor of defendant, terminate Docket No. 50, and close the file.

> The order ends by restating the **conclusion** and **decision** in clear terms.

**IT IS SO ORDERED.**

## C. JURY INSTRUCTIONS

Once trial testimony, objections, and closing arguments are complete, the judge typically hands over the decision making to the men and women sitting in the jury box. Our justice system gives these ordinary citizens extraordinary authority: They can decide guilt or innocence, freedom or death, or they can make millions of dollars change hands.

Jurors receive no legal training. Their objective approach to answering the ultimate questions in a case is the foundation of the American justice system. But they do not answer those legal questions entirely on their own. The judge will instruct the jurors on the law and on how to assess the facts that they have heard and apply the legal rules. These jury instructions are meant to carefully guide the jury's decision.

Attorneys commonly submit proposed instructions for the judge to consider and, outside of the jury's earshot, debate the particular wording. Rulings on erroneous jury instructions can make once-victorious cases crumble. Take, for example, the fraud and extortion conviction of former Virginia governor Robert McDonnell, who appealed based on how the jury instructions defined a single term.[23] The government accused McDonnell of committing an "official act" in exchange for loans and gifts, so he wanted the term "official act" defined narrowly.[24] The trial judge disagreed, leaving room for a successful appeal and a unanimous Supreme Court opinion that overturned McDonnell's conviction in 2016.

The mistake in the jury instructions, Chief Justice John G. Roberts wrote, meant that McDonnell may have been convicted for conduct that is not unlawful. Even so, Chief Justice Roberts noted, "[t]here is no doubt that this case is distasteful; it may be worse than that. But our concern is not with tawdry tales of Ferraris, Rolexes, and ball gowns. It is instead with the broader legal implications of the Government's boundless interpretation of the federal bribery statute."[25] Jury instructions can present the final words of a case, so each word, each interpretation, and each point must be precise.

### Types of Jury Instructions

1. Preliminary Instructions
2. Final Instructions
3. Standardized Instructions
4. Special Instructions

---

23. *McDonnell v. United States*, 136 S. Ct. 2355 (2016).
24. *Id.* at 2361.
25. *Id.* at 2375.

Judges always charge the jury at the end of a trial, but they also may instruct juries at the beginning or in the middle. These earlier instructions vary based on the nature of case, the demands and length of a trial, preliminary rulings, and the preferences of the judge and jurisdiction. Many judges will begin a trial with these "preliminary instructions" to outline the trial process. They may choose to add instructions at this point about jurors' duties and the types of evidence that will be presented.

With the preliminary instructions, judges also might instruct jurors on their upcoming deliberations and the substantive law relating to the specific legal claims in the case—although many judges save these directives for the end of trial. Throughout the trial, judges may repeat or add to these instructions to remind jurors to be mindful of their duties. Those reminders are especially common for lengthy or high-profile cases where jurors must avoid the media or when jurors are sequestered.

Overall, the preliminary instructions aim to explain jurors' role in the trial and ward off grounds for mistrials and appeals, such as a juror visiting the scene of a crime. The following excerpt from a standard preliminary instruction used in Maine federal courts shows the level of detail in these preliminary instructions:

> To insure fairness, you as jurors must obey the following rules:
>
> First, do not talk among yourselves about this case, or about anyone involved with it, until the end of the case when you go to the jury room to decide on your verdict; . . .
>
> Fifth, do not read any news stories or articles about the case or about anyone involved with it, or listen to any radio or television reports about the case or about anyone involved with it;
>
> Sixth, do not do any research on the internet about anything in the case or consult blogs or dictionaries or other reference materials, and do not make any investigation about the case on your own;
>
> Seventh, do not discuss the case or anyone involved with it, or your status as a juror on any social media or look up any of the participants there.
>
> Eighth, if you need to communicate with me simply give a signed note to the [court security officer] to give to me.... [26]

With these specific instructions, the judge explains to jurors how they should approach the trial and how they should act in and out of court.

---

26. United States District Court for the District of Maine, Revisions to Pattern Criminal Jury Instructions for the District Courts of the First Circuit, at 19 (2016), http://www.med. uscourts.gov/pdf/crpjilinks.pdf.

Later, at the close of trial, judges will charge the jury with final instructions—whether they instructed jurors at the start or they are instructing jurors for the first time. These final jury instructions identify the issues, claims, and defenses in the case. They describe the relevant law and help jurors understand the step-by-step process for reaching their verdict.

For both preliminary and final jury instructions, judges and the parties may choose to use ready-made standardized instructions. Most states and federal circuits have standardized instructions, sometimes called pattern or model jury instructions for specific claims and defenses.[27]

But when the standardized instructions lack the detail necessary to describe a claim or fail to describe the current state of the law, attorneys may propose special instructions.[28] The parties debate the specifics of these special instructions, and the judge decides on a version to adopt. So "special instructions" refer to instructions that add specificity, clarity, or additions to the standardized or model instructions.

Attorneys regularly propose special instructions in complex litigation or in cases where claims involve overlapping areas of law. As an example, one case that involved both negligence and water law principles was reversed because the trial judge failed to use a special instruction.[29] One party claimed that her neighbor was responsible for property damage after heavy rains and flooding because the neighbor's landscaping changed the natural flow of water.[30]

The appeals court found that traditional negligence principles—and therefore the traditional instruction—was insufficient to describe the case.[31] The judge should have added a special instruction on a basic principle in water law—that property owners have a duty "to take reasonable care to avoid injury to adjacent property through the flow of surface waters."[32] This special instruction would have filled in the blanks left by the standardized instructions. That filling-in-the-blanks is a large part of what writing jury instructions is all about.

---

27. Jan Bissett & Margi Heinen, *Accurately Instructed in the Law*, 94 Mich. B.J. 28 (2015) (adding that jury instructions also may be called "jury charges" or "requests to charge").

28. Cristina Alonso, *Young Lawyer's Corner: Advice on Jury Instructions and Verdict Forms*, ABA Section of Litigation (Sept. 24, 2012), http://apps.americanbar.org/litigation/committees/appellate/email/summer2012/summer2012-0912-jury-instructions-verdict-forms-young-lawyer.html.

29. *Gdowski v. Louie*, 101 Cal. Rptr. 2d 609, 612 (2000); *see also* Elisabeth Frater, *Special Instructions: Improperly Drafted Special Jury Instructions May Result in a Reversal of Judgment*, 35 L.A. Law. 25, 27-28 (2012).

30. *Id.*

31. *Id.*

32. *Id.*

```
┌──────────────────────────────────────────────┐
│            Writing Jury Instructions           │
│  1. Review the pleadings and outline the claims. │
│  2. Compile instructions from all sources.     │
│  3. Master your subject and present a neutral  │
│     approach.                                  │
│  4. Supplement where needed.                   │
│  5. Organize the instructions logically.       │
│  6. Proofread for plain language.              │
└──────────────────────────────────────────────┘
```

## 1. Review the Pleadings and Outline the Claims

Judges frequently assign judicial clerks the task of writing jury instructions. The assignment usually means compiling, adapting, and rewriting—not crafting each line from scratch. Begin by constructing an outline of the case. Start by reviewing the case materials. Reread the complaint, which describes the causes of action; review any responsive pleadings for defenses; and check the depositions, affidavits, and other factual materials for legal theories or key terms. Finally, consult the pretrial order,[33] which sets out rulings and stipulations from before the trial began. Use these documents to construct an outline of what the jury must decide.

## 2. Compile Instructions from All Sources

Next, compile the potential instructions—from the parties, from the judge, and from your jurisdiction. The parties may have submitted their own versions of the standardized instructions and proposed special instructions. Judges also might have a cache of customary instructions,[34] which they have compiled from previous cases addressing similar issues.[35]

> RESEARCH TIP:
> To find standardized jury instructions for your case, follow these four steps:
> 1. Identify your jurisdiction.
> 2. Using online databases, like Westlaw and LexisNexis, narrow your search to "secondary sources" and then to "jury instructions."
> 3. Browse the listing and select your jurisdiction's standardized instructions.
> 4. Search for your subject matter, claims, and defenses.

---

33. Jennifer Sheppard, *The "Write" Way: A Judicial Clerk's Guide to Writing for the Court*, 38 U. Balt. L. Rev. 73 (2008).

34. *Id.*

35. Fed. Judicial Ctr., *Chambers Handbook for Judges' Law Clerks and Secretaries*, at 149-50

In nearly all jurisdictions, standardized and model instructions provide at least a baseline. Many states have approved standardized jury instructions. The Judicial Council of California has approved official civil jury instructions and verdict forms known by the acronym CACI.[36] Like many approved forms, their use is not mandatory but "strongly encouraged."[37] Other jurisdictions merely suggest instructions, like the aptly named Pennsylvania Suggested Instructions.

In the federal system, judges and attorneys use the Federal Judicial Center's pattern civil and criminal jury instructions for each circuit. Other sources include the Federal Jury Practice and Instructions, the Modern Federal Jury Instructions, and form books that include jury instructions for specialized areas of law, like patent and antitrust law.[38]

## 3. Master Your Subject and Present a Neutral Approach

Once you have assembled your sources, it's time to master each point of law in the case. That's not as daunting as it sounds. The standardized instructions provide a primer on each subject area of the law. Take, for example, the standardized instruction for a defamation claim from the Massachusetts Superior Court Civil Practice Jury Instructions:

IN GENERAL

The plaintiff has brought a suit against the defendant charging [him/her] with libel and/or slander, which is a type of defamation. Libel refers to written words that are false and defamatory, while slander refers to spoken words that are false and defamatory.

ELEMENTS—DEFAMATION OF A PRIVATE PERSON

In order to prevail on [his/her] claim for defamation, the plaintiff must prove to you by a preponderance of the evidence each of the following elements:

1. the defendant published a [false and] defamatory statement of and concerning the plaintiff;

2. the defendant

   (a) knew that the statement was false; or

   (b) acted in reckless disregard as to whether the statement was true or false; or

   (c) acted negligently in failing to ascertain whether the statement was true or false before publishing it; and

---

36. Judicial Council of California Civil Jury Instructions (2013).
37. California Rule of Court 2.1050 (2017).
38. Sheppard, *supra* note 33.

3. the defamatory statement either caused the plaintiff economic loss or was of the type that is actionable without proof of economic loss.

I will instruct you on each of these elements.[39]

These instructions explain each element in a straightforward list. They continue by defining key terms, including publication and defamatory. They also contain extensive footnotes to supporting case law and practice notes—which makes them look a lot like a secondary source you might consult when you start researching an area of law.

A federal handbook for judicial clerks advises that "jury instructions require complete mastery of the subject."[40] By using all of the sources at your disposal—from the case materials to the available instructions—you can master your subject area and construct jury instructions that will describe step by step what the jurors need to know to reach a decision.

As you fine-tune the instructions, consider that the instructions proposed by attorneys will at least subtly aim to help their side win. The final instructions cannot favor either side in their wording or directions. Instead, the instructions should guide the jury with objective wording to neutrally approach their deliberations.

## 4. Supplement Where Needed

Having a deep understanding of the issues and subject area is key because many standard instructions require more specificity and more explanation. Some instructions are generic and follow a fill-in-the-blank format. The pattern instruction on negligence in New York, for example, provides a universal explanation of "reasonably foreseeable danger" but then cautions that the instructions "should be related to the particular facts of the case" and should refer to the language from another section of the pattern instructions "where appropriate."[41] That means the judge, law clerk, or the parties must supplement the existing instructions in any negligence case.

Deciding whether to supplement the instructions you have assembled is a case-by-case decision. To figure out whether and how to adapt and expand existing instructions, consider the following: (1) the level of detail in a standardized instruction, (2) the complexity of a case, (3) any recent changes to the law, and (4) the additions proposed by the parties in special instructions. Then, construct a step-by-step guide of each point of law that the jurors need to understand to reach their decision. Consider that you may need to supplement the instructions with definitions and explanations of the claims, defenses, and damages.

---

39. Mass. Sup. Ct. Civ. Practice Jury Instr. § 6.1-2 (2014).
40. *Chambers Handbook, supra* note 35, at 149.
41. N.Y. Pattern Jury Instr. Civil § 2:12 (2016).

In addition to describing the relevant law, final jury instructions cover general rules and procedures. The following outline describes the typical parts of a complete set of final jury instructions. The model jury instructions at the end of this section show examples of most of these parts.

---

### Common Parts of Final Jury Instructions

1. General Rules
   a. Concerning jurors' duties
   b. Explaining how jurors should use their notes
   c. Explaining the burden of proof
   d. Explaining what is and what is not evidence
   e. Explaining credibility of witnesses
   f. Explaining how to consider jurors' questions of witnesses
   g. Explaining how to address lawyers' objections
2. Relevant Law
   a. Explaining  legal rules for each legal claim
   b. Explaining defenses
   c. Explaining damages
   d. Defining key terms
3. General Procedures for Deliberations
   a. Explaining how to communicate with judge
   b. Explaining requirements for unanimity

---

## 5.  Organize the Instructions Logically

Because most cases involve more than one issue, theory, or defense, jury instructions will have multiple parts. They can span a few pages or a few dozen. And because the judge reads the instructions aloud to the jury, reciting every word can take anywhere from a half-hour to several hours.[42]

Imagine listening to an hours-long lecture of jury instructions, and the need for clarity and an easy-to-follow organization becomes obvious. Consider your organization on three levels: the organization of the document as a whole, of each subject, and of each sentence.

---

42. Nancy S. Marder, *Bringing Jury Instructions into the Twenty-First Century*, 81 Notre Dame L. Rev. 449, 491 (2006).

First, develop a plan for the overall organization. Use an introduction or a roadmap to outline the subject areas to come. Then, provide clear subject headings for each part. Rules require attorneys' proposed instructions to clearly mark each section with a description and number at the top.[43] The following excerpt shows two separate instructions that led to a $140 million victory in 2016 for Terry Gene Bollea, better known as Hulk Hogan. Bollea sued Gawker Media on invasion of privacy and other claims in a case that pitted privacy against press freedom.[44]

---

### INSTRUCTION #23

#### INVASION OF PRIVACY BY INTRUSION UPON SECLUSION

The issues for you to decide on Plaintiff's claim for invasion of privacy based on intrusion are:

(1) Whether the Defendants, in posting the **VIDEO**, wrongfully intruded into a place where plaintiff had a reasonable expectation of privacy, and, if so,

(2) Whether posting the **VIDEO** would outrage of cause mental suffering, shame, humiliation or hurt feelings to a person of ordinary sensibilities.

### INSTRUCTION #24

#### INVASION OF PRIVACY BASED ON RIGHT OF PUBLICITY

The issues for you to decide on Plaintiff's claim for invasion of privacy based on common law right of publicity are:

(1) Whether the Defendants, in posting the **VIDEO** on Gawker.com, used Plaintiff's name or likeness for a commercial or advertising purpose; and if so,

(2) Whether Plaintiff gave his consent to Defendants to use his image or likeness.

*The instructions begin with numbered and descriptive headings.*

*The instructions use key legal terms and plain language to explain specifically what the jury must decide.*

*With each issue listed separately, and with each element numbered, the instructions highlight each change in subject and the specific elements required to prove each claim.*

---

After organizing the overall document, the second step is to look at the organization for each subject—each claim, each defense, and each definition. Keep in mind that the overall goal is to explain to the jury how to

---

43. *Chambers Handbook, supra* note 35, at 148 ("Counsel are instructed that each paragraph of a requested instruction be typed on a separate piece of plain, white, letter-sized paper with the description at the top and numbered, for example, as Plaintiff's Requested Jury Instruction No. 1…."). In practice, judges may combine paragraphs for readability.

44. Jury Instructions, *Bollea v. Gawker Media LLC*, No. 12012447CI-011 (Fla. 6th Cir. Mar. 18, 2016).

apply the law to the facts. Use numbered lists and bullet points to organize key information. Try to enumerate the "elements of a violation, theory, or defense so that the jurors can approach a decision step-by-step," as the federal judicial clerk handbook advises.[45] Also, make sure the instructions are not referencing abstract statements of the law but instead directly relate to the circumstances of the case.[46]

The third step in organizing jury instructions is to examine each sentence and word, making sure each one is short, simple, and straightforward. Detail specific facts, and use names instead of pronouns to keep every reference clear. When citing relevant statutes and legal rules, quote any essential language, but be wary of legalese and paraphrase legal rules if possible.[47]

A single incorrect word or confusing term could mean reversal. An appellate court in New Jersey, for example, recently required a new trial in a criminal case because the judge repeatedly used "and/or" to define what the jury was obligated to determine.[48] The court said the term was "so confusing and misleading as to engender great doubt about whether the jury was unanimous with respect to some part or all aspects of its verdict."[49] Try to use clear, straightforward language with positive, not negative wording to make the instructions clear and precise and avoid any potential misunderstanding.

Finally, review your punctuation, keeping in mind that every word will be read aloud by the judge. Commas, sentence breaks, and em dashes can create helpful pauses. Also, show what words should be emphasized with capital, bold, and underlined letters. Note how in the previous example, the instructions consistently use the word "VIDEO" and emphasize it with bold, capital letters.

The next excerpt from the jury instructions in the Hulk Hogan case shows how to organize the instructions for one claim, intentional infliction of emotional distress. Consider that the terms used in describing the elements—extreme and outrageous conduct and severe emotional distress—might seem ordinary, but because they each have a precise legal meaning, the judge takes the time to carefully define each one.

---

45. *Chambers Handbook, supra* note 35, at 149.
46. Kevin M. Fong & John M. Grenfell, *Crafting Jury Instructions to Win Trials and Appeals*, The Practical Litigator, Jan. 2009, at 39.
47. *Chambers Handbook, supra* note 35, at 149.
48. *State v. Gonzalez*, 130 A.3d 1250, 1255 (N.J. Super. Ct. App. Div. 2016).
49. *Id.*

---

**INSTRUCTION #25**

**ISSUES ON INTENTIONAL INFLICTION OF EMOTIONAL DISTRESS**

The issues for you to decide on Plaintiff's claim for intentional infliction of emotional distress are:

(1)     Whether the Defendants engaged in extreme and outrageous conduct in posting the **VIDEO** on Gawker.com; and, if so,

(2)     Whether the Defendants acted either with the intent to cause Plaintiff severe emotional distress, or acted with reckless disregard of the high probability of causing Plaintiff severe emotional distress; and if so,

(3)     Whether Plaintiff in fact suffered severe emotional distress; and if so

(4)     Whether that extreme and outrageous conduct was a legal cause of severe emotional distress.

I will now define some of these terms for you now:

Extreme and outrageous conduct is behavior, which, under the circumstances, goes well beyond all possible bounds of decency and is regarded as shocking, atrocious, and utterly intolerable in a civilized community.

Emotional distress is severe when it is of such intensity or duration that no ordinary person should be expected to endure it.

*Annotations in margin:*
— A simple heading and straightforward introduction begins this new subject area.

— With a numbered list of elements using the words "and, if so" to combine them, the judge makes clear that jurors must find each element of the claim for the plaintiff to succeed.

— Detailed definitions—and a simple introduction to them—describe key legal terms.

---

## 6. Proofread for Plain Language

Once you have sharpened the organization of the jury instructions at every level, the final step before the judge reads them to the jury is proofreading. Read the instructions aloud—not just to fix punctuation, catch typos, and refine awkward wording—but to make sure jurors can easily understand each section and each sentence. Consider that the goal of the instructions is to explain the law "in a way that makes sense" and "in language that a high school student could understand."[50]

Getting jury instructions right is an ongoing challenge. U.S. Supreme Court Justice Sandra Day O'Connor once complained that jurors are too often given "a virtually incomprehensible set of instructions and sent into the jury room to reach a verdict in a case they may not understand much better than they did before the trial began."[51]

---

50. *Chambers Handbook, supra* note 35, at 149.
51. *See* James D. Wascher, *The Long March Toward Plain English Jury Instructions*, 19 CBA Rec. 50 (2005).

Jurors may understand only half the information in their instructions.[52] One study found that many jurors did not know the definitions of key legal terms, like inference, impeach, proximate cause, and circumstantial.[53] And another study found that a majority of jurors thought that preponderance of the evidence "meant a slow, careful pondering of the testimony and exhibits."[54]

Legalese and confusing terms abound, so jurors—like law students in that lengthy lecture class—can glaze over when hearing instructions and miss key information. When writing instructions, think back to before your first day of law school, when you did not know even what a legal citation was, and prepare jury instructions that use plain, simple language.[55] Use the following checklist as a guide.

## Checklist for Writing Jury Instructions

- ☐ Use an easy-to-follow organization with numbered headings.
- ☐ Begin with a clear introduction or roadmap outlining the subject areas to come.
- ☐ Use numbered lists to keep claims, elements, and other information straight.
- ☐ Use consistent terms.
- ☐ Use short, simple sentences.
- ☐ Use positive, not negative words.
- ☐ Use active voice.
- ☐ Avoid unclear pronouns in reference to parties. (Note: "You" is correct and conversational when addressing the jury.)
- ☐ Use concrete, rather than abstract, terms.
- ☐ Use parallel construction of separate elements, clauses, and phrases to help listeners understand and remember the information.
- ☐ Avoid terms that might be confusing to listeners: homonyms (words that sound alike) and words with more than one meaning.
- ☐ Rewrite legalese, jargon, and uncommon words.
- ☐ Define any term you would not have known before going to law school and any term that has a precise legal meaning.

---

52. *Id.*
53. *Id.*
54. *Id.*
55. *See, e.g., Chambers Handbook, supra* note 35, at 148-49.

## D. MODEL JURY INSTRUCTIONS WITH ANNOTATIONS

U.S. District Judge Amul R. Thapar gave the following instructions to explain how jurors should address two claims—nuisance and trespass—in an action against a coal processing plant. The plaintiffs alleged that a layer of black, soot-like coal dust collected on their homes and yards, interfering with their lives and damaging their properties.[56]

---

56. *Barnette v. Grizzly Processing, LLC*, 809 F. Supp. 2d 636, 640 (E.D. Ky. 2011).

Jury Instruction, *Boyd v. Grizzly Processing, LLC*[57]

**Final Jury Instructions**

Now that you have heard all of the evidence, it becomes my duty to give you the instructions of the Court concerning the law applicable to this case. It is your duty as jurors to follow the law as I shall state it to you, and the facts as you shall find them from the evidence. You are not to single out one instruction alone as stating the law but must consider the instructions as a whole.

*The judge begins with a broad overview and a* **roadmap** *of the four parts of the instructions that follow.*

These instructions will be in four parts: first, some general rules that define and control your duties as jurors; second, the rules of law that you must apply in deciding whether each plaintiff has proved its case; third, some general rules that should govern your deliberations; and lastly, several verdict forms consisting of separate interrogatories which must be answered by you during your deliberations. A copy of these instructions will be available for you in the jury room.

*These* **general rules** *address questions relevant to most trials. Other issues in this part that are omitted from this excerpt include (1) how to treat jurors' notes, (2) how to view testimony, (3) what is evidence and how to view it, (4) how jurors can pose questions during deliberations, and (5) how to treat the lawyers' objections.*

### PART I—GENERAL RULES CONCERNING JURORS DUTIES
### INSTRUCTION NO. 1

Regardless of any opinion you may have as to what the law ought to be, it would be a violation of your sworn duty to base a verdict upon any other view of the law than that given in the Instructions of the Court—just as it would be a violation of your sworn duty, as judges of the facts, to base a verdict upon anything but the evidence in the case. Nothing I say in these Instructions is to be taken as an indication that I have an opinion about the facts of the case, or what that opinion is. It is not my function to determine the facts, but rather yours. You have been chosen and sworn as jurors in this case to try the issues of fact presented by the allegations of the complaint of the Plaintiffs. You are to perform this duty without bias or prejudice as to any party. Our system of law does not permit jurors to be governed by sympathy, prejudice, or public opinion. All of the parties and the public expect that you will carefully and impartially consider all the evidence in the case, follow the law as stated by the Court, and reach a just verdict, regardless of the consequences.

\* \* \*

### INSTRUCTION NO. 4
### BURDEN OF PROOF; PREPONDERANCE OF THE EVIDENCE

*The judge explains each part of the juror's deliberations, including how to view the evidence in light of the burdens and legal standards.*

The burden is on each plaintiff in a civil action such as this to prove every essential element of his or her claim by a "preponderance of the evidence." A preponderance of the evidence means such evidence as, when considered and

---

57. These instructions are condensed from Jury Instruction, *Boyd v. Grizzly Processing, LLC*, No. 10-77-ART, 2012 WL 4043404 (E.D. Ky. 2012).

compared with that opposed to it, has more convincing force and produces in your mind a belief that what is sought to be proved is more likely true than not true. In other words, to establish a claim by a "preponderance of the evidence" merely means to prove that the claim is more likely so than not so.

In determining whether any fact in issue has been proved by a preponderance of the evidence, the jury may consider the testimony of all the witnesses, regardless of who may have called them, and all exhibits received in evidence, regardless of who may have produced them. If the proof should fail to establish any essential element of each Plaintiff's claim by a preponderance of the evidence, the jury should find for the Defendants as to that claim.

\* \* \*

### PART II—RULES OF LAW
### INSTRUCTION NO. 15

I will now instruct you as to the claims of each party to the case and the law governing the case.

> Instructions on the law can follow standardized instruction forms, but they should be customized for the particular case.

### INSTRUCTION NO. 16
### DUST NUISANCE CLAIMS

Some of the Plaintiffs allege that dust from the Defendants' operations is a nuisance. These Plaintiffs are Eric and Cara Hall and Wanda L. Caudill.

In order for a Plaintiff to recover on a claim of nuisance, he or she must demonstrate, by a preponderance of the evidence, that Grizzly Processing and/or Frasure Creek caused unreasonable interference with the use and enjoyment of that Plaintiff's property. Specifically, a Plaintiff must prove both of the following:

> The instructions detail the **elements of each claim** and which party must prove the element.

1) that the presence of dust from the Defendants' operations caused unreasonable and substantial annoyance to the Plaintiff in the use and enjoyment of his or her property; AND

2) that the presence of such dust would have caused a substantial annoyance to a person of ordinary health and normal sensitivities occupying the property.

In determining whether such annoyance or interference, if any, is unreasonable, you shall take into consideration all of the circumstances of the case as shown by the evidence, including the lawful nature and location of the facility; the manner in which the facility was operated; the importance and influence of the facility on the growth and prosperity of the community; the kind, volume, and duration of the presence of dust created by the facility, if any; the respective situations of the parties; and the character and development of the neighborhood and locality in which a Plaintiff's property is located, including but not confined to existing zoning laws and regulations applicable to the Plaintiff's property.

> Here, the judge gives **additional specifics** on how the jurors should determine if the elements are met.

*A second claim appears with a second heading and a numbered list of elements. The language and structure aid the jurors' understanding.*

*The instructions on damages are omitted. In some cases, a judge would give these instructions in a bifurcated way—only after the jurors find the preceding elements to be met.*

*The closing sections give helpful reminders to the jury and help set the tone for deliberations.*

## INSTRUCTION NO. 17
### TRESPASS

Almost all of the Plaintiffs in this case allege that both Defendants have trespassed on their properties. However, Michael L. and Sabrina Boyd do not allege that Grizzly Processing trespassed on their 129 Court Street address (the Dental Office). They allege that only Frasure Creek trespassed on this property.

In order for a Plaintiff to recover on a claim of trespass, he or she must prove all of the following elements by a preponderance of the evidence:

1) the Plaintiff held title to or had a possessory interest in the property at the time of the alleged trespass; AND

2) the Defendants' operations released dust that caused damage to the Plaintiff's property; AND

3) the dust entered the Plaintiff's property without permission or invitation.

If you find that a Plaintiff has failed to prove any of these propositions by a preponderance of the evidence, then your verdict must be for Grizzly Processing and/or Frasure Creek on the Plaintiff's trespass claim.

\* \* \*

## INSTRUCTION NO. 26

Remember that you must make your decision based only on the evidence that you saw and heard here in court. Do not try to gather any information about the case on your own while you are deliberating.

For example, do not conduct any experiments inside or outside the jury room; do not bring any books, like a dictionary, or anything else with you to help you with your deliberations; do not conduct any independent research, reading, or investigation about the case, such as getting on the Internet to find out more about the case, and do not visit any of the places that were mentioned during the trial.

Make your decision based only on the evidence that you saw and heard here in Court.

## INSTRUCTION NO. 27

Let me finish up by repeating something that I said to you earlier. Nothing that I have said or done during this trial was meant to influence your decision in any way. You must decide for yourselves if each Plaintiff has proven his or her case.

# CHAPTER

# WRITING AN
# APPELLATE OPINION

The nature of injustice is that we may not always see it in our own times. The generations that wrote and ratified the Bill of Rights and the Fourteenth Amendment did not presume to know the extent of freedom in all of its dimensions, and so they entrusted to future generations a charter protecting the right of all persons to enjoy liberty as we learn its meaning. When new insight reveals discord between the Constitution's central protections and a received legal stricture, a claim to liberty must be addressed.

—U.S. Supreme Court Justice Anthony Kennedy
in *Obergefell v. Hodges*.[1]

An appellate court is the place for second chances. And plenty of people need those second chances in our legal system—like the people with the now-famous last names of Brown, Gideon, Miranda, Tinker, and Roe. Trial courts mess up sometimes, and it's up to the appellate courts to fix the mistakes and correct injustices. That's what happened when the U.S. Court of Appeals for the Fifth Circuit heard the appeal of five college students who were expelled from a state college without a hearing because they attended one protest. The trial court said the expulsion was constitutional,[2] but the appeals court righted the wrong, chastising the lower court and college for arbitrarily exercising their power over the students.[3]

---

1. 135 S. Ct. 2584, 2598 (2015).
2. *Dixon v. Ala. State Bd. of Educ.*, 186 F. Supp. 945, 952 (M.D. Ala. 1960), *rev'd*, 294 F.2d 150 (5th Cir. 1961).
3. *Dixon v. Ala. State Bd. of Educ.*, 294 F.2d 150, 157 (5th Cir. 1961).

Appellate courts review lower court rulings and write opinions detailing the reasons to affirm or reverse. But the words in an opinion do so much more: They balance inequalities, preserve order, punish crimes, and protect basic rights. A judge's clerks and interns often help research and draft opinions, so you could have the chance to help write these words and shape opinions early in your law school career.

Judges write and publish appellate opinions to explain the court's rationale and show consistency in the law by following and setting precedent. They also want to communicate with the parties, their attorneys, and the public. Some opinions are unsigned—these "per curiam" opinions are released by a few judges who make up an appellate panel or the entire court, and they tend to be brief. But most opinions are signed by the judge who authors the opinion. They can be short, reviewing a single trial court ruling, but they're often more intricate, following years of litigation and answering complex and important legal questions.

You'll go about writing an appellate opinion in much the same way as a research memo, bench memo, or trial court order. All of these judicial documents present a fair view of the facts and the law and detail a sound legal analysis. They also follow a logical organization, like IRAC or CREAC (acronyms for Issue or Conclusion, Rule and Explanation, Analysis, Conclusion). But memos and opinions have one major difference: While a bench memo recommends how a case should come out, an appellate opinion provides the answer authoritatively. An opinion will not use qualifying language, like "probably" or "likely" in its analysis or conclusion. Instead, it will definitively state a holding that answers the question on appeal.

---

### Writing an Appellate Opinion

1. Identify the Issues
2. Outline and Draft Each Section
3. Proofread to Perfection

---

## A. HOW TO WRITE AN APPELLATE OPINION

### 1. Identify the Issues

The first step in writing an opinion, as with everything else in life, is to make sure you know what you're talking about. Fortunately, with an appeals case, you should have everything you need in front of you, starting with the parties' briefs and the record.

The appellate record could have numerous documents from the lower court, like deposition transcripts, affidavits, a trial transcript, and lower court orders. These documents require a careful reading—and rereading—to grasp the nuances of the case before you. You'll also need to do your own research and analysis, using the authorities cited in the parties' briefs as a starting point. The goal throughout the research, analysis, and writing process is to ensure that you help the court consider the facts objectively, apply the law fairly, and reach an impartial decision.

Start your review of the case by identifying the issues, which you'll find in the question presented or issue statement in the parties' briefs. All briefs begin with a question presented of some form. The exact style and title vary among courts—some court rules require an "Issue Presented" or "Statement of the Issues." But whatever the name, this statement should describe the issue that the appellate court needs to review. The dueling questions in the next example show how parties present the same issue but frame it in their own terms.

### Petitioner's Question Presented

Whether the Florida Supreme Court has decided an important federal question in a way that conflicts with the established Fourth Amendment precedent of this Court by holding that an alert by a well-trained narcotics-detection dog certified to detect illegal contraband is insufficient to establish probable cause for the search of a vehicle?[4]

### Respondent's Question Presented

Does a handler's perception of a dog's alert automatically create probable cause under the Fourth Amendment to search a vehicle without a warrant when the dog had an expired drug-detector certification with a different handler and the dog's reliability with its current handler is not established?[5]

These questions reveal two issues in the case: whether the state had probable cause to search and whether the dog was reliable. U.S. Supreme Court Justice Elena Kagan addressed each of those issues in turn in her majority opinion in *Florida v. Harris*.[6]

---

4. Brief for Petitioner at *i, *Florida v. Harris*, 133 S. Ct. 1050 (2013) (No. 11-817), 2012 WL 3027354.

5. Brief for Respondent at *i, *Florida v. Harris*, 133 S. Ct. 1050 (2013) (No. 11-817), 2012 WL 3716865.

6. 133 S. Ct. 1050 (2013).

## 2. Outline and Draft Each Section

### a. Review Samples, Create a Template, and Start with the Case Caption

> ### Common Parts of an Appellate Opinion
>
> 1. Case Caption
> 2. Introduction
> 3. Standard of Review
> 4. Background
> 5. Discussion with IRAC or CREAC Analysis of Each Issue
> 6. Decision

Courts use different formats for their opinions depending on preference and the type of case. Each opinion typically includes a case caption, an introduction, a description of the standard of review, a background section, a discussion with an IRAC- or CREAC-style analysis of each issue, and a final conclusion with the court's decision. Depending on the complexity of each of these sections, an opinion may include headings, along with subheadings within the sections.

When getting ready to write an appellate opinion, review several examples from your judge and your court to create an exact template—from the case caption to the final decision. Opinions are public records, and you can find opinions from many courts on the courts' websites[7] and through services like Westlaw and LexisNexis. Keep in mind that most of the opinions in law school casebooks are excerpts, so they don't accurately reflect the many sections in a traditional opinion.

### b. Introduction

The introduction describes what the case is about. It introduces the parties, procedural history, key facts, legal issues, and the court's holding. These openings are usually only a few sentences or a few paragraphs, so the challenge is summing up key information concisely and completely. That's

---

7. For example, the U.S. Supreme Court's latest opinions can be found here: http://www.supremecourt.gov/opinions/slipopinions.aspx. A simple Internet search brings up these sites for other courts' orders and opinions: Examples include Massachusetts, www.massreports.com/SlipOps/Default.aspx, and Texas, www.supreme.courts.state.tx.us/historical/recent.asp.

what Justice Kagan does in the next example from the Fourth Amendment case, *Florida v. Harris.*

> In this case, we consider how a court should determine if the "alert" of a drug-detection dog during a traffic stop provides probable cause to search a vehicle. The Florida Supreme Court held that the State must in every case present an exhaustive set of records, including a log of the dog's performance in the field, to establish the dog's reliability. *See* 71 So. 3d 756, 775 (2011). We think that demand inconsistent with the "flexible, common-sense standard" of probable cause. *Illinois v. Gates*, 462 U.S. 213, 239 (1983).[8]

— The introduction begins with the issue, then the more specific holding from the lower court. It ends with a concise conclusion.

For cases tackling multiple issues, the challenge is condensing a complicated case to its essence. The next introduction, authored by U.S. Circuit Judge Adalberto J. Jordan, effectively hints at the overall conclusion, rather than detailing the entire five-part holding in the case. It grabs the reader's attention with a few intriguing facts, squeezes in a quick summary of the holding, and orients the reader to what's to come.

> For about eight years, James Edward Hoefling, Jr. lived on his 29-foot sailboat in state waters off the South Florida coast. In August of 2010, however, City of Miami marine patrol officers seized the sailboat and had it destroyed. According to Mr. Hoefling—who sued the City and its officers under 42 U.S.C. § 1983, federal maritime law, and state law—they did so unlawfully, without justification and without notice.

— The opening lines describe the parties, the key facts, and the core legal issue.

> Mr. Hoefling appeals from the district court's dismissal of his second amended complaint in its entirety. After a review of the record, and with the benefit of oral argument, we conclude that the district court got some things right and some things wrong. We therefore affirm in part, reverse in part, and remand for further proceedings.[9]

— After a reference to the procedural history, the court sums up the holding in broad terms.

The level of detail in an introduction varies, depending on the judge's style preference and the case itself. Some cases warrant more facts and context at the start, and some judges want to add policy or emotional appeals to set up the holding or to highlight the errors made below. In the next example, U.S. Supreme Court Justice Neil M. Gorsuch, as a U.S. circuit judge, chooses facts that stir empathy for the petitioner and the few civil liberties he still has.

> Andrew Yellowbear will probably spend the rest of his life in prison. Time he must serve for murdering his daughter. With that much lying behind and still before him, Mr. Yellowbear has found sustenance in his faith. No one doubts the sincerity of his religious beliefs or that they are the

---

8. 133 S. Ct. 1050 (2013).
9. *Hoefling v. Miami*, 811 F.3d 1271, 1274 (11th Cir. 2016).

> reason he seeks access to his prison's sweat lodge—a house of prayer and meditation the prison has supplied for those who share his Native American religious tradition. Yet the prison refuses to open the doors of that sweat lodge to Mr. Yellowbear alone, and so we have this litigation. While those convicted of crime in our society lawfully forfeit a great many civil liberties, Congress has (repeatedly) instructed that the sincere exercise of religion should not be among them—at least in the absence of a compelling reason. In this record we can find no reason like that.[10]

The *Yellowbear* introduction could have addressed the religious liberty issue more directly. But Justice Gorsuch chose instead to acknowledge the emotions that the case invokes. The result is a memorable opening that tells of the strain between Yellowbear's situation and his inability to practice his faith. The setup creates a powerful undercurrent for the rest of the opinion.

In contrast to this sympathetic approach, the next introduction shows the judge's impatience with the parties and their "shenanigans." U.S. Circuit Judge Diane P. Wood showcases a conversational, no-nonsense style in this opening.

> Deals are the stuff of legislating. Although logrolling may appear unseemly some of the time, it is not, by itself, illegal. Bribes are. This case requires us once again to decide whether some shenanigans in the Illinois General Assembly and governor's office crossed the line from the merely unseemly to the unlawful. It involves a subject we have visited in the past: two industries that compete for gambling dollars. *See Empress Casino Joliet Corp. v. Balmoral Racing Club, Inc.*, 651 F.3d 722 (7th Cir. 2011) (en banc). In 2006 and 2008, former Governor Rod Blagojevich signed into law two bills (to which we refer as the '06 and '08 Acts) that imposed a tax on certain in-state casinos of 3 percent of their revenue and placed the funds into a trust for the benefit of the horseracing industry. Smelling a rat, the plaintiff casinos brought suit under the federal Racketeering Influenced and Corrupt Organizations Act (RICO), 18 U.S.C. § 1964, alleging that the defendants, all members of the horseracing industry, had bribed the governor to ensure that the bills were enacted. Viewing the evidence in the light most favorable to the plaintiffs (and of course not vouching for anything), we conclude that there was enough to survive summary judgment on the claim that the governor agreed to sign the '08 Act in exchange for a bribe. We therefore reverse in part and remand for further proceedings on that part of the case.[11]

---

10. *Yellowbear v. Lampert*, 741 F.3d 48, 51-52 (10th Cir. 2014).
11. *Empress Casino Joliet Corp. v. Johnston*, 763 F.3d 723, 725 (7th Cir. 2014).

In some cases, judges will go even further to inject some narrative flair in their opinions. The following opening to a dissent from a denial of certiorari written by U.S. Supreme Court Chief Justice John G. Roberts has drawn attention for its crime-noir style and creativity. Even so, the introduction provides all the necessary information: the nature of the case, the parties, the key facts, the issue, the procedural history, and Chief Justice Roberts' conclusion.

> North Philly, May 4, 2001. Officer Sean Devlin, Narcotics Strike Force, was working the morning shift. Undercover surveillance. The neighborhood? Tough as a three-dollar steak. Devlin knew. Five years on the beat, nine months with the Strike Force. He'd made fifteen, twenty drug busts in the neighborhood.
>
> Devlin spotted him: a lone man on the corner. Another approached. Quick exchange of words. Cash handed over; small objects handed back. Each man then quickly on his own way. Devlin knew the guy wasn't buying bus tokens. He radioed a description and Officer Stein picked up the buyer. Sure enough: three bags of crack in the guy's pocket. Head downtown and book him. Just another day at the office.
>
> That was not good enough for the Pennsylvania Supreme Court, which held in a divided decision that the police lacked probable cause to arrest the defendant. The court concluded that a "single, isolated transaction" in a high-crime area was insufficient to justify the arrest, given that the officer did not actually see the drugs, there was no tip from an informant, and the defendant did not attempt to flee. I disagree with that conclusion, and dissent from the denial of certiorari. A drug purchase was not the only possible explanation for the defendant's conduct, but it was certainly likely enough to give rise to probable cause.[12]

This opinion is memorable—and a rarity. Chief Justice Roberts used a dissent, and not a precedent-setting majority opinion, to show off his writing panache. He also chose a criminal case that involves a serious issue but not life-and-death consequences. Still, the example shows when and how you can infuse legal writing with wit and imagination.

### c. Standard of Review

Once a case reaches an appellate court, the question before the court is not exactly the same as when the trial court decided it. The standard of review determines how much deference the appellate court should give to the

---

12. *Pennsylvania v. Dunlap*, 555 U.S. 964, 964 (2008) (Roberts, C.J., dissenting).

**RESEARCH TIP:**
To identify and under-
stand the standard
of review, start with
secondary sources for
your jurisdiction. Appel-
late practice manuals
for state and federal
courts, for instance, will
explain the standard's
scope and provide help-
ful citations to primary
authorities.

lower court's judgment. Because the trial court acts as the finder of fact, appellate courts are required to defer to the trial court's findings in some ways.

The abuse of discretion standard, for instance, means that the appellate court reverses only if the decision below was based on an erroneous conclusion of law or where the record contains no evidence that the judge could have rationally based the decision on.[13] In contrast, the *de novo* standard requires the appellate court to show no deference to the lower court's finding and to apply the same standard as the trial court, reviewing the judgment anew.[14]

To figure out the standard of review in your case, begin by reviewing the parties' briefs. Then, even when the parties do not dispute the standard of review, check their work with your own research to confirm that the standard cited by the parties is correct.

To start your research, consider that most trial court decisions are one of three types: (1) decisions of law, (2) discretionary decisions, and (3) decisions of fact. On appeal, the first type—decisions of law—are reviewed *de novo*. The second type—discretionary decisions—are reviewed under the highest standard: abuse of discretion.

Decisions of fact, the third type, also face a high standard of review on appeal. Because trial courts are the triers of fact, appellate courts show deference to trial courts' factual findings and review them under the clear error standard.[15] That means that factual findings "whether based on oral or documentary evidence, shall not be set aside unless clearly erroneous, and due regard shall be given to the opportunity of the trial court to judge of the credibility of the witnesses."[16]

Because the standard of review determines how the appeals court analyzes the facts and law, describing it before the background or discussion section makes sense. The next example details the common *de novo* standard of review.

## Standard of Review

The *de novo* standard means — that the appeals court will apply the same standard as the trial court, so this section starts by citing Rule 12(b)(6).

"We review *de novo* the trial court's dismissal of a complaint pursuant to Super. Ct. Civ. R. 12(b)(6)," and "apply the same standard as the trial court, meaning we accept the allegations of the complaint as true." *Comer v. Wells Fargo Bank, N.A.*, 108 A.3d 364, 371 (D.C. 2015). "To survive a motion to dismiss, a complaint must set forth sufficient facts

---

13. *See, e.g., Admasu v. 7-11 Food Store No. 11731G/21926D*, 108 A.3d 357, 361 (D.C. 2015).
14. *See, e.g., McCall v. D.C. Hous. Auth.*, 126 A.3d 701, 704 (D.C. 2015).
15. *House v. Bell*, 547 U.S. 518, 559 (2006); Fed. R. Civ. P. 52(a).
16. *House*, 547 U.S. at 559.

to establish the elements of a legally cognizable claim," *Woods v. District of Columbia*, 63 A.3d 551, 552-53 (D.C. 2013), containing "sufficient factual matter, accepted as true, to 'state a claim to relief that is plausible on its face.'" *Ashcroft v. Iqbal*, 556 U.S. 662, 678 (2009) (citing *Bell Atl. Corp. v. Twombly*, 550 U.S. 544, 555 (2007).[17]

*—Next, the opinion uses key language from two seminal cases.*

### d. Background

The background section tells the story of the case. It answers six basic questions about the case: Who are the parties? What happened? And where, when, why, and how did it happen?

These questions should lead you to discover all the legally significant facts. And you'll need to include all of them because omitting a key fact could affect the way that courts apply and interpret precedent. Also consider that this section tells the story of the case. Even when the case involves years of legal wrangling and the record includes boxes of documents, the background story needs to be just that—a well-told story with sparing detail. This is a section where a narrative style comes more naturally, so take advantage of the chance to spin a tale about what's most important in the case: the issues, the actions, the setting, and the people.

Start by figuring out what facts the holding depends on, and add any other facts needed for context. Take into account the parties' version of events, while keeping in mind the judge's obligation to view the case objectively. For cases without a complex or lengthy history, a judge may choose to weave all of the legally significant facts and procedural history into the introduction or analysis. But when the relevant facts of a case are particularly involved, use a separate background section with a heading. The story should be organized logically, usually by chronology. It should have short, focused paragraphs with topic sentences and transitions that guide the story of the case.

The next example by U.S. Circuit Judge Alex Kozinski details the facts and context behind a long-shot presidential candidate's constitutional complaints—and nothing more. Judges are often tackling lengthy factual histories, so shrinking this section to the basic story will take editing and time.

#### Background

Like Stephen Colbert before her, Peta Lindsay didn't want to become president of the United States. She just wanted to run. To that end, she sought a place on the 2012 presidential primary ballot for the Peace and Freedom Party. She properly filed her nomination papers

*—The story starts with a pop culture reference and the introduction of the appellant.*

---

17. *McCall*, 126 A.3d at 704-05.

*Here, Judge Kozinski resolves a discrepancy to move the story forward.*

and, as required by California law, was generally recognized as a candidate for that party. *See* Cal. Elec. Code § 6720. (In her brief, Lindsay refers to Election Code section 6041. But that section pertains to the Democratic Party. We therefore assume that she means to refer to section 6720, which pertains to the Peace and Freedom Party.)

*A transition introduces what happens next.*

Nevertheless, when California Secretary of State Debra Bowen distributed the certified list of the candidates generally recognized to be seeking their parties' nominations, Lindsay discovered that her name wasn't on it. *See* Cal. Elec. Code §§ 6722, 6951. At twenty-seven years of age, Lindsay wasn't constitutionally eligible to *be* president. *See* U.S. Const. art. II, § 1, cl. 5. But was she eligible to *run?*

*The story ends with a summary of the initial lawsuit and what led to this appeal.*

Lindsay claims she was, and so brings suit seeking vindication of her rights under the First Amendment, the Equal Protection Clause of the Fourteenth Amendment, and the Twentieth Amendment. She is joined by one of her supporters and the Peace and Freedom Party. For convenience, we will generally refer only to her.

The district court dismissed the case with prejudice and Lindsay appeals. Because the case is "capable of repetition, yet evading review," it is not moot. *See Fed. Election Comm'n v. Wis. Right to Life, Inc.*, 551 U.S. 449, 462-64 (2007).[18]

A good story makes you want to keep reading, and that's what Judge Kozinski's lively writing does here. You can read the complete opinion—with annotations describing how it's put together—at the end of this chapter.

**WRITING TIP:**
On the U.S. Supreme Court, most of the justices use the CREAC format most of the time. Chief Justice John G. Roberts and Justices Anthony Kennedy and Sonia Sotomayor occasionally use the IRAC format instead of CREAC. The late Justice Antonin Scalia always opted for IRAC. Both formats effectively convey the justices' reasoning in their opinions.

### e. Discussion

The discussion section of an opinion details the law and rationale for a decision. This section uses a logical organization, like IRAC or CREAC, for each legal issue. If the opinion addresses more than one legal issue, the opinion usually includes some form of a roadmap or umbrella paragraph to introduce the multiple issues, and it often has headings to indicate each section to help the reader follow along.

The U.S. Supreme Court and others use roman numerals to mark each section of an opinion, while some judges add short phrases. The typical format for Chief Justice Roberts is the following:

• An introduction follows the heading, "CHIEF JUSTICE ROBERTS delivered the opinion of the Court";

---

18. *Lindsay v. Bowen*, 750 F.3d 1061, 1062-63 (9th Cir. 2014).

- Section I describes the background, facts, and procedural history (possibly with subheadings of A, B, and so forth);
- Section II describes the issue and explains the law (the first parts of IRAC);
- Section III explains the parties' arguments and the Court's analysis; and
- The decision is presented in a section set apart from the previous section with three asterisks and ending with, "It is so ordered."

As an alternative, some judges prefer to title each section of their opinions with short phrases about the topics or with headings similar to point headings in appellate briefs. A basic outline for a discussion with topic headings that addresses multiple issues could look similar to the following example. The headings Judge Kozinski used in the opinion[19] are in bold.

Case caption

Introduction

  **I. BACKGROUND**

  **II. DISCUSSION**

    1. **Speedy Trial Act**

    2. **Motion to Reopen**

      a. **Surprise**

      b. **Discovery**

      c. **Prejudice**

Decision

### i. *Roadmap*

A roadmap helps everything that comes after it make sense. When an opinion addresses more than one legal issue, a roadmap explains how those issues relate to each other. Also called an umbrella section, a roadmap usually has one to a few short paragraphs. It typically includes an overall conclusion or issue statement, the overarching rule for a case, and some kind of summary of what's to come. The next example does just that. Written by U.S. Circuit Judge Frank Easterbrook, the opinion's first paragraph introduces the case and facts, and the second gives the roadmap of the opinion's three key points.

> This suit began 28 years ago and has been to the Supreme Court three times. *Nat'l Org. for Women, Inc. v. Scheidler*, 510 U.S. 249 (1994); *Scheidler v. Nat'l Org. for Women, Inc.*, 537 U.S. 393 (2003); *Scheidler v. Nat'l Org. for Women, Inc.*, 547 U.S. 9 (2006). All defendants who stuck

—The introduction begins with a broad summary. While string cites are generally not favored, this triple cite emphasizes the repetitive nature of the litigation.

---

19. *United States v. Hernandez-Meza*, 720 F.3d 760, 769-70 (9th Cir. 2013).

it out to the end (some settled) prevailed across the board. They applied for costs under 28 U.S.C. § 1920 and were awarded most of what they sought—but not until District Judge Coar held the request under advisement for three years and then retired, after which the case was transferred to District Judge Norgle. He awarded a total $63,391.45, modest for a suit that entailed discovery, a long trial, many motions in the district court, and appellate proceedings that span a generation. The costs amount to less than $2,300 per year of litigation.

*The roadmap starts by noting what the opinion will not address.*

*The three issues are in a numbered list. Then, a transition provides a simple description of the opinion's organization.*

Plaintiffs dispute some of the district judge's decisions about particular items, but we do not perceive either a clear error of fact or an abuse of discretion and have no more to say about those matters. Plaintiffs also offer three reasons why defendants should get nothing: (1) they took too long to request costs; (2) they did not establish that the transcripts and copies were "necessarily obtained for use in the case" as § 1920 requires; and (3) they did not nudge Judge Coar to rule before he retired. We consider these in turn.[20]

### ii. IRAC or CREAC Analysis of the Issues

The longest and most important part of any opinion—the discussion section—details the law and analysis for each legal issue. Most opinions follow a logical organization, usually IRAC or CREAC, for each issue. The format should feel familiar, but the authoritative tone might take some practice. Try reading the work of a few judges you admire for inspiration. The next example—the closing from Chief Justice Roberts' majority opinion in *Snyder v. Phelps*—is an excellent place to start.

> Westboro believes that America is morally flawed; many Americans might feel the same about Westboro. Westboro's funeral picketing is certainly hurtful and its contribution to public discourse may be negligible. But Westboro addressed matters of public import on public property, in a peaceful manner, in full compliance with the guidance of local officials. The speech was indeed planned to coincide with Matthew Snyder's funeral, but did not itself disrupt that funeral, and Westboro's choice to conduct its picketing at that time and place did not alter the nature of its speech.
>
> Speech is powerful. It can stir people to action, move them to tears of both joy and sorrow, and—as it did here—inflict great pain. On the facts before us, we cannot react to that pain by punishing the speaker.

---

20. *Nat'l Org. for Women, Inc. v. Scheidler*, 750 F.3d 696, 697-98 (7th Cir. 2014).

As a Nation we have chosen a different course—to protect even hurtful speech on public issues to ensure that we do not stifle public debate. That choice requires that we shield Westboro from tort liability for its picketing in this case.

The judgment of the United States Court of Appeals for the Fourth Circuit is affirmed.

*It is so ordered.*[21]

## Issue or Conclusion

You are now at the opening line for the heart of the opinion. You can start with an issue or a conclusion, depending on how much you want and need to describe up front. U.S. Supreme Court Justice Antonin Scalia began his discussions with an issue statement. The next two issue statements, in his last published opinion, introduce the two sections in the discussion in *Kansas v. Carr.*[22]

> We first turn to the Kansas Supreme Court's contention that the Eighth Amendment required these capital sentencing courts to instruct the jury that mitigating circumstances need not be proved beyond a reasonable doubt.

> We turn next to the contention that a joint capital sentencing proceeding in the Carrs' cases violated the defendants' Eighth Amendment right to an "individualized sentencing determination."

Other judges choose to provide more context and a conclusion, like the following artful example from U.S. Circuit Judge Raymond Kethledge. This conclusion paragraph begins a one-issue opinion that analyzes a term in an insurance contract.

> There are good reasons not to call an opponent's argument "ridiculous," which is what State Farm calls Barbara Bennett's principal argument here. The reasons include civility; the near-certainty that overstatement will only push the reader away (especially when, as here, the hyperbole begins on page one of the brief); and that, even where the record supports an extreme modifier, "the better practice is usually to lay out the facts and let the court reach its own conclusions." *Big Dipper Entm't, L.L.C. v. City of Warren*, 641 F.3d 715, 719 (6th Cir. 2011). But here the biggest reason is more simple: the argument that State Farm derides as ridiculous is instead correct.[23]

---

21. *Snyder v. Phelps*, 562 U.S. 443, 460-61 (2011).
22. 136 S. Ct. 633, 641, 644 (2016) (citation omitted).
23. *Bennett v. State Farm Mut. Auto. Ins. Co.*, 731 F.3d 584, 584-85 (6th Cir. 2013).

**WRITING TIP:**
An opinion is "an expla-
nation of what the law
is," says Chief Justice
John G. Roberts. He
instructs that readers
of an opinion should
"be able to look at an
opinion and leave it
with some understand-
ing [for now] and . . .
certainly for the future
as well."[24]

Note the commanding voice in each of these examples. This part of the discussion and every part that follows should have no hedging or qualifying language. "Seems to be," "probably," and "likely" don't fit with the confident voice required to render a decision.

## Rule and Explanation of Law

The rule and explanation of law can be a single sentence or span pages in an opinion. When organizing a complex rule section, start with the broadest rule and move to the more specific rules. The next example shows how to begin with the highest author-ity, then detail a particular protection, and then provide more specific examples.

The Fourth Amendment's key language is quoted, followed by an interpretation from a seminal case.

— The Fourth Amendment, as applied to the states by way of the Four-teenth Amendment protects "[t]he right of the people to be secure in their persons, houses, papers, and effects, against unreasonable searches and seizures." U.S. Const. amend. IV. For our purposes, a Fourth Amendment search occurs "when the government violates a subjective expectation of privacy that society recognizes as reason-able." *Kyllo v. United States*, 533 U.S. 27, 33 (2001).

Next comes the explanation of the historical nature of the protection.

The explanation then nar-rows its focus to the Fourth Amendment's specific protec-tion of conversations.

Examples of the varied protections of private conversations from three cases help illustrate the rule.

— Almost 50 years ago, the Supreme Court held that a "'conversation' [is] within the Fourth Amendment's protections," and that "the use of electronic devices to capture it [is] a 'search' within the meaning of the Amendment." *See Berger v. New York*, 388 U.S. 41, 51 (1967) (invalidating a New York statute that authorized the electronic inter-ception of private conversations by the police (through recording de-vices installed in various offices) pursuant to a court order, on the ground that the procedures for obtaining the order were insufficient to comply with the Warrants Clause of the Fourth Amendment). In a number of cases following *Berger*, the Supreme Court similarly ruled that the warrantless electronic interception of private conversations by the government violates the Fourth Amendment. *See Katz v. United States*, 389 U.S. 347, 353-59 (1967) (warrantless interception of con-versation conducted from public phone booth in case involving use of wires to make bets or wagers); *United States v. U.S. Dist. Ct. for E. Dist. of Mich.*, 407 U.S. 297, 318-21 (1972) (warrantless interception

This series of parentheticals describes specific examples of the Court's protection of private conversations.

of calls in case involving domestic threat to national security—a plot to bomb the office of the Central Intelligence Agency); *Mitchell v. Forsyth*, 472 U.S. 511, 531-34 (1985) (warrantless wiretap of anti-war group

---

24. Interview by Bryan A. Garner with Chief Justice John G. Roberts, 13 Scribes J. Legal Writing 8 (2010).

which had made plans to blow up heating tunnels connecting office buildings in Washington, D.C.).

*Mitchell*, while granting qualified immunity to the Attorney General because the warrantless wiretapping at issue there had been authorized prior to Katz, explained that *Katz* "held that no recognized exception to [the Fourth Amendment's] warrant requirement could justify warrantless wiretapping in an ordinary criminal case." *Mitchell*, 472 U.S. at 531. These cases stand for the now-unremarkable proposition that, because society recognizes as reasonable an expectation of privacy for confidential conversations between individuals, the government needs a warrant to intercept or record such conversations.[25]

— A description of how *Mitchell* interprets another seminal case leads to an overarching summary of the warrant requirement, which completes the explanation of the law.

## Analysis

The analysis applies the law to the facts of the case. This section should describe the arguments that support the decision, without equivocation. But it may also describe the losing party's arguments or the reasons why the lower court's decision or the dissent is wrong. The next excerpt of an analysis shows a common organization: First, Judge Kethledge describes the appellant's winning argument. Next, he takes on one of the appellee's arguments and reaches the opposite conclusion.

The argument that State Farm calls "ridiculous" is that Bennett was an occupant of the [Ford] Fusion per the policy's terms. Under Ohio law, courts construe insurance agreements "in accordance with the same rules as other written contracts." *Hybud Equip. Corp. v. Sphere Drake Ins. Co.*, 597 N.E.2d 1096, 1102 (Ohio 1992). Here, as a matter of ordinary English usage, one might be skeptical that Bennett was an "occupant" of the Fusion during the time she was on its hood. Occupants are normally inside vehicles, not on them. But the parties to a contract can define its terms as they wish; and State Farm has done so here. Its policy for the Fusion defines "occupying" as "in, on, entering or alighting from." And the parties have stipulated that Bennett was on the Fusion—specifically, on its hood—and that she "suffered further bodily injuries" while she was there. Per the policy's terms, therefore, Bennett was an "occupant" of the vehicle and thus entitled to coverage for those additional injuries.

— The analysis begins by describing Bennett's argument, then states the rule.

— Next, the judge applies the law and common understanding to the relevant contract term.

— After describing the analysis, the judge wraps up with a brief conclusion on this point.

State Farm offers some arguments in response. It argues that other courts have held that pedestrians were not "occupants" of the vehicles that struck them and hence that we should hold the same. The argument is a common one in coverage disputes: that courts have inter-

— The second paragraph describes a counterargument from the appellee.

---

25. *Gennusa v. Canova*, 748 F.3d 1103, 1109-10 (11th Cir. 2014) (some citations omitted).

<table>
<tr>
<td>

Next the analysis briefly references the relevant law.

</td>
<td>

— preted a certain "type" of provision a certain way in other cases, and that we ought to interpret the same "type" of provision the same way in ours. But "we do not construe contractual provisions in gross." *Abercrombie & Fitch Co. v. Fed. Ins. Co.*, 370 Fed. App'x 563, 573 (6th Cir. 2010) (dissenting opinion). Instead we interpret each contract individually, according to its terms. Here, in one of the cases that State Farm cites, the court did not mention any definition of the term "occupy" in the policy itself and thus gave the term its ordinary meaning.

</td>
</tr>
<tr>
<td>

Then, by applying the law to the contract provision, the judge describes why the facts here require a different outcome.

</td>
<td>

— *See Williams v. Bache*, 2000 WL 1533897, at \*2-3 (Ohio Ct. App. Oct. 11, 2000). We cannot do the same in this case, since the policy does define the term. In other cases that State Farm cites, the plaintiff was adjacent to or under the covered vehicle, rather than on it. *See, e.g., Estate of Richerson ex rel. Richerson v. Cincinnati Ins. Co.*, 264 P.3d 1087, 1088 (2011) (truck backed over decedent); *Rednour v. Hastings Mut. Ins. Co.*, 468 Mich. 241, 661 N.W.2d 562, 563 (2003) (plaintiff was changing a tire). So those cases are distinguishable on their facts.[26]

</td>
</tr>
</table>

### f. Decision

The end of an opinion gets the most attention. Lawyers and clients will jump to the end to find out how their case came out; journalists will look there for a quote or sound bite; others want to know how the opinion might affect the law. This final section has all the answers. It formalizes the analysis and conclusion on each issue by stating the court's holding. In the next example penned by Justice Scalia in *Kansas v. Carr*, he ends the majority opinion as many courts do, with common language that describes whether the court affirms or reverses and remands with instructions for the lower court.

> The judgments of the Supreme Court of Kansas are reversed, and these cases are remanded for further proceedings not inconsistent with this opinion.
>
> It is so ordered.

Because the holding sets precedent, it needs to clearly describe the scope of the court's decision. The next example from a criminal case, written by Judge Kozinski, does that and more.

> We vacate the conviction and remand for an evidentiary hearing into whether the prosecution's failure to disclose the certificate in discovery or at any point before the proofs had closed was willful. If it was willful, the district court shall impose appropriate sanctions. The district court

---

26. *Bennett*, 731 F.3d at 585.

shall, in any event, dismiss the illegal reentry count of the indictment on account of the STA violation, with or without prejudice, depending on its weighing of the relevant factors. *See* 18 U.S.C. § 3162(a)(2); *United States v. Lewis*, 349 F.3d 1116, 1121-22 (9th Cir. 2003).

We are perturbed by the district court's handling of the reopening issue. The court persisted in giving a reason for allowing the government to reopen that was contradicted by the record, despite defense counsel's repeated attempts to point out the error. The court also ignored defendant's twice-raised Rule 16 objection and made a questionable ruling regarding defendant's Speedy Trial Act claim.

"Whether or not [the district judge] would reasonably be expected to put out of his mind" his previous rulings, and "without ourselves reaching any determination as to his ability to proceed impartially, to preserve the appearance of justice, ... we conclude reassignment is appropriate," and we so order. *See Ellis v. U.S. Dist. Ct.*, 356 F.3d 1198, 1211 (9th Cir. 2004) (en banc).

**VACATED and REMANDED.** This panel retains jurisdiction over any further appeals in this case.[27]

While some conclusions are straightforward, some chastise the lower court, as Judge Kozinski's does. And some chastise the parties. Take the next example from the prolific U.S. Circuit Judge Richard Posner. He held that a student, who was suspended after school officials found marijuana in his dorm room, suffered no due process or Fourth Amendment deprivations.

In short, the case is near frivolous, the decision to sue the two student inspectors offensive, and the most surprising feature of the entire episode is the exceptional lenity with which a state university (in a state that does not allow medicinal, let alone recreational, use of marijuana) treated a brazen violator of its rules of conduct and of the criminal law. But as we noted some years ago, "the danger that without the procedural safeguards deemed appropriate in civil and criminal litigation public universities will engage in an orgy of expulsions is slight. The relation of students to universities is, after all, essentially that of customer to seller." *Osteen v. Henley*, 13 F.3d at 226. And if we may judge from the happy ending of the marijuana bust for Medlock, the customer is indeed always right.

Affirmed.[28]

---

27. *Hernandez-Meza*, 720 F.3d at 769-70.
28. *Medlock v. Trs. of Ind. Univ.*, 738 F.3d 867, 873-74 (7th Cir. 2013).

## 3. Proofread to Perfection

An appellate opinion represents not just the work of the judge or justice who authors the opinion but the work of the entire court. So making sure that the analysis and writing are flawless is vital. Grammatical errors in contracts can cost parties millions, and errors in opinions cost courts credibility. As Justice Gorsuch noted in a case that hinged on what he called a "punctuation peccadillo," grammatical errors "are syntactical sins righteously condemned by English teachers everywhere."[29] Judges share the sentiment.

The editing process for an appellate opinion is intense. Several judicial clerks and judges may work together on numerous drafts to refine the analysis before declaring it sound. Once the editing phase is complete, the judges and clerks for the entire court might review and proofread the opinion. Your proofreading should check every detail, reviewing every paragraph, every citation, every letter, every space, and every punctuation mark for spelling, grammar, style, and format. The goal is to turn out an accurate, sound, and well-written opinion that helps maintain the integrity of the judicial process. Use the following checklist to guide your revision.

### Checklist for Writing an Appellate Opinion

- ☐ In the caption, check the party names, case number, judge's name, court name, and date for accuracy.
- ☐ Choose an effective overall organization, using topic headings, point headings, or roman numerals to clearly identify the main sections: introduction, background, legal standard, discussion, and decision.
- ☐ Provide a succinct and helpful introduction describing the issue or conclusion and necessary context.
- ☐ In the background section, detail the legally significant facts and procedural history in narrative form, and cast the facts according to the standard of review.
- ☐ In the standard of review section, describe the relevant rules and case law according to the facts and issue in the case.
- ☐ Follow a logical organization for the discussion—addressing each question with an IRAC or CREAC structure and using introductory roadmap paragraphs and subheadings where appropriate.
- ☐ Approach the analysis objectively, detailing why one party's arguments prevail and why the other party's arguments lose.
- ☐ State the decision authoritatively.

---

29. *Payless Shoesource, Inc. v. Travelers Cos.*, 585 F.3d 1366, 1368 (10th Cir. 2009).

☐ Revise the memo for large-scale organizational issues, checking to make sure that topic sentences reflect each paragraph's substance.
☐ Proofread to ensure correct grammar, punctuation, style, and citations.

## B. MODEL APPELLATE OPINION WITH ANNOTATIONS

The appellate opinion provided in full on the next several pages shows how to develop an effective and well-written opinion. Judge Kozinski affirms the dismissal of a case that raises three distinct constitutional questions.

750 F.3d 1061

United States Court of Appeals for the Ninth Circuit.

Peta LINDSAY; Richard Becker; Peace and Freedom Party,
Plaintiffs–Appellants,

v.

Debra BOWEN, in her official capacity as Secretary of the State of California,
Defendant–Appellee.

Filed May 6, 2014.

**OPINION**

KOZINSKI, Chief Judge:

Like Stephen Colbert before her, Peta Lindsay didn't want to become president of the United States. She just wanted to run. To that end, she sought a place on the 2012 presidential primary ballot for the Peace and Freedom Party. She properly filed her nomination papers and, as required by California law, was generally recognized as a candidate for that party. *See* Cal. Elec. Code § 6720. (In her brief, Lindsay refers to Election Code section 6041. But that section pertains to the Democratic Party. We therefore assume that she means to refer to section 6720, which pertains to the Peace and Freedom Party.)

Nevertheless, when California Secretary of State Debra Bowen distributed the certified list of the candidates generally recognized to be seeking their parties' nominations, Lindsay discovered that her name wasn't on it. *See* Cal. Elec. Code §§ 6722, 6951. At twenty-seven years of age, Lindsay wasn't constitutionally eligible to *be* president. *See* U.S. Const. art. II, § 1, cl. 5. But was she eligible to *run*?

Lindsay claims she was, and so brings suit seeking vindication of her rights under the First Amendment, the Equal Protection Clause of the Fourteenth Amendment and the Twentieth Amendment. She is joined by one of her supporters and the Peace and Freedom Party. For convenience, we will generally refer only to her.

The district court dismissed the case with prejudice and Lindsay appeals. Because the case is "capable of repetition, yet evading review," it is not moot. *See* Fed. Election Comm'n v. Wis. Right to Life, Inc., 551 U.S. 449, 462-64 (2007).

## I. First Amendment Claims

Although regulation of who can appear on the ballot "inevitably affects" free speech, association and voting rights, *Anderson v. Celebrezze*, 460 U.S. 780, 788 (1983), we uphold restrictions that impose only a "[l]esser burden[ ]" on those rights so long as they are reasonably related to the state's "important regulatory interest [ ]," *Timmons v. Twin Cities Area New Party*, 520 U.S. 351, 358 (1997).

---

*Margin notes:*

The **caption** includes the parties' names, the date, and the judge's name. It will also include a case number.

An **introduction** begins colorfully at the start of the story.

The opening section condenses the introduction, background, and roadmap into a few short paragraphs. The **background** section tells the story of the case chronologically and covers the basic questions of who, what, where, when, why, and how.

This sentence sums up Lindsay's three constitutional claims, giving a **roadmap** of the three sections in the discussion.

This transition sets up the court's jurisdiction and the subsequent discussion.

For the first of three issues in the discussion, Judge Kozinski identifies the **issue** in the heading, followed by the **rule** statement, using a simplified **IRAC** structure.

Age requirements, like residency requirements and term limits, are "neutral candidacy qualification[s]...which the State certainly has the right to impose." *Bates v. Jones*, 131 F.3d 843, 847 (9th Cir. 1997) (en banc); *see also Rubin v. City of Santa Monica*, 308 F.3d 1008, 1014 (9th Cir. 2002) (restrictions aren't severe when they are "generally applicable, even-handed, [and] politically neutral"). Distinctions based on undisputed ineligibility due to age do not "limit political participation by an identifiable political group whose members share a particular viewpoint, associational preference or economic status." *Bates*, 131 F.3d at 847 (quoting *Anderson*, 460 U.S. at 793). They simply recognize the lines that the Constitution already draws. Any burden on Lindsay's speech and association rights is therefore minimal.

*This paragraph explains the law by describing the purpose of the requirement.*

*A transition sets up the analysis and conclusion.*

This burden is amply justified by California's asserted interest in "protecting the integrity of the election process and avoiding voter confusion." *See Timmons*, 520 U.S. at 364-65. Lindsay alleges neither that Secretary Bowen prevented other Peace and Freedom Party candidates from running nor that she interfered with Lindsay's or the party's ability to advocate for the party's platform. *See Anderson*, 460 U.S. at 791 n. 12. She argues primarily that Secretary Bowen's refusal to place her on the presidential primary ballot denied her and her party the "right to present and support an alternative to the two-party system." But there is neither any "fundamental right to run for public office," *NAACP v. Jones*, 131 F.3d 1317, 1324 (9th Cir. 1997), nor any right "to use the ballot itself to send a particularized message," *Timmons*, 520 U.S. at 363. That "a particular individual may not appear on the ballot as a particular party's candidate does not severely burden that party's associational rights." *Id.* at 359. Lindsay and the party have ways of promoting their policy agenda other than placing Lindsay's name on the ballot, such as encouraging voters to write her name in. Moreover, the voting rights of Lindsay's supporter were not severely burdened by Lindsay's exclusion from the ballot. *See Burdick v. Takushi*, 504 U.S. 428, 440 n. 10 (1992).

*The **analysis** continues the traditional IRAC structure. Judge Kozinski describes Lindsay's arguments and refutes each one, using case law for support.*

Lindsay also claims that the Secretary lacked authority to keep her off the primary ballot. She points to California Election Code section 6720, which states that the Secretary "shall place the name of a candidate upon the Peace and Freedom Party presidential preference ballot when [he] has determined that the candidate is generally advocated for or recognized throughout the United States or California as actively seeking the presidential nomination." Lindsay is free to bring such a claim in state court but it has no bearing on this lawsuit, which is based entirely on federal law.

*Here, Judge Kozinski details another of Lindsay's arguments, then decisively explains why it cannot succeed.*

Nor is this a case where a candidate's qualifications were disputed. Everyone agrees that Lindsay couldn't hold the office for which she was trying to run. Lindsay therefore could never have been a legitimate contender for the presidency, and there's no doubt that "a State has an interest, if not a duty, to protect the integrity of its political processes from frivolous or fraudulent candidacies." *See Bullock v. Carter*, 405 U.S. 134, 145 (1972). Holding that

*Judge Kozinski details an additional weakness in Lindsay's position, in the lead-up to the conclusion.*

Secretary Bowen couldn't exclude Lindsay from the ballot, despite her admission that she was underage, would mean that anyone, regardless of age, citizenship or any other constitutional ineligibility would be entitled to clutter and confuse our electoral ballot. Nothing in the First Amendment compels such an absurd result.

*The analysis ends with a convincing **conclusion** that's justified in part because the opposite holding lacks sense.*

## II. Equal Protection Claim

Lindsay claims an Equal Protection Clause violation; she says that she "is similarly situated to the other candidates...because she qualified for and won the support of the Peace and Freedom Party." To the extent this is an argument that state officials can't draw distinctions between candidates who are clearly ineligible to become president and those who aren't, it fails: "The Constitution does not require things that are different in fact or opinion to be treated in law as though they were the same." *Plyler v. Doe*, 457 U.S. 202, 216 (1982); *see also Am. Party of Tex. v. White*, 415 U.S. 767, 781 (1974). Those who can't legally assume office, even if elected, are undeniably different from those who can. Because including ineligible candidates on the ballot could easily cause voter confusion, treating ineligible candidates differently from eligible ones is rationally related to the state's interest in maintaining the integrity of the election process. *See Ventura Mobilehome Cmtys. Owners Ass'n v. City of San Buenaventura*, 371 F.3d 1046, 1055 (9th Cir. 2004).

*Judge Kozinski addresses the second issue in the discussion with a **CREAC** format, beginning with this powerful **conclusion**.*

*The **rule** from Plyler comes next, followed by an **explanation** of the law, with details from a supporting case.*

Lindsay also seems to argue that Secretary Bowen used age as a mere pretext to "singl[e] out a minor party and a particular candidate, the only African American female candidate for the Presidency...and [that the Secretary] exercised no such usurped authority, for other candidates for the Presidency, such as major party primary candidates and other similarly situated individuals." But she offers no proof, beyond conclusory allegations of discrimination, that the Secretary had any such ulterior motive. *See Ashcroft v. Iqbal*, 556 U.S. 662 (2009); *Bell Atl. Corp. v. Twombly*, 550 U.S. 544, 555-56 (2007). While claiming that similarly situated candidates were treated differently than she was, Lindsay can't identify a single person who appeared on the California ballot despite admitting that he wasn't qualified. *See N. Pacifica LLC v. City of Pacifica*, 526 F.3d 478, 486 (9th Cir. 2008); *Ventura*, 371 F.3d at 1055.

*This **analysis** section continues similarly to the first, with a description of Lindsay's major points, followed by a reasoned explanation of why they cannot survive a motion to dismiss.*

Lindsay points to 2008 presidential candidate John McCain, who some considered to be ineligible to hold office because he was born outside the United States. But, at worst, McCain's eligibility was disputed. He never *conceded* that he was ineligible to serve, and it was generally assumed that he could. The Secretary does not violate the Equal Protection Clause by excluding from the ballot candidates who are indisputably ineligible to serve, while listing those with a colorable claim of eligibility. Because those two groups stand on a different footing, the Secretary is entitled to exclude the former while including the latter. *See Robinson v. Bowen*, 567 F. Supp. 2d 1144, 1146-47 (N.D. Cal. 2008); *Keyes v. Bowen*, 117 Cal. Rptr. 3d 207, 214-16 (Cal. Ct. App. 2010).

*Here, Judge Kozinski describes an analogy that Lindsay made, then explains why it fails, using factual discrepancies and case law for support.*

### III. Dormant Twentieth Amendment Claim

The Twentieth Amendment provides that, "if the President elect shall have failed to qualify, then the Vice President elect shall act as President until a President shall have qualified; and the Congress may by law provide for the case wherein neither a President elect nor a Vice President elect shall have qualified." U.S. Const. amend. XX, § 3. Lindsay argues that this amendment prohibits states from determining the qualifications of presidential candidates.

It's far from clear that the Twentieth Amendment gives rise to a private right of action. *Cf. Golden State Transit Corp. v. City of L.A.*, 493 U.S. 103, 107 (1989) (Supremacy Clause doesn't create any enforceable rights). But, even if it does, nothing in the Twentieth Amendment states or implies that Congress has the *exclusive* authority to pass on the eligibility of candidates for president. The amendment merely grants Congress the authority to determine how to proceed *if* neither the president elect nor the vice president elect is qualified to hold office, a problem for which there was previously no express solution. *See* 75 Cong. Rec. 3831 (1932) (statement of Rep. Cable). Candidates may, of course, become ineligible to serve after they are elected (but before they start their service) due to illness or other misfortune. Or, a previously unknown ineligibility may be discerned after the election. The Twentieth Amendment addresses such contingencies. Nothing in its text or history suggests that it precludes state authorities from excluding a candidate with a known ineligibility from the presidential ballot.

**AFFIRMED.**

---

Judge Kozinski disposes of the third claim in a succinct **IRAC** here, with the issue identified in the heading, followed by the **rule** statement.

The **analysis** again explains why Lindsay's position must be rejected.

A **conclusion** ends the discussion, stating why the dismissal should be affirmed.

CHAPTER

# WRITING DISSENTS
# AND CONCURRENCES

Dissents can be fierce and fiery. They candidly explain why the outcome should be different, if not now, then in the future. A judge who disagrees with the majority opinion writes a dissent to detail why the majority got it wrong. Though they're not binding, dissents explain and publicize the losing side's rationale. In this way, dissents can persuade future courts to adopt their reasoning and overturn precedent.

U.S. Supreme Court Justice Oliver Wendell Holmes earned his reputation as the "Great Dissenter" because his minority opinions did just that. His 1919 dissent in *Abrams v. United States* helped reshape the way the country thought about free speech rights. His stirring defense of the First Amendment, with statements like "we should be eternally vigilant against attempts to check the expression of opinions that we loathe,"[1] still resonates today.

A concurring opinion, or concurrence, also can showcase the author's writing prowess. As with a dissent, one judge writes a concurrence, but other judges may join in. Judges write concurring opinions to offer a different rationale for a decision. For instance, the U.S. Supreme Court held in *Florida v. Jardines* that police cannot bring a drug-sniffing dog to a home's front porch because the Fourth Amendment protects that part of the property.[2] In a concurring opinion, U.S. Supreme Court Justice Elena Kagan agreed with the majority's rationale about property rights, but she argued that a

---

1. *Abrams v. United States*, 250 U.S. 616, 630 (1919) (Holmes, J., dissenting).
2. *Florida v. Jardines*, 133 S. Ct. 1409 (2013).

dog with specialized training also violated the homeowner's personal privacy under the Fourth Amendment.[3] The case, she wrote, could have come out in the homeowner's favor on either ground.[4]

Concurrences and dissents can be a short paragraph or span dozens of pages. But many of these minority opinions follow a familiar organizational structure known by the acronym CREAC.[5] They begin with a conclusion explaining the reason for writing separately, followed by a statement of the rule, an explanation of the law, and an account of the author's analysis. They end with a decisive conclusion. U.S. Supreme Court Justice Samuel Alito's short dissent in a case about restricting a judicial candidate's speech shows how these CREAC parts fit together.

Justice ALITO, dissenting.

*Justice Alito opens with a broad **conclusion** stating his position.*

— I largely agree with what I view as the essential elements of the dissents filed by Justices SCALIA and KENNEDY. The Florida rule before us regulates speech that is part of the process of selecting those who wield the power of the State. Such speech lies at the heart of the protection provided by the First Amendment. The Florida rule regulates that speech based on content and must therefore satisfy strict scrutiny. This means that it must be narrowly tailored to further a compelling state interest. Florida has a compelling interest in making sure that its courts decide cases impartially and in accordance with the law and that its citizens have no good reason to lack confidence that its courts are performing their proper role. But the Florida rule is not narrowly tailored to serve that interest.

*He then states the strict scrutiny **rule** and **explains** what it means for this case.*

*He sums up his analysis here to explain his **reason for writing separately**.*

*The **analysis** gets off to a forceful start with a biting analogy.*

— Indeed, this rule is about as narrowly tailored as a burlap bag. It applies to all solicitations made in the name of a candidate for judicial office—including, as was the case here, a mass mailing. It even applies to an ad in a newspaper. It applies to requests for contributions in any amount, and it applies even if the person solicited is not a lawyer, has never had any interest at stake in any case in the court in question, and has no prospect of ever having any interest at stake in any litigation in that court. If this rule can be characterized as narrowly tailored, then narrow tailoring has no meaning, and strict scrutiny, which is essential to the protection of free speech, is seriously impaired.

*The **analysis** incorporates **facts** throughout. Here, it details the reasons why the majority's holding is too broad.*

*A detailed **conclusion** explains how the majority should have shaped its holding.*

— When petitioner sent out a form letter requesting campaign contributions, she was well within her First Amendment rights. The Florida Supreme Court violated the Constitution when it imposed a financial

---

3. *Id.* at 1418-20 (Kagan, J. concurring).
4. *Id.*
5. See pages 17-18 in Chapter 4 for a complete explanation of the CREAC structure.

penalty and stained her record with a finding that she had engaged in unethical conduct. I would reverse the judgment of the Florida Supreme Court.[6]

Justice Alito's tone is sharp, as is common for dissents. Because other judges sign on to the majority opinion, it represents a harmonious or conciliatory approach. A dissent frees the writer to express a more individual interpretation of the law. For that reason, judges in dissents use first-person, singular pronouns, as Justice Alito does in his final sentence. Meanwhile, majority opinions speak for the Court and use the plural, first-person pronouns "we" and "our." Concurrences can use either, depending on whether the judge is expressing an individual view or supporting the majority approach.

Concurrences and dissents can have all the same parts as an appellate opinion, including a description of the standard of review and the facts. That's especially true if the standard is in dispute or if a dissenting judge wants to highlight certain facts that the majority opinion might have minimized. But many dissents and concurrences, like Justice Alito's in the First Amendment case, use the majority opinion as a jumping-off point and focus their words only on a specific point of contention. This chapter will show you how to write each part of a concurrence or dissent, using examples of both types of minority opinions, to guide your writing.

> **WRITING TIP:** Dissents are more interesting, according to Justice Antonin Scalia, "because they can be more the expression of the man or woman who writes them. You don't have to get permission from somebody else to put in a vivid metaphor or something like that."[7]

## A. COMMON PARTS OF A DISSENT OR CONCURRENCE

---

### Common Parts of a Dissent or Concurrence

1. Conclusion and Reason for Writing Separately
2. Rule and Explanation of the Law
3. Analysis with Incorporated Facts
4. Conclusion Describing Desired Outcome

---

6. *Williams-Yulee v. Fla. Bar*, 135 S. Ct. 1656, 1687-88 (2015) (Alito, J., dissenting).

7. Interview by Bryan A. Garner with Justice Antonin Scalia, 13 Scribes J. Legal Writing 64 (2010).

## 1. Conclusion and Reason for Writing Separately

The first step in writing a concurrence or dissent is to ask an overarching question: Is writing separately necessary? U.S. Supreme Court Chief Justice John G. Roberts aims for his Court to speak with one voice and avoid dissenting opinions whenever possible.[8] He encourages lengthy discussions among the justices at conference—the weekly meeting where the justices meet to talk about and vote on cases. And he has often achieved unanimity by encouraging the justices to craft a holding on the narrowest of grounds.[9]

Decades ago when U.S. Supreme Court Justice Ruth Bader Ginsburg was a federal appellate judge, she also argued that judges should show more restraint before writing separately.[10] In support, U.S. Circuit Judge Richard Posner reasoned that it might "sometimes be prudent to acquiesce provisionally" or "at least long enough to see how the majority's rule works."[11]

These comments reveal dedication to the back-and-forth discussions that occur among judges and their judicial clerks before a court publishes a minority opinion. Judges who are writing the majority opinion work with judges who might be considering a dissent or concurrence to try to accommodate their concerns. At all appellate courts, judges meet regularly to discuss their cases and try to build consensus.

If they fail, drafting a minority opinion can create another round of negotiations. Judges share drafts of their concurrences and dissents with the other judges and judicial clerks at their courts. A well-reasoned minority opinion could sway the other judges to change their position, effectively making a dissent or concurrence the new majority opinion. Or a minority opinion might persuade the author of the majority opinion to adjust the reasoning or holding in the opinion, leading to unanimous opinion.

Achieving unanimity can be a numbers game. With three-judge panels at intermediate courts of appeals, a single judge switching sides or altering a position can shift the balance. At state supreme courts, where the number of justices ranges from five to nine, convincing one or two justices might be all it takes to create consensus.

Even when judges continue to disagree, they still work together before publishing their majority and minority opinions by sharing drafts. This collaboration helps make the final products better. It also allows judges to sharpen their positions and reasoning.

---

8. Cass R. Sunstein, *Unanimity and Disagreement on the Supreme Court*, 100 Cornell L. Rev. 769 (2015).

9. *See, e.g.*, Nina Totenberg, *Roberts' Court Produces More Unanimous Opinions*, NPR (May 22, 2006), http://www.npr.org/templates/story/story.php?storyId=5421326

10. Ruth Bader Ginsburg, *Remarks on Writing Separately*, 65 Wash. L. Rev. 133 (1990).

11. *Id.* at 149.

When negotiations for unanimity fail, the first step in writing a concurrence or dissent is to ask a few more questions: What is the majority opinion missing? Is the holding too broad or too limited? Is the rationale shortsighted or faulty in other ways?

Judges rely on their judicial clerks and interns for help drafting their dissents and concurrences in the same way they rely on them for majority opinions. To begin, try to narrow the focus to a specific issue so you can craft a concise and precise conclusion. A good conclusion in a dissent or concurrence should have three parts: (1) a precise statement of the issue; (2) the reason for writing separately; and (3) a reason to support the dissenting or concurring view.

Conclusion statements bookend dissents and concurrences. These statements work as a thesis, so it's helpful to consider them together, even if you rewrite them through the drafting process. Notice how U.S. Supreme Court Justice Stephen Breyer's conclusions in the next example work together to first describe and then elaborate on the issue in a First Amendment case. He introduces the specific issue in the opening conclusion, explains his reason for writing separately, then provides more detail in the closing conclusion.

### Justice BREYER, concurring.

I agree with the Court and join its opinion. That opinion restricts its analysis here to the matter raised in the petition for certiorari, namely, Westboro's picketing activity. The opinion does not examine in depth the effect of television broadcasting. Nor does it say anything about Internet postings. The Court holds that the First Amendment protects the picketing that occurred here, primarily because the picketing addressed matters of "public concern."

While I agree with the Court's conclusion that the picketing addressed matters of public concern, I do not believe that our First Amendment analysis can stop at that point.

### [Closing Conclusion]

To uphold the application of state law in these circumstances would punish Westboro for seeking to communicate its views on matters of public concern without proportionately advancing the State's interest in protecting its citizens against severe emotional harm. Consequently, the First Amendment protects Westboro. As I read the Court's opinion, it holds no more.[12]

---

12. *Snyder v. Phelps*, 562 U.S. 443, 461, 462-63 (Breyer, J., concurring).

Justice Breyer's conclusions achieve three things: First, he describes the issue and the reason for writing separately. Second, he states his position, giving his answer on the legal question. And finally, he provides a specific reason to support his decision. Justice Kagan follows the same pattern in the next pair of conclusions from her dissent in a case about a police stop.

> Justice KAGAN, with whom Justice GINSBURG joins, dissenting.
>
> If a police officer stops a person on the street without reasonable suspicion, that seizure violates the Fourth Amendment. And if the officer pats down the unlawfully detained individual and finds drugs in his pocket, the State may not use the contraband as evidence in a criminal prosecution. That much is beyond dispute. The question here is whether the prohibition on admitting evidence dissolves if the officer discovers, after making the stop but before finding the drugs, that the person has an outstanding arrest warrant. Because that added wrinkle makes no difference under the Constitution, I respectfully dissent.
>
> [Closing conclusion]
>
> Because the majority thus places Fourth Amendment protections at risk, I respectfully dissent.[13]

Justice Kagan starts by framing the issue. She then skillfully weaves in what she sees as the most important fact—that the officer didn't know about the outstanding warrant until after the illegal stop—to support her conclusion. Her final statement broadly describes why she opposes the majority's decision and why she wrote separately.

In the next example, Chief Justice Roberts goes beyond the law to use policy and emotion to argue that young people can be sentenced to mandatory life sentences under the Constitution. The majority held that defendants who were under 18 when they committed their crimes cannot be sentenced to life sentences because the Constitution forbids "cruel and unusual punishments." Chief Justice Roberts acknowledges the heartbreaking consequences for his position but contends that the Court cannot answer such questions of morality.

> Chief Justice ROBERTS, with whom Justice SCALIA, Justice THOMAS, and Justice ALITO join, dissenting.
>
> Determining the appropriate sentence for a teenager convicted of murder presents grave and challenging questions of morality and social policy. Our role, however, is to apply the law, not to answer such questions. The pertinent law here is the Eighth Amendment to the Constitution, which prohibits "cruel and unusual punishments." Today, the Court in-

---

13. *Utah v. Strieff*, 136 S. Ct. 2056, 2071, 2074 (2016) (Kagan, J., dissenting).

vokes that Amendment to ban a punishment that the Court does not itself characterize as unusual, and that could not plausibly be described as such. I therefore dissent.

[Closing conclusion]

It is a great tragedy when a juvenile commits murder—most of all for the innocent victims. But also for the murderer, whose life has gone so wrong so early. And for society as well, which has lost one or more of its members to deliberate violence, and must harshly punish another. In recent years, our society has moved toward requiring that the murderer, his age notwithstanding, be imprisoned for the remainder of his life. Members of this Court may disagree with that choice. Perhaps science and policy suggest society should show greater mercy to young killers, giving them a greater chance to reform themselves at the risk that they will kill again. But that is not our decision to make. Neither the text of the Constitution nor our precedent prohibits legislatures from requiring that juvenile murderers be sentenced to life without parole. I respectfully dissent.[14]

These examples show three distinct ways to effectively craft conclusions. Justice Breyer hones in on the breadth of the majority's holding, Justice Kagan interweaves essential facts, and Chief Justice Roberts injects policy and emotion. But all explain the precise issue and the reason why they split from their colleagues to write separately.

## 2. Rule and Explanation of the Law

Even where the majority opinion meticulously explains the rules and law, a concurrence or dissent should add to it. The explanation section in a concurrence or dissent does not need a comprehensive recital of all the rules—that's what the majority opinion does. Instead, it should highlight the parts of the law that relate to the judge's difference in opinion. In this way, a judge has the freedom to shift readers' understanding of the law, to help us understand the nuances and interpretations of the law in a different way.

The majority opinion in the case about juveniles' life sentences quotes the Eighth Amendment's prohibition of "cruel and unusual punishments" and key cases that interpret it.[15] Chief Justice Roberts' dissent doesn't repeat these rules but instead focuses on language from cases that boost his argument. He begins the explanation section by concentrating on the need for an objective analysis, which he argues the majority failed to do.

---

14. *Miller v. Alabama*, 132 S. Ct. 2455, 2477, 2482 (2012) (Roberts, C.J., dissenting) (citation omitted).

15. *Id.* at 2460, 2463.

The **rule** section narrows the — focus to objective indicia to support the conclusion that the practice of sentencing juveniles to life without parole is not "unusual" under the Eighth Amendment.

The dissent cites many of the — same cases as the majority, but here, it introduces and explains an additional case, *Gregg*, to bolster the objective analysis argument.

When determining whether a punishment is cruel and unusual, this Court typically begins with "'objective indicia of society's standards, as expressed in legislative enactments and state practice.'" *Graham v. Florida*, 560 U.S. 48, 61 (2010); *see also, e.g.*, *Kennedy v. Louisiana*, 554 U.S. 407, 422 (2008); *Roper v. Simmons*, 543 U.S. 551, 564 (2005). We look to these "objective indicia" to ensure that we are not simply following our own subjective values or beliefs. *Gregg v. Georgia*, 428 U.S. 153, 173 (1976) (joint opinion of Stewart, Powell, and Stevens, JJ.). Such tangible evidence of societal standards enables us to determine whether there is a "consensus against" a given sentencing practice. *Graham*, 560 U.S. at 60. If there is, the punishment may be regarded as "unusual." But when, as here, most States formally require and frequently impose the punishment in question, there is no objective basis for that conclusion.

The dissent quotes language — from *Estelle* that the majority opinion used to set up the argument against the majority's interpretation.

The explanation concludes by — describing how the majority overstepped.

Our Eighth Amendment cases have also said that we should take guidance from "evolving standards of decency that mark the progress of a maturing society." *Ante*, at 2463 (quoting *Estelle v. Gamble*, 429 U.S. 97, 102 (1976). Mercy toward the guilty can be a form of decency, and a maturing society may abandon harsh punishments that it comes to view as unnecessary or unjust. But decency is not the same as leniency. A decent society protects the innocent from violence. A mature society may determine that this requires removing those guilty of the most heinous murders from its midst, both as protection for its other members and as a concrete expression of its standards of decency. As judges we have no basis for deciding that progress toward greater decency can move only in the direction of easing sanctions on the guilty.[16]

The organization of the explanation section in a concurrence or dissent is the same as that in other legal documents. It begins with the broadest rule, then provides more specific interpretations and examples. A broader rule or description of the law typically begins each paragraph, acting as a topic sentence.

Chief Justice Roberts starts his first paragraph with a broad rule about objective indicators from case law, followed by more specific rules. His second paragraph introduces another broad rule—about evolving standards of decency, followed by examples, and ending with his individual view of how judges should apply the rules. The explanation is persuasive, authoritative, and sets up the analysis that comes next.

---

16. *Id.* at 2477-78.

### 3. Analysis with Incorporated Facts

### a. Style and Substance

The style and substance of the analysis section in a majority opinion, concurrence, and dissent look and sound different. Judges use a distinct tone and approach for each. While the analysis in a majority opinion is straightforward, a concurrence uses a more appeasing tone to explain a tweak or addition to the majority's approach. Take, for example, this agreeable line in a Justice Kagan concurrence: "The Court today treats this case under a property rubric; I write separately to note that I could just as happily have decided it by looking to Jardines' privacy interests."[17]

The tone is that of a peacemaker. The majority did not agree with Justice Kagan's analysis that privacy rights should prevail in this case. But the outcome is the same, so her position is not defensive and neither is her tone.

A concurrence, therefore, uses a tone that supports the majority opinion. U.S. Supreme Court Justice Anthony Kennedy uses the first two lines of this concurrence to defend the majority against the dissent: "It seems to me appropriate, in joining the Court's opinion, to add these few remarks. At the outset it should be said that the Court's opinion does not have the breadth and sweep ascribed to it by the respectful and powerful dissent."[18]

A dissent, though, is disagreeable by nature. And some judges take their disagreements to fiery extremes. U.S. Supreme Court Justice Antonin Scalia was well known for stinging rebukes. In one dissent, he wrote that he would rather "hide my head in a bag" than join the majority and that the Court "has descended from the disciplined legal reasoning of John Marshall and Joseph Story to the mystical aphorisms of the fortune cookie."[19] In another, he quipped, "The Court must be living in another world. Day by day, case by case, it is busy designing a Constitution for a country I do not recognize."[20]

The next excerpts of analysis sections show how judges differ in their tones to put forth points in a concurrence versus a dissent. Both follow similar organizations: A broad thesis statement begins the analysis section, summarizing a major point. That's followed by additional points in support. Topic sentences summarize each new point at the start of paragraphs to set up specific examples and analyses. Transitions, like "in sum" and "finally," guide the reader along to each point.

---

17. *Jardines*, 133 S. Ct. at 1418.

18. *Burwell v. Hobby Lobby Stores, Inc.*, 134 S. Ct. 2751, 2785 (2014) (Kennedy, J., concurring).

19. *Obergefell v. Hodges*, 135 S. Ct. 2584, 2630, n.22 (2015) (Scalia, J., dissenting).

20. *Bd. of Cty. Comm'rs, Wabaunsee Cty., Kan. v. Umbehr*, 518 U.S. 668, 711 (1996) (Scalia, J., dissenting).

In the first example, U.S. Circuit Judge Ojetta R. Thompson concurs with a cautionary note. She writes that the case's prolonged journey through the court system has left her "with a queasy confidence in the decision."[21] Still, her firm tone defends the majority position.

Judge Thompson organizes her reasoning to support the majority's holding around two points: a lack of evidence and the totality of circumstances. She begins with a broad summary—or thesis statement—of why she supports the decision below, which found a prosecutor had a non-discriminatory reason to strike a juror. She then details four examples supporting the lack of evidence, before moving to her second point.

| | |
|---|---|
| A direct **thesis statement** on the lack of **facts** and evidence begins this analysis paragraph. | — This case is devoid of extrinsic evidence of racial discrimination. We do not, for example, have trial notes from the prosecutor indicating that race played a role in jury selection. We do not have evidence that the prosecutor manipulated trial procedures in an attempt to influence |
| The judge then details four specifics—no notes, no manipulation, no tradition, and no pretext—to describe the lack of evidence. | — the racial makeup of the jury. *See, e.g., Miller-El v. Dretke*, 545 U.S. 231, 253-55 (2005) (commenting on the prosecutor's use of a "jury shuffle" to keep black members of the venire at the back of the line). Nor is there evidence of a longstanding tradition of racial discrimination in the use of peremptory challenges in the prosecutor's office or evidence that prosecutors were encouraged to exercise peremptories so as to |
| Citations with the signal "see" and parentheticals show how each of the four reasons supports the thesis of this analysis. | — keep minorities off the jury. *See id.* at 263-66 (taking into account a particular county's "specific policy of systematically excluding blacks from juries"). And nothing in the record clearly demonstrates that the prosecutor's proffered reason for accepting Juror No. 243 but not Juror No. 261 was pretextual. *See id.* at 240-52, 255-63 (comparing |
| Parentheticals from two cases support her final point on pretext, adding supportive facts and rationale from the cases. | — the prosecution's treatment and questioning of black versus white venire members at voir dire and concluding that "the implication of race in the prosecutors' choice of questioning cannot be explained away"); *see also Snyder*, 552 U.S. at 485 (concluding that the justification offered by the prosecutor was pretextual after conducting a comparative juror analysis). |
| The judge uses a clear transition—"in sum"—to signal that she's wrapping up the analysis on her first point. | — In sum, whether the prosecutor's strike of Juror No. 261 violated *Batson* comes down entirely to his credibility in explaining his strikes that day and, in particular, why he did not challenge Juror No. 243. We have said time and time again that making credibility determinations |
| The judge concludes her support of the first point by detailing the practical limitations of appellate review. | — is a job for the district court, not something for us to do looking at a cold record. Absent other evidence in the record pointing to racial discrimination, we simply cannot say that the district judge clearly erred in accepting the prosecutor's explanation and upholding the peremptory challenge. This holds true even if any one (or all) of us, sitting as the trial judge, might have reached a contrary conclusion. |

---

21. *Sanchez v. Roden*, 808 F.3d 85, 93 (1st Cir. 2015) (Thompson, J., concurring).

Finally, because a trial judge faced with a *Batson* challenge must consider the totality of the circumstances, it is appropriate for us to acknowledge them here. Although we are unable to say the district judge clearly erred in finding that the prosecutor's strike was not motivated by Juror No. 261's race, the end result is that all young, black men and young men of color in the venire—indeed all those who resembled Dagoberto Sanchez—found themselves dismissed at the behest of their own government. No other group of prospective jurors received such treatment.

—She then uses a transition—"finally"—to signal her last point and describes her analysis of the totality of the circumstances with a clear topic sentence.

The facts in this record certainly raise the judicial antennae. But given the standard of review, I can do no more than register my discomfort at having to affirm the denial of habeas relief even though the best evidence as to whether or not a *Batson* violation occurred—the prosecutor's contemporaneous explanation—has been irretrievably lost to us.[22]

—In this **conclusion**, the judge restates her concern, referencing the broad habeas issue and detailing her central reason.

Judge Thompson's rationale tries to help justify what might be viewed as a poor decision by the majority. Her tone is supportive and straightforward. The tone in the next dissent excerpt, however, is meant to provoke. In the analysis, Justice Scalia blasts the majority opinion point by point. Here, he addresses whether the Affordable Care Act's three key reforms apply in every state, as the majority held.

This reasoning suffers from no shortage of flaws. To begin with, "even the most formidable argument concerning the statute's purposes could not overcome the clarity [of] the statute's text." *Kloeckner v. Solis*, 133 S. Ct. 596, 607, n. 4 (2012). Statutory design and purpose matter only to the extent they help clarify an otherwise ambiguous provision. Could anyone maintain with a straight face that § 36B is unclear? To mention just the highlights, the Court's interpretation clashes with a statutory definition, renders words inoperative in at least seven separate provisions of the Act, overlooks the contrast between provisions that say "Exchange" and those that say "Exchange established by the State," gives the same phrase one meaning for purposes of tax credits but an entirely different meaning for other purposes, and (let us not forget) contradicts the ordinary meaning of the words Congress used. On the other side of the ledger, the Court has come up with nothing more than a general provision that turns out to be controlled by a specific one, a handful of clauses that are consistent with either understanding of establishment by the State, and a resemblance between the tax-credit provision and the rest of the Tax Code. If that is all it takes to make something ambiguous, everything is ambiguous.

—After describing the majority's reasoning, Justice Scalia disputes the majority's finding that the Act's words must be understood as part of a larger statutory purpose. He begins with a broad and biting thesis statement.

—Strong verbs punctuate major points: suffers, matter, clashes, renders, overlooks, and contradicts.

---

22. *Id.* at 93-97 (footnote omitted).

He then reaches back to an 1819 case to dispute the Court's analysis of the purpose.

— Having gone wrong in consulting statutory purpose at all, the Court goes wrong again in analyzing it. The purposes of a law must be "collected chiefly from its words," not "from extrinsic circumstances." *Sturges v. Crowninshield*, 4 L. Ed. 529 (1819) (Marshall, C.J.). Only by concentrating on the law's terms can a judge hope to uncover the scheme *of the statute*, rather than some other scheme that the judge thinks desirable. Like it or not, the express terms of the Affordable Care Act make only two of the three reforms mentioned by the Court applicable

Justice Scalia uses sarcasm to create a dismissive tone, with phrases like "It is perfectly possible."

— in States that do not establish Exchanges. It is perfectly possible for them to operate independently of tax credits. The guaranteed-issue and community-rating requirements continue to ensure that insurance companies treat all customers the same no matter their health, and the individual mandate continues to encourage people to maintain coverage, lest they be "taxed."[23]

While the tone of a dissent is sharp, it does not need to be so biting. Years of experience may allow judges to develop a more flippant or sarcastic tone that wouldn't be proper for a rookie judge—or a judicial clerk. In the next excerpt, Texas Supreme Court Justice Don Willett showcases a more reasonable, yet still resolute, approach. His dissent argues that the court should hear a case that allowed the state to seize a man's pickup truck. He weaves colorful, historical references throughout the dissent to contend that the court needs to revisit the constitutional analysis of the civil forfeiture law.

Justice Willett uses a broad **thesis statement** to describe a policy concern.

— Texas, like the federal government and other states, has dramatically expanded the use of civil forfeiture. But as asset forfeiture grows, so grows the risk of abuse—what some call "policing for profit." Across America, cash-strapped governments at all levels increasingly rely on civil forfeiture to boost revenue—to fund operations, buy new equip-

Instead of citations within the text, Justice Willett uses footnotes (omitted here), allowing his narrative to flow more smoothly.

— ment, and so on. Government budgeteers relish multiple spigots, and money from confiscated property provides an irresistible profit incentive. But the intersection of power and profit is a troubling one. When agency budgets grow dependent on asset forfeiture, not as an occasional windfall or supplement but as indispensable revenue to fund basic operations, constitutional liberties are unavoidably imperiled. Unsurprisingly, a cottage industry has emerged to advise law enforcement how to boost their asset-seizing potential.

Here, he switches from the general argument to the more emotional, individual argument.

— One wonders if our colonial ancestors, transported to 2014, would be astonished—watching government seize, then sell, the property of guiltless citizens who have not been charged with any crime, much

---

23. *King v. Burwell*, 135 S. Ct. 2480, 2502-03 (2015) (Scalia, J., dissenting).

less convicted of one. And unsurprisingly, civil forfeiture, once focused on the illicit goodies of rich drug dealers, now disproportionately ensnares those least capable of protecting themselves, poor Texans who usually capitulate without a fight because mounting a defense is too costly.

Funding government is important. Safeguarding the constitutional rights of Texans is more important. Fundamental rights should never be sacrificed with nonchalance.[24]

*—He wraps up with simple, candid language that urges the court to take the case.*

### b. Incorporated Facts

Throughout these examples, the authors effectively incorporate key facts to buoy their reasoning. Justice Willett discusses examples of government seizures to rile readers and stir sympathy. Justice Scalia refers generally to the reforms and later goes into how customers are affected. Judge Thompson details the lack of facts supporting a charge of racial discrimination. She then describes the facts in distinguishable cases to support her conclusion—that the record in the case is not just cold but empty.

Because majority opinions detail the background and essential facts of a case, the minority opinion can focus instead on the reasoning—highlighting only those facts essential to the concurrence or dissent. Judges writing minority opinions are not constrained to follow the sometimes rigid structure of a majority opinion. How many facts a judge uses and how they are incorporated into the analysis depends on the subject and on the judge. As U.S. Circuit Judge Ruggero J. Aldisert has noted, "[a] writer has greater literary freedom in preparing a concurring or dissenting opinion than does the majority opinion writer."[25]

## 4. Conclusion Describing Desired Outcome

The freedom a judge has in drafting a concurrence or dissent is evident from beginning to end. And dissents and concurrences end the way most judicial documents do—with a conclusion. The closing conclusion should describe the desired outcome and fit with the opening conclusion, but without duplication. Together, the conclusions should define the issue, describe the reason for writing separately, and detail the supporting rationale. In the next pair of conclusions, U.S. Supreme Court Justice Neil M. Gorsuch, as a U.S. circuit judge, takes advantage of his literary freedom by quoting Charles Dickens.

---

24. *El-Ali v. Texas*, 428 S.W.3d 824, 828 (Tex. 2014) (Willett, J., dissenting) (footnotes omitted).

25. Ruggero J. Aldisert, *Opinion Writing* 157 (3d ed. 2012).

GORSUCH, Circuit Judge, dissenting.

If a seventh grader starts trading fake burps for laughs in gym class, what's a teacher to do? Order extra laps? Detention? A trip to the principal's office? Maybe. But then again, maybe that's too old school. Maybe today you call a police officer. And maybe today the officer decides that, instead of just escorting the now compliant thirteen year old to the principal's office, an arrest would be a better idea. So out come the handcuffs and off goes the child to juvenile detention. My colleagues suggest the law permits exactly this option and they offer ninety-four pages explaining why they think that's so. Respectfully, I remain unpersuaded.

[Closing conclusion]

**WRITING TIP:**
"Literature, poetry, popular culture and other art forms can be worked effectively into opinion writing," writes Judge Ruggero J. Aldisert. "Not only are they expressive and engaging, but they reflect the mores and customs of the culture of which they are a part."[27]

Often enough the law can be "a ass—a idiot," Charles Dickens, *Oliver Twist* 520 (Dodd, Mead & Co. 1941) (1838)—and there is little we judges can do about it, for it is (or should be) emphatically our job to apply, not rewrite, the law enacted by the people's representatives. Indeed, a judge who likes every result he reaches is very likely a bad judge, reaching for results he prefers rather than those the law compels. So it is I [who] admire my colleagues today, for no doubt they reach a result they dislike but believe the law demands—and in that I see the best of our profession and much to admire. It's only that, in this particular case, I don't believe the law happens to be quite as much of a ass as they do. I respectfully dissent.[26]

Aspiring to write like Dickens is a stretch for any judge. But here, Justice Gorsuch blends a coarse phrase from a Dickens character with the refined tone of a judicial opinion. Bowing to tradition, Justice Gorsuch ends with the customary three words: "I respectfully dissent."

## B. FINALIZE AND PROOFREAD

Throughout the writing and editing process of a dissenting or concurring opinion, judges share drafts among their colleagues. That's in part because they hope their written argument will sway a colleague to side with their view, potentially swapping the minority for the majority opinion. But it's also because judges want to make sure they issue all opinions free of error—in everything from constructing sentences to detailing the law and describing their arguments.

---

26. *A.M. v. Holmes*, 830 F.3d 1123, 1169, 1170 (10th Cir. 2016).
27. Aldisert, *supra* note 25, at 240.

The last steps in polishing a concurrence or dissent are the same as those for other judicial documents. The document should be free of typos, awkward wording, and grammatical, style, and citation errors. The analysis should be sound and add something of value to the majority opinion. The final rounds of editing a concurrence or dissent also give authors one more chance to polish their prose and add some individual or literary flair—because in the end, this minority opinion offers the best stage for it.

### Checklist for Writing a Dissent or Concurrence

☐ Follow a logical CREAC organization.

☐ Identify the reason for writing separately and the issue to address.

☐ Begin with a conclusion that states (1) the issue, (2) the reason for writing separately, and (3) a reason supporting the minority position.

☐ Explain the relevant law by highlighting essential components and not by repeating the majority opinion's comprehensive explanation.

☐ Detail the analysis point by point, explaining why the majority's rationale is misguided, incomplete, or incorrect.

☐ Incorporate key facts throughout the analysis to buoy your arguments.

☐ Organize the analysis with a broad thesis statement to start, with topic sentences to summarize the main point of each paragraph, and with transitions to guide readers along the points.

☐ Use a reasonable and resolute tone, even when expressing disagreement with the majority.

☐ State the final conclusion authoritatively, describing the desired outcome.

☐ Revise the minority opinion first for large-scale organizational issues, checking to make sure that each of the CREAC sections flows to the next and that topic sentences reflect each paragraph's substance.

☐ Proofread to ensure correct grammar, punctuation, style, and citations.

## C. MODEL CONCURRENCE AND DISSENT WITH ANNOTATIONS

The examples of a concurrence and a dissent on the next pages show how two writers—Justices Breyer and Kagan—share their minority views in original ways. The minority opinions showcase razor-sharp hypotheticals and convincing descriptions. Justice Kagan throws in a baseball reference to dissect the majority opinion strike by strike.

## CONCURRENCE EXAMPLE

*Snyder v. Phelps*[28]

Justice BREYER, concurring.

*Justice Breyer begins by describing the key parts of the majority opinion that he wants to address to explain his **reason for writing** separately.*

I agree with the Court and join its opinion. That opinion restricts its analysis here to the matter raised in the petition for certiorari, namely, Westboro's picketing activity. The opinion does not examine in depth the effect of television broadcasting. Nor does it say anything about Internet postings. The Court holds that the First Amendment protects the picketing that occurred here, primarily because the picketing addressed matters of "public concern."

*He states a clear **conclusion** to describe how he would change the constitutional analysis.*

While I agree with the Court's conclusion that the picketing addressed matters of public concern, I do not believe that our First Amendment analysis can stop at that point. A State can sometimes regulate picketing, even picketing on matters of public concern. *See Frisby v. Schultz*, 487 U.S. 474 (1988). Moreover, suppose that A were physically to assault B, knowing that the assault (being newsworthy) would provide A with an opportunity to transmit to the public his views on a matter of public concern. The constitutionally protected nature of the end would not shield A's use of unlawful, unprotected means. And in some circumstances the use of certain words as means would be similarly unprotected. *See Chaplinsky v. New Hampshire*, 315 U.S. 568 (1942) ("fighting words").

*He illustrates the conclusion with a hypothetical and highlights the **rule** about "fighting words" that is central to his concurrence's main point: that the majority opinion applies only to the picketing activity—and not necessarily to other verbal attacks.*

The dissent recognizes that the means used here consist of speech. But it points out that the speech, like an assault, seriously harmed a private individual. Indeed, the state tort of "intentional infliction of emotional distress" forbids only conduct that produces distress "so severe that no reasonable man could be expected to endure it," and which itself is "so outrageous in character, and so extreme in degree, as to go beyond all possible bounds of decency, and to be regarded as atrocious, and utterly intolerable in a civilized community." *Harris v. Jones*, 380 A.2d 611, 614, 616 (1977) (internal quotation marks omitted). The dissent requires us to ask whether our holding unreasonably limits liability for intentional infliction of emotional distress—to the point where A (in order to draw attention to his views on a public matter) might launch a verbal assault upon B, a private person, publicly revealing the most intimate details of B's private life, while

*Here, Justice Breyer uses another hypothetical to help **explain** his understanding of the majority's holding.*

knowing that the revelation will cause B severe emotional harm. Does our decision leave the State powerless to protect the individual against invasions of, *e.g.*, personal privacy, even in the most horrendous of such circumstances?

As I understand the Court's opinion, it does not hold or imply that the State is always powerless to provide private individuals with necessary protection. Rather, the Court has reviewed the underlying facts in detail, as will sometimes prove necessary where First Amendment values and state-protected (say,

28. 562 U.S. 443, 461-63 (2011) (Breyer, J., concurring).

privacy-related) interests seriously conflict. *Cf. Fla. Star v. B.J. F.*, 491 U.S. 524, 533 (1989); *Bose Corp. v. Consumers Union of U.S., Inc.*, 466 U.S. 485, 499 (1984). That review makes clear that Westboro's means of communicating its views consisted of picketing in a place where picketing was lawful and in compliance with all police directions. The picketing could not be seen or heard from the funeral ceremony itself. And Snyder testified that he saw no more than the tops of the picketers' signs as he drove to the funeral. To uphold the application of state law in these circumstances would punish Westboro for seeking to communicate its views on matters of public concern without proportionately advancing the State's interest in protecting its citizens against severe emotional harm. Consequently, the First Amendment protects Westboro. As I read the Court's opinion, it holds no more.

Justice Breyer's **analysis** highlights that the majority opinion applies only to the picketing activity. The church also posted verbal attacks on the Internet.

Justice Breyer incorporates key **facts** about the picketing here.

The closing restates the **conclusion**.

## DISSENT EXAMPLE

*Utah v. Strieff* [29]

Justice KAGAN, with whom Justice GINSBURG joins, dissenting.

*Justice Kagan begins by describing the issue and her **reason for writing separately** in clear terms, then stating a **conclusion**.*

If a police officer stops a person on the street without reasonable suspicion, that seizure violates the Fourth Amendment. And if the officer pats down the unlawfully detained individual and finds drugs in his pocket, the State may not use the contraband as evidence in a criminal prosecution. That much is beyond dispute. The question here is whether the prohibition on admitting evidence dissolves if the officer discovers, after making the stop but before finding the drugs, that the person has an outstanding arrest warrant. Because that added wrinkle makes no difference under the Constitution, I respectfully dissent.

*She then states the **rule** at the heart of her disagreement with the majority.*

This Court has established a simple framework for determining whether to exclude evidence obtained through a Fourth Amendment violation: Suppression is necessary when, but only when, its societal benefits outweigh its costs. *See ante*, at 2060-61; *Davis v. United States*, 564 U.S. 229, 237 (2011). The exclusionary rule serves a crucial function—to deter unconstitutional police conduct. By barring the use of illegally obtained evidence, courts reduce the temptation for police officers to skirt the Fourth Amendment's requirements. *See James v. Illinois*, 493 U.S. 307, 319 (1990). But suppression of evidence also "exacts a heavy toll": Its consequence in many cases is to release a criminal without just punishment. *Davis*, 564 U.S at 237. Our decisions have thus endeavored to strike

*The **explanation** follows, setting up her argument for why the evidence should not have been admissible in this case—because it creates "unfortunate incentives" for the police.*

a sound balance between those two competing considerations—rejecting the "reflexive" impulse to exclude evidence every time an officer runs afoul of the Fourth Amendment, *id.* at 238, but insisting on suppression when it will lead to "appreciable deterrence" of police misconduct. *Herring v. United States*, 555 U.S. 135, 141 (2009).

This case thus requires the Court to determine whether excluding the fruits of Officer Douglas Fackrell's unjustified stop of Edward Strieff would significantly deter police from committing similar constitutional violations in the future. And as the Court states, that inquiry turns on application of the "attenuation doctrine," *ante*, at 2061-62—our effort to "mark the point" at which the discovery of evidence "become[s] so attenuated" from the police misconduct that the deterrent benefit of exclusion drops below its cost. *United States v. Leon*, 468 U.S.

*The **explanation** continues, highlighting the three factors for analysis.*

897, 911 (1984). Since *Brown v. Illinois*, 422 U.S. 590, 604-605 (1975), three factors have guided that analysis. First, the closer the "temporal proximity" between the unlawful act and the discovery of evidence, the greater the deterrent value of suppression. *Id.* at 603. Second, the more "purpose[ful]" or "flagran[t]" the police illegality, the clearer the necessity, and better the chance, of preventing similar misbehavior. *Id.* at 604. And third, the presence (or absence) of

---

29. 136 S. Ct. 2056, 2071-74 (2016) (Kagan, J., dissenting) (footnotes omitted) (some citations omitted).

"intervening circumstances" makes a difference: The stronger the causal chain between the misconduct and the evidence, the more exclusion will curb future constitutional violations. *Id.* at 603-04. Here, as shown below, each of those considerations points toward suppression: Nothing in Fackrell's discovery of an outstanding warrant so attenuated the connection between his wrongful behavior and his detection of drugs as to diminish the exclusionary rule's deterrent benefits.

In resolute terms, Justice Kagan decisively outlines why none of the facts support suppression, providing a **thesis** for her **analysis**.

Start where the majority does: The temporal proximity factor, it forthrightly admits, "favors suppressing the evidence." *Ante*, at 2062. After all, Fackrell's discovery of drugs came just minutes after the unconstitutional stop. And in prior decisions, this Court has made clear that only the lapse of "substantial time" between the two could favor admission. *Kaupp v. Texas*, 538 U.S. 626, 633 (2003) (*per curiam*); *see, e.g., Brown*, 422 U.S. at 604 (suppressing a confession when "less than two hours" separated it from an unlawful arrest). So the State, by all accounts, takes strike one.

Throughout the analysis, Justice Kagan incorporates key **facts**, like this one about the timing of the stop, to support her points.

She attacks the analysis point by point, calling her first "strike" here for the first factor.

Move on to the purposefulness of Fackrell's conduct, where the majority is less willing to see a problem for what it is. The majority chalks up Fackrell's Fourth Amendment violation to a couple of innocent "mistakes." *Ante*, at 2063. But far from a Barney Fife-type mishap, Fackrell's seizure of Strieff was a calculated decision, taken with so little justification that the State has never tried to defend its legality. At the suppression hearing, Fackrell acknowledged that the stop was designed for investigatory purposes—*i.e.*, to "find out what was going on [in] the house" he had been watching, and to figure out "what [Strieff] was doing there." And Fackrell frankly admitted that he had no basis for his action except that Strieff "was coming out of the house." *Id.* at 17. Plug in Fackrell's and Strieff's names, substitute "stop" for "arrest" and "reasonable suspicion" for "probable cause," and this Court's decision in *Brown* perfectly describes this case:

Colorful references, like "a Barney Fife-type mishap" drive home her points.

Simple, direct, and active verbs make Justice Kagan's writing flow: "Move on," "chalks up," and "plug in" are just a few in this paragraph.

> [I]t is not disputed that [Fackrell stopped Strieff] without [reasonable suspicion]. [He] later testified that [he] made the [stop] for the purpose of questioning [Strieff] as part of [his] investigation…. The illegality here…had a quality of purposefulness. The impropriety of the [stop] was obvious. [A]wareness of that fact was virtually conceded by [Fackrell] when [he] repeatedly acknowledged, in [his] testimony, that the purpose of [his] action was 'for investigation': [Fackrell] embarked upon this expedition for evidence in the hope that something might turn up. 422 U.S. at 592, 605 (some internal punctuation altered; footnote, citation, and paragraph break omitted).

This long quote highlights language from a key case, essential to the majority opinion, to pull the reader in a different direction.

In *Brown*, the Court held those facts to support suppression—and they do here as well. Swing and a miss for strike two.

Finally, consider whether any intervening circumstance "br[oke] the causal chain" between the stop and the evidence. *Ante*, at 2062. The notion of such a disrupting event comes from the tort law doctrine of proximate causation. *See*

After calling strike two, Justice Kagan transitions to the third factor. This easy-to-follow **organization** leads to an easy-to-follow argument.

*Bridge v. Phoenix Bond & Indemnity Co.*, 553 U.S. 639, 658-659 (2008) (explaining that a party cannot "establish [ ] proximate cause" when "an intervening cause break[s] the chain of causation between" the act and the injury); Kerr, Good Faith, New Law, and the Scope of the Exclusionary Rule, 99 Geo. L.J. 1077, 1099 (2011) (Fourth Amendment attenuation analysis "looks to whether the constitutional violation was the proximate cause of the discovery of the evidence"). And as in the tort context, a circumstance counts as intervening only when it is unforeseeable—not when it can be seen coming from miles away. *See* W. Keeton, D. Dobbs, B. Keeton, & D. Owen, Prosser and Keeton on Law of Torts 312 (5th ed. 1984). For rather than breaking the causal chain, predictable effects (*e.g.*, X leads naturally to Y leads naturally to Z) are its very links.

And Fackrell's discovery of an arrest warrant—the only event the majority thinks intervened—was an eminently foreseeable consequence of stopping Strieff. As Fackrell testified, checking for outstanding warrants during a stop is the "normal" practice of South Salt Lake City police. *See State v. Topanotes*, 76 P.3d 1159, 1160 (describing a warrant check as "routine procedure" and "common practice" in Salt Lake City). In other words, the department's standard detention procedures—stop, ask for identification, run a check—are partly designed to find outstanding warrants. And find them they will, given the staggering number of such warrants on the books. *See generally ante*, at 2067-68 (SOTOMAYOR, J., dissenting). To take just a few examples: The State of California has 2.5 million outstanding arrest warrants (a number corresponding to about 9 percent of its adult population); Pennsylvania (with a population of about 12.8 million) contributes 1.4 million more; and New York City (population 8.4 million) adds

To get to "strike three," Justice Kagan uses secondary sources and statistics.

another 1.2 million. So outstanding warrants do not appear as bolts from the blue. They are the run-of-the-mill results of police stops—what officers look for when they run a routine check of a person's identification and what they know will turn up with fair regularity. In short, they are nothing like what intervening circumstances are supposed to be. Strike three.

She sums up her main concern here—the "unfortunate incentives" for police—and emphasizes it with a hypothetical.

The majority's misapplication of *Brown's* three-part inquiry creates unfortunate incentives for the police—indeed, practically invites them to do what Fackrell did here. Consider an officer who, like Fackrell, wishes to stop someone for investigative reasons, but does not have what a court would view as reasonable suspicion. If the officer believes that any evidence he discovers will be inadmissible, he is likely to think the unlawful stop not worth making—precisely the deterrence the exclusionary rule is meant to achieve. But when he is told of today's decision? Now the officer knows that the stop may well yield admissible evidence: So long as the target is one of the many millions of people in this country with an outstanding arrest warrant, anything the officer finds in a search is fair game for

The dissent's **conclusion** details why the majority's holding is harmful to the Constitution, and it describes the desired outcome. It closes with the three customary words, again indicating respect.

use in a criminal prosecution. The officer's incentive to violate the Constitution thus increases: From here on, he sees potential advantage in stopping individuals without reasonable suspicion—exactly the temptation the exclusionary rule is supposed to remove. Because the majority thus places Fourth Amendment protections at risk, I respectfully dissent.

CHAPTER

# JUDGES' WRITING STYLES

Judges are writers first. And many write exceptionally well, lacing their prose with artful passages, vivid descriptions, stinging rebukes, and clever turns of phrase. What's even more remarkable is that they do this while crafting the law.

The goal of great legal writing has always been plain language. James Madison called for concise, straightforward language in drafting the U.S. Constitution, writing that it "will be of little avail to the people that the laws are made by men of their own choice if the laws be so voluminous that they cannot be read, or so incoherent that they cannot be understood." That's not an easy task—and anyone who has read a few opinions from the last 200 years knows that it's not always achieved.

The law is complicated, and writing about it in plain language is one of the legal writer's biggest challenges. This chapter celebrates some of the many examples of good judicial writing. While each example shows many qualities of good writing, the examples are organized into six strategies that all legal writers can emulate to improve their own prose.

---

### Six Tips to Write Like the Best

1. Tell a Story
2. Keep It Short
3. Avoid Jargon
4. Show with Examples
5. Start with a Bang
6. Persuade with Power

---

## A. TELL A STORY

Behind every court case is a story, with real people and real emotion and real conflict. The more the story shines through the legal complexities, the better the writing and the more convincing the point. The next examples show how you can focus on the facts, strip a story of legalese, and tell that story in plain language. Plain doesn't mean boring. It means free of jargon and clichés and stilted phrases. It means that readers can focus on what's important because they don't have to take the time to figure out the meaning behind a word, sentence, or paragraph.

The first excerpt, from a dissent by Pennsylvania Supreme Court Justice Michael Musmanno, describes a bull charging at a woman. The scene helps justify why the woman should win her negligence lawsuit, even though the bull did not physically touch her, as the law requires.

> Like those human beings who believe that fame and fortune always lie in some land distant from their own, the cows of the Dale Andrews farm in West Salem, Mercer County, were not satisfied to browse and chew their cuds in their own pasture. They were certain that in the fields across the highways which bordered their owner's domain, the grass was greener, the earth fresher, the trees shadier, and the skies above bluer. Thus from time to time they would leave their own preserves and invade the Bosley farm on the other side of the road where, with the spirit of bovine buccaneers, they devoured their neighbor's corn and wheat, destroyed his vegetable gardens, knocked over young peach trees, damaged the apple orchard, mangled berry bushes, and eventually departed, leaving behind them a wide swath of ruin destruction. They sometimes went away of their own accord, but frequently they had to be driven back to their home territory by the Bosleys.
>
> On the morning of April 10, 1950,…they came, eight of them, with reinforcements. They brought along their boy friend, a 1500-pound Hereford white-faced bull.…
>
> Mr. Hereford and Mrs. Bosley saw each other at the same time. Mrs. Bosley screamed, and the truculent Hereford lowered his head to charge. Terror-stricken, Mrs. Bosley tried to run, but, as in a bad dream one cannot flee although disaster is at one's heels, she froze to the spot.…
>
> Although the bull was about 25 feet away from Mrs. Bosley when she first beheld him charging toward her, she ran some "five steps" before she collapsed. Allowing for at least two feet for each step, it becomes evident that the bull was within 10 to 15 feet of Mrs. Bosley before his course was diverted. It is enough merely to visualize a snorting, charging bull with impaling horns only a dozen feet away, to grasp at once

the magnitude of Mrs. Bosley's fright and the extent of the terror to which she was subjected.[1]

This dissent could have focused on the law and the reasons for an exception to the physical contact rule. But instead, the vivid account shows just how close the bull came to Mrs. Bosley, and it helps sell Judge Musmanno's argument that the rule needs tweaking.

Some cases might seem blessed with more innately entertaining facts, and maybe a charging bull would help any story. But legal writers can become storytellers when writing about any case. In the next excerpt, U.S. Supreme Court Justice Robert H. Jackson uses just a few facts from the case to bring the defendant to life and spin a gripping tale.

> **WRITING TIP:**
> Find a writer you admire to emulate. For Chief Justice John G. Roberts and Justice Elena Kagan, that writer is Justice Robert H. Jackson. Justice Antonin Scalia was also a fan: "He was a wonderful writer, had flow, vividness; he could make a point with such force."[2]

Korematsu was born on our soil, of parents born in Japan. The Constitution makes him a citizen of the United States by nativity and a citizen of California by residence. No claim is made that he is not loyal to this country. There is no suggestion that apart from the matter involved here he is not law-abiding and well disposed. Korematsu, however, has been convicted of an act not commonly a crime. It consists merely of being present in the state whereof he is a citizen, near the place where he was born, and where all his life he has lived.

Even more unusual is the series of military orders which made this conduct a crime. They forbid such a one to remain, and they also forbid him to leave. They were so drawn that the only way Korematsu could avoid violation was to give himself up to the military authority. This meant submission to custody, examination, and transportation out of the territory, to be followed by indeterminate confinement in detention camps.

A citizen's presence in the locality, however, was made a crime only if his parents were of Japanese birth. Had Korematsu been one of four—the others being, say, a German alien enemy, an Italian alien enemy, and a citizen of American-born ancestors, convicted of treason but out on parole—only Korematsu's presence would have violated the order. The difference between their innocence and his crime would result, not from anything he did, said, or thought, different than they, but only in that he was born of different racial stock.

Now, if any fundamental assumption underlies our system, it is that guilt is personal and not inheritable. Even if all of one's antecedents

---

1. *Bosley v. Andrews*, 142 A.2d 263, 267-68 (1958) (Musmanno, J., dissenting).
2. Interview by Bryan A. Garner with Justice Antonin Scalia, 13 Scribes J. Legal Writing 64 (2010).

had been convicted of treason, the Constitution forbids its penalties to be visited upon him, for it provides that "no Attainder of Treason shall work Corruption of Blood, or Forfeiture except during the Life of the Person attained." Article 3, § 3, cl. 2. But here is an attempt to make an otherwise innocent act a crime merely because this prisoner is the son of parents as to whom he had no choice, and belongs to a race from which there is no way to resign. If Congress in peace-time legislation should enact such a criminal law, I should suppose this Court would refuse to enforce it.[3]

Meaningful examples, like the parallels Justice Jackson draws to alien enemies from other countries, underpin his dissent. Good characters can do the same for a story, even when they're inanimate. In the next excerpt, U.S. Circuit Judge Diane Wood exploits the facts in a copyright infringement case and injects some subtle humor. She describes dolls, which are the subject of the suit, as characters, as if they were players in a work of fiction.

Meet Pull My Finger® Fred. He is a white, middle-aged, overweight man with black hair and a receding hairline, sitting in an armchair wearing a white tank top and blue pants. Fred is a plush doll and when one squeezes Fred's extended finger on his right hand, he farts. He also makes somewhat crude, somewhat funny statements about the bodily noises he emits, such as "Did somebody step on a duck?" or "Silent but deadly."

Fartman could be Fred's twin. Fartman, also a plush doll, is a white, middle-aged, overweight man with black hair and a receding hairline, sitting in an armchair wearing a white tank top and blue pants. Fartman (as his name suggests) also farts when one squeezes his extended finger; he too cracks jokes about the bodily function. Two of Fartman's seven jokes are the same as two of the ten spoken by Fred. Needless to say, Tekky Toys, which manufactures Fred, was not happy when Novelty, Inc., began producing Fartman, nor about Novelty's production of a farting Santa doll sold under the name Pull-My-Finger Santa.

Tekky sued for copyright infringement, trademark infringement, and unfair competition and eventually won on all claims. The district court awarded $116,000 based on lost profits resulting from the copyright infringement, $125,000 in lost profits attributable to trademark infringement, and $50,000 in punitive damages based on state unfair competition law. The district court then awarded Tekky $575,099.82 in attorneys' fees. On appeal, Novelty offers a number of arguments for why it should not be held liable for copyright infringement, argues that

---

3. *Korematsu v. United States*, 323 U.S. 214, 242-44 (1944) (Jackson, J., dissenting).

Illinois's punitive damages remedy for unfair competition is preempted by federal law, and contends that the attorneys' fees awarded by the district court should have been capped according to Tekky's contingent-fee arrangement with its attorneys. For the reasons set forth below, we affirm.[4]

With the crux of the Fartman-Fred dispute focused on attorneys' fees, Judge Wood chose not to focus the start of her opinion on Fartman's argument, which revolved around the preemption of "Illinois's punitive damages remedy for unfair competition." That's enough to lull any reader to sleep. Instead, she shifts focus to tell the story behind those fees, effectively and entertainingly setting up why they're justified.

Judge Wood's use of humor is restrained and therefore effective. Regardless of the subject matter, a judge should approach each issue, each party, and each case with respect. That rule is especially true for judicial clerks and interns, who are learning to follow a judge's style and preferences. Patricia M. Wald, a former chief judge for the D.C. Circuit Court of Appeals, explains that too much humor can degrade the serious work of the judiciary: "The law is not a sport, and legal opinions should not be a vehicle for showing how clever we are."[5] So humor, when subtle, can inject interest in an opinion, but legal writers should take care that it's not overdone.

## B.  KEEP IT SHORT

Legal writers too often take 20 words to say something when 10 will do. Writing about complicated legal issues in plain language might require twice the editing as writing about the issues in a convoluted way. But the payoff for concise, plain writing is that the reader will figure out what you're saying in half the time—and probably understand it better too.

To prove this point, U.S. Circuit Judge Richard Posner once wrote an article that took a 3,237-word opinion by a district judge and slashed it to 602 words.[6] For anyone keeping track, that's a cut of more than 80 percent of the words in the original. His chief reasons were that the opinion lacked focus, forethought, and editing. Judge Posner's aim was to inspire others to think hard about what they are writing and revise their documents until the content is precise and the style is readable and clear.

The next few examples show how effective judicial writing can be when judges keep it short. Good legal writers use short paragraphs, short sen-

---

4. *JCW Invs., Inc. v. Novelty, Inc.*, 482 F.3d 910, 912-13 (7th Cir. 2007).
5. Patricia M. Wald, *"How I Write" Essays*, 4 Scribes J. Legal Writing 55, 62-63 (1993).
6. Richard A. Posner, *Reflections on Judging* 260 (2013).

tences, and short words to explain the law in an approachable way. Describing a good test for choosing the right word to use, U.S. Supreme Court Justice Antonin Scalia said, "[I]f you used the word at a cocktail party, would people look at you funny? You talk about *the instant case* or *the instant problem*. That's ridiculous. It's legalese. *This* case would do very well."[7]

The memorable closing lines from U.S. Supreme Court Justice Anthony Kennedy's majority opinion in *Obergefell v. Hodges*, which granted same-sex couples the right to marry, average just 16 words per sentence.

> No union is more profound than marriage, for it embodies the highest ideals of love, fidelity, devotion, sacrifice, and family. In forming a marital union, two people become something greater than once they were. As some of the petitioners in these cases demonstrate, marriage embodies a love that may endure even past death. It would misunderstand these men and women to say they disrespect the idea of marriage. Their plea is that they do respect it, respect it so deeply that they seek to find its fulfillment for themselves. Their hope is not to be condemned to live in loneliness, excluded from one of civilization's oldest institutions. They ask for equal dignity in the eyes of the law. The Constitution grants them that right.
>
> The judgment of the Court of Appeals for the Sixth Circuit is reversed.[8]

The dissents follow in concise fashion. The dissent by U.S. Supreme Court Chief Justice John G. Roberts ends with a short paragraph that uses repetition and a series of short sentences (averaging less than eight words each) to forcefully make his point.

**WRITING TIP:**
Chief Justice John G. Roberts looks for good pacing, "whether it's a thick biography of one of the founding fathers or the latest by Elmore Leonard. . . . The pacing—bringing the reader along at the particular speed you want, for the effect you want—is, I think, very important."[10]

> If you are among the many Americans—of whatever sexual orientation—who favor expanding same-sex marriage, by all means celebrate today's decision. Celebrate the achievement of a desired goal. Celebrate the opportunity for a new expression of commitment to a partner. Celebrate the availability of new benefits. But do not celebrate the Constitution. It had nothing to do with it.[9]

Chief Justice Roberts' first line sets up a powerful sequence. The repetition in each line creates a rhythm. And the staccato length of each sentence propels the reader forward.

Writers can speed up the pace of their writing or add a punch by mixing in short sentences like this. Justice Scalia was a mas-

---

7. Interview by Garner with Justice Scalia, *supra* note 2, at 58.
8. *Obergefell v. Hodges*, 135 S. Ct. 2584, 2608 (2015).
9. *Id.* at 2626 (Roberts, C.J., dissenting).
10. Interview by Bryan A. Garner with Chief Justice John G. Roberts Jr., 13 Scribes J. Legal Writing 40 (2010).

ter at injecting a pithy line or two, especially in his dissents. True to form, the closing in his *Obergefell* dissent punctuates two longer sentences with a couple snappy ones:

> Our Constitution—like the Declaration of Independence before it—was predicated on a simple truth: One's liberty, not to mention one's dignity, was something to be shielded from—not provided by—the State. Today's decision casts that truth aside. In its haste to reach a desired result, the majority misapplies a clause focused on "due process" to afford substantive rights, disregards the most plausible understanding of the "liberty" protected by that clause, and distorts the principles on which this Nation was founded. Its decision will have inestimable consequences for our Constitution and our society.[11]

All legal writers have a point to make, and the best writers know they can make an impact with a mix of short sentences and short words. The lines, "They ask for equal dignity in the eyes of the law," "It had nothing to do with it," and "Today's decision casts that truth aside," make the reader pay attention.

Consider the reader when constructing paragraphs, drafting sentences, and choosing words. No reader wants to see a wall of text—with a paragraph spanning more than a page. And no reader wants to start reading a sentence without being able to see the end of it. Long sentences lead to run-ons, subject-verb disagreement, and confusion. Picking long words because they sound more impressive also won't do. "But" works just as well as "however." "And" works for "additionally," "moreover," and "furthermore." And "about" works in place of "regarding" or "concerning."

U.S. Supreme Court Justice Elena Kagan shuns these overly complex adverbs and connectors in favor of simple language. In the next excerpt, she starts a series of sentences with short conjunctions and speeds up the pace. The use of "so" especially shows how she and other judges are consistently becoming more conversational in their writing.

> And then Marvel stumbled across Brulotte, the case at the heart of this dispute. In negotiating the settlement, neither side was aware of *Brulotte*. But Marvel must have been pleased to learn of it. *Brulotte* had read the patent laws to prevent a patentee from receiving royalties for sales made after his patent's expiration. So the decision's effect was to sunset the settlement's royalty clause.[12]

Writing concisely—and conversationally—about a complex case takes many rounds of editing. When Judge Posner condensed the opinion to 600

---

11. 135 S. Ct. at 2639-40 (Scalia, J., dissenting).
12. *Kimble v. Marvel Entm't, LLC*, 135 S. Ct. 2401, 2406 (2015) (citations and footnotes omitted).

words, he cut many details extraneous to the core issue, such as the defendant's address and the date of the arrest and search.[13] The next example shows a similarly militant approach to compressing a case to its essence. The opening by U.S. Circuit Judge Frank Easterbrook tackles a case that spans nearly three decades. He clips it to a core narrative.

> This suit began 28 years ago and has been to the Supreme Court three times. All defendants who stuck it out to the end (some settled) prevailed across the board. They applied for costs under 28 U.S.C. § 1920 and were awarded most of what they sought—but not until District Judge Coar held the request under advisement for three years and then retired, after which the case was transferred to District Judge Norgle. He awarded a total $63,391.45, modest for a suit that entailed discovery, a long trial, many motions in the district court, and appellate proceedings that span a generation. The costs amount to less than $2,300 per year of litigation.
>
> Plaintiffs dispute some of the district judge's decisions about particular items, but we do not perceive either a clear error of fact or an abuse of discretion and have no more to say about those matters. Plaintiffs also offer three reasons why defendants should get nothing: (1) they took too long to request costs; (2) they did not establish that the transcripts and copies were "necessarily obtained for use in the case" as § 1920 requires; and (3) they did not nudge Judge Coar to rule before he retired. We consider these in turn.[14]

The description of this protracted case is most remarkable for what it doesn't have. It's not littered with detailed history or unnecessary descriptions of the conflict. It has no intensifiers, like clearly and obviously. It has no qualifiers, like rather or quite. It doesn't have multiple negatives. And it doesn't have any common wordy phrases, like "in order to" or "it is important to consider" or "the fact that." The opinion reveals only what's necessary in skillfully simple language, until the crisp closing lines: "This litigation has lasted far too long. At last it is over."

Writers use wordy phrases as crutches to warm up to their main point. Cutting a wordy phrase, like "it is important to note that" or "it would be helpful to consider," can make any sentence more direct. These wordy warm-ups often begin with "there is" or the undefined pronoun "it." Use this chart as a guide to help cut wordy warm-ups from your writing.

---

13. Posner, *supra* note 6.
14. *Nat'l Org. for Women, Inc. v. Scheidler*, 750 F.3d 696, 697-98 (7th Cir. 2014) (citations omitted).

### Wordy Warm-Ups[15]

- Arguably
- As noted above
- In light of the fact that
- In order to
- It could be argued that
- It is
- It is clear
- It is crucial to consider
- It is important to note that
- It is worth considering
- It is generally recognized that
- It is interesting to consider
- It is to be noted
- It might be said that
- It must be recognized that
- It seems
- It seems likely that
- It should also be noted
- It would appear that
- It would be helpful to consider
- The fact that
- There are/is/was/were
- There is little doubt that
- With regard/respect to

## C. AVOID JARGON

When you start law school, you're told that you're learning a new language. In many ways, you are. But too often legal writers use Latin and jargon to prop up poor writing and convoluted explanations. It doesn't have to be that way.

It's true that the law has plenty of jargon that you'll need to learn, like *de novo* and *res ipsa loquitur*. And while *res ipsa loquitur* translates from Latin to the beautifully simple phrase, "the thing speaks for itself," it has a precise meaning in tort law.

As a negligence claim, *res ipsa loquitur* allows a jury to infer negligence when an accident occurs. In one well-known case, the jury inferred that K-Mart was negligent under the *res ipsa loquitur* doctrine when a heavy display rack toppled onto a woman "for no apparent reason."[16] The judge who wrote the K-Mart opinion couldn't translate a term of art like *res ipsa loquitur* into plain language because an opinion wouldn't make sense without this term of art.

But many legal terms appear in legal writing for show and should be translated into plain language. Here are some examples of what to cut:

- Outdated formalities — "now comes," "further affiant sayeth naught"
- Redundancies — "null and void," "each and every"
- Archaic words — "aforementioned," "hereinabove," "herewith," "whereof"

---

15. Jill Barton & Rachel H. Smith, *The Handbook for the New Legal Writer* 111 (2014).
16. *K-Mart Corp. v. Gipson*, 563 N.E.2d 667, 670 (1990).

- Uncommon titles—"lessor," "lessee," "testatrix"
- Most Latin terms—translate a phrase like inter alia to "among other things"
- Overly long words and phrases—"firstly," "pursuant to," "in order to," "in the event of."

As a simple test to avoid overwrought language, consider whether you would use the term or phrase in everyday conversation, and if you wouldn't, swap it for simple English. This next example takes on legalese explicitly. While U.S. Circuit Judge Ojetta R. Thompson uses two terms of art—actual malice and reckless disregard—she labels them as legalese before explaining these elements in a defamation claim. The writing is direct and concise and begins like a novel, with the heading of "prologue."

### PROLOGUE

Campaigning for public office sometimes has the feel of a contact sport, with candidates, political organizations, and others trading rhetorical jabs and sound-bite attacks in hopes of landing a knockout blow at the polls. It is not for the thin-skinned or the faint-hearted, to use two apropos clichés. And because political speech is the life-breath of democracy, the First Amendment—applied to the states via the Fourteenth—bars public figures from recovering damages under state defamation laws unless they show that the defamer acted with "actual malice," legalese that might suggest ill will or evil motive to the uninitiated but really means knowledge of falsity or reckless disregard for the truth. Cases define "reckless disregard" variously as a defamer's having "'serious doubts'" about a statement's falsity, or "actually" having "a 'high degree of awareness of . . . probable falsity,'" or suspecting falsity and purposefully—not just negligently—avoiding the truth.

All this makes it quite obvious that defamation law does not require that combatants for public office act like war-time neutrals, treating everyone evenhandedly and always taking the high road. Quite the contrary. Provided that they do not act with actual malice, they can bad-mouth their opponents, hammering them with unfair and one-sided attacks—remember, speaking out on political issues, especially criticizing public officials and hopefuls for public office, is a core freedom protected by the First Amendment and probably presents "the strongest case" for applying "the *New York Times* rule." And absent actual malice, more speech, not damages, is the right strike-back against superheated or false rhetoric.

Today's appeal—targeting speech critical of a candidate's performance in public office and challenging the dismissal of his defamation-based complaint for failure to state a claim—brings these principles into bold relief. Finding no reversible error in the judge's careful opinion, we affirm. The story follows.[17]

## D. SHOW WITH EXAMPLES

Show, don't tell. It's a common canon for novelists, screenwriters, journalists, poets, speechwriters—and legal writers. And it's especially important for legal writers. Telling a judge that you should win because your case is exactly like another doesn't work. The other side can simply state the opposite to refute your position. You need to show the judge why your case is like another and how it fits with the law. The same is true for judges when writing opinions because they need to show the parties and the public why their decision is just.

The excerpts so far in this chapter have come to life through examples—of a charging bull, alien enemies in World War II, a doll that passes gas just like another doll. These examples help lead the reader to the judge's conclusion, showing why the outcome is correct. In the next excerpt, U.S. Circuit Judge Alex Kozinski leads a dissent with a string of examples to show why, in a case between a robot impostor and Wheel of Fortune celebrity Vanna White, the robot should win.

> Saddam Hussein wants to keep advertisers from using his picture in unflattering contexts. Clint Eastwood doesn't want tabloids to write about him. Rudolf Valentino's heirs want to control his film biography. The Girl Scouts don't want their image soiled by association with certain activities. George Lucas wants to keep Strategic Defense Initiative fans from calling it "Star Wars." Pepsico doesn't want singers to use the word "Pepsi" in their songs. Guy Lombardo wants an exclusive property right to ads that show big bands playing on New Year's Eve. Uri Geller thinks he should be paid for ads showing psychics bending metal through telekinesis. Paul Prudhomme, that household name, thinks the same about ads featuring corpulent bearded chefs. And scads of copyright holders see purple when their creations are made fun of....
>
> Overprotecting intellectual property is as harmful as underprotecting it. Creativity is impossible without a rich public domain. Nothing today, likely nothing since we tamed fire, is genuinely new: Culture, like science and technology, grows by accretion, each new creator building

---

17. *Schatz v. Republican State Leadership Comm.*, 669 F.3d 50, 52 (1st Cir. 2012) (internal citations and footnotes omitted).

on the works of those who came before. Overprotection stifles the very creative forces it's supposed to nurture.[18]

The facts of a case can help you paint a picture to show your reader what it's about. Real-world examples, like the ones Judge Kozinski uses here, also work. So too do hypothetical examples, as Justice Kagan proves with her refined prose in the next concurrence excerpt.

> For me, a simple analogy clinches this case—and does so on privacy as well as property grounds. A stranger comes to the front door of your home carrying super-high-powered binoculars. He doesn't knock or say hello. Instead, he stands on the porch and uses the binoculars to peer through your windows, into your home's furthest corners. It doesn't take long (the binoculars are really very fine): In just a couple of minutes, his uncommon behavior allows him to learn details of your life you disclose to no one. Has your "visitor" trespassed on your property, exceeding the license you have granted to members of the public to, say, drop off the mail or distribute campaign flyers? Yes, he has. And has he also invaded your "reasonable expectation of privacy," by nosing into intimacies you sensibly thought protected from disclosure? *Katz v. United States*, 389 U.S. 347, 360 (1967) (Harlan, J., concurring). Yes, of course, he has done that too.

> That case is this case in every way that matters.[19]

Judges can take a paragraph or more to craft an example—hypothetical or otherwise. But sometimes they do so in a single sentence. Here, Judge Posner creates a dramatic image in the reader's mind and quickly makes his point:

> To take the period of limitations from one statute and the accrual date from another, however, is like grafting a giraffe's head onto an alligator's body.[20]

Simply stated, the analogy helps the reader see the point with just a few words. Justice Jackson pulls off the same feat here by deftly summing up the major flaw in a case:

> We granted certiorari, and in this Court the parties changed positions as nimbly as if dancing a quadrille.[21]

---

18. *White v. Samsung Elecs. Am., Inc.*, 989 F.2d 1512, 1512-13 (9th Cir. 1993) (footnotes omitted).

19. *Florida v. Jardines*, 133 S. Ct. 1409, 1418 (2013).

20. *Singletary v. Cont'l Ill. Nat'l Bank & Trust Co. of Chi.*, 9 F.3d 1236, 1242 (7th Cir. 1993).

21. *Ortloff v. Willoughby*, 345 U.S. 83, 87 (1953).

A fan of Justice Jackson's, Chief Justice Roberts explains why Justice Jackson's approach works: "You read one of his opinions, and it makes an impression on you—not just the law, but the felicity of expression and the breadth of analogy and reference. And at the same time, it has a very plainspoken approach to it. You don't have to be a lawyer to read one of Justice Jackson's opinions and understand exactly what he's saying. And that's very valuable."[22]

## E. START WITH A BANG

Every writer wants the reader to keep going after the opening line. The first words are meant to hook, tease, or introduce readers to something that's worth their time. Author Stephen King writes that the "opening line should invite the reader to begin the story. It should say: 'Listen. Come in here. You want to know about this.'"[23] A good opinion should do the same.

U.S. Supreme Court Justice Samuel Alito commands the reader to listen in the next opening. His wrath, directed at the lower courts, can be felt throughout his majority opinion—and tugs at the reader to feel the same way.

> This case is about a little girl (Baby Girl) who is classified as an Indian because she is 1.2 percent (3/256) Cherokee. Because Baby Girl is classified in this way, the South Carolina Supreme Court held that certain provisions of the federal Indian Child Welfare Act of 1978 required her to be taken, at the age of 27 months, from the only parents she had ever known and handed over to her biological father, who had attempted to relinquish his parental rights and who had no prior contact with the child. The provisions of the federal statute at issue here do not demand this result.[24]

Plenty of opinions can read like high-drama novellas. Cases revolve around characters, themes, conflict, and carefully crafted plots. The best judicial writers exploit these opportunities, writing in a way that's engaging enough to compel even the most reluctant reader to keep going. Readers of Justice Alito's *Baby Girl* opinion want to know why she was taken and what happens next. So too do readers of the next opening, where U.S.

---

22. Interview by Garner with Chief Justice Roberts, supra note 10, at 9.

23. Joe Fassler, *Why Stephen King Spends "Months and Even Years" Writing Opening Sentences,* The Atlantic, July 23, 2013, http://www.theatlantic.com/entertainment/archive/2013/07/why-stephen-king-spends-months-and-even-years-writing-opening-sentences/278043/.

24. *Adoptive Couple v. Baby Girl*, 133 S. Ct. 2552, 2556-57 (2013).

Circuit Judge Irving L. Goldberg quotes Ecclesiastes to masterfully turn a tax case about fertilizer deductions into a compelling read.

> "To every thing there is a season, and a time to every purpose under the heaven: A time to be born, and a time to die; a time to plant, and a time to pluck up that which is planted;" a time to purchase fertilizer, and a time to take a deduction for that which is purchased. In this appeal from a Tax Court decision, we are asked to determine when the time for taking a fertilizer deduction should be.[25]

Judge Goldberg could have played it straight—and boring. But he chose to create a lyrical opening that asks the reader to keep going—if only to see if he can keep up the poetic style. Judges don't have to invent drama to animate their opinions. In the next example, then-New York Chief Judge Benjamin Cardozo builds up the suspense to the inevitable accident in describing a 1929 amusement park ride.

> The defendant, Steeplechase Amusement Company maintains, an amusement park at Coney Island, N. Y. One of the supposed attractions is known as "the Flopper." It is a moving belt, running upward on an inclined plane, on which passengers sit or stand. Many of them are unable to keep their feet because of the movement of the belt, and are thrown backward or aside.[26]

Plenty of cases won't have facts as naturally compelling as a ride on "the Flopper." And some cases easily offer up those facts—but only for one side. That can work, but what if the party that doesn't have a great story to tell has the law on its side? That was U.S. District Judge Amul R. Thapar's challenge in a case that pitted an employee who suffered a stroke and loss of eyesight against his employer. Judge Thapar detailed the employee's plight with empathy—his 20 years of dedicated service that ended when he fell ill and was placed on disability leave. But in granting summary judgment for the employer, Judge Thapar created a story for the employer as well by looking to the big picture.

> Specialty retailers have it rough these days. Big-box stores and internet vendors can offer one-stop shopping, more-convenient ordering, and lower prices. But there is something that those competitors cannot offer: face-to-face service. It is often the only thing. To have any hope of remaining competitive in that kind of marketplace, specialty retailers need to forge strong, in-person bonds with customers. That is what Sherwin-Williams, a specialty paint retailer, tries to do.[27]

---

25. *Schenk v. Comm'r of Internal Revenue*, 686 F.2d 315, 316 (5th Cir. 1982).
26. *Murphy v. Steeplechase Amusement Co.*, 166 N.E. 173, 173-74 (1929).
27. *Wagner v. Sherwin-Williams Co.*, No. CV 14-178-ART, 2015 WL 5174130, at *1 (E.D. Ky. Sept. 2, 2015).

It can be tricky to champion an American Fortune 500 company over the little guy in the typical David-Goliath showdown. But the context that Judge Thapar creates helps bolster his holding. Like any other writer, a judge can use various devices to make an opinion more interesting and more vibrant. These examples by Judge Thapar and others have shown how to use emotion, characters, playful language, suspense, and context to craft winning stories. The openings make the reader want to keep going—not just to find out the answer but also because they're just good reads.

## F.  PERSUADE WITH POWER

While focusing on good writing can help any opinion, the purpose is still to persuade. The best judges do both. The final examples in this chapter show how to pack a persuasive punch—using common themes like protecting democracy from corruption, upholding precedent, and casting wrath on the mistakes of lower courts (or your fellow justices). All of them draw on the shared values that make the country and its judicial system what it is.

In the first example here, Justice Kagan takes on political corruption in a dissent. She uses strong verbs: plague, ignore, and languish. And she casts her hypothetical with convincing terms, like bargains and cancerous effect. All of it leads to the simple conclusion that the majority's holding just won't work.

> Imagine two States, each plagued by a corrupt political system. In both States, candidates for public office accept large campaign contributions in exchange for the promise that, after assuming office, they will rank the donors' interests ahead of all others. As a result of these bargains, politicians ignore the public interest, sound public policy languishes, and the citizens lose confidence in their government.
>
> Recognizing the cancerous effect of this corruption, voters of the first State, acting through referendum, enact several campaign finance measures previously approved by this Court. They cap campaign contributions; require disclosure of substantial donations; and create an optional public financing program that gives candidates a fixed public subsidy if they refrain from private fundraising. But these measures do not work.[28]

Judges often reserve their strongest language for their dissents. A majority opinion needs to represent the majority view, and that can call for a

---

28. *Arizona Free Enter. Club's Freedom Club PAC v. Bennett*, 564 U.S. 721, 755 (2011) (Kagan, J. dissenting).

more toe-the-line approach. But sometimes judges lay into lower courts or the parties. Take the next example from Judge Kozinski. He skewers the Department of Justice in the opening lines of his majority opinion. The writing compels readers down the page, if only to see what other punches he might land on the government.

> Suspect that giant film distributors like Columbia, Paramount and Twentieth Century-Fox had fallen prey to Raymond Syufy, the canny operator of a chain of Las Vegas, Nevada, movie theatres, the United States Department of Justice brought this civil antitrust action to force Syufy to disgorge the theatres he had purchased in 1982-84 from his former competitors. The case is unusual in a number of respects: The Department of Justice concedes that moviegoers in Las Vegas suffered no direct injury as a result of the allegedly illegal transactions; nor does the record reflect complaints from Syufy's bought-out competitors, as the sales were made at fair prices and not precipitated by any monkey business; and the supposedly oppressed movie companies have weighed in on Syufy's side. The Justice Department nevertheless remains intent on rescuing this platoon of Goliaths from a single David.[29]

Judge Kozinski uses playful references like "monkey business" and "platoon of Goliaths." But a light touch is not always appropriate. For cases tasked with addressing serious crimes and fundamental rights, judges historically have used emotion and a shared desire to protect the nation's core values as an underlying theme to support their position. In the next example, Texas Supreme Court Justice Don Willett draws on a case from 1882 to frame a case that's focused on a seemingly innocuous practice today—eyebrow threading.

> *To understand the emotion which swelled my heart as I clasped this money, realizing that I had no master who could take it from me—that it was mine—that my hands were my own, and could earn more of the precious coin.... I was not only a freeman but a free-working man, and no master Hugh stood ready at the end of the week to seize my hard earnings.*

Frederick Douglass's irrepressible joy at exercising his hard-won freedom captures just how fundamental—and transformative—economic liberty is. Self-ownership, the right to put your mind and body to productive enterprise, is not a mere luxury to be enjoyed at the sufferance of governmental grace, but is indispensable to human dignity and prosperity....

This case raises constitutional eyebrows because it asks building-block questions about constitutional architecture—about how we as Texans govern ourselves and about the relationship of the citizen to the State.

---

29. *United States v. Syufy Enters.*, 903 F.2d 659, 661 (9th Cir. 1990).

This case concerns far more than whether Ashish Patel can pluck unwanted hair with a strand of thread. This case is fundamentally about the American Dream and the unalienable human right to pursue happiness without curtsying to government on bended knee. It is about whether government can connive with rent-seeking factions to ration liberty unrestrained, and whether judges must submissively uphold even the most risible encroachments.[30]

Justice Willett masterfully uses an old but revered precedent to broaden a seemingly simple case about eyebrow threading into one that's about the American Dream. He mixes a spirited line—"This case raises constitutional eyebrows"—with an undeniably serious one—"the unalienable human right to pursue happiness without curtsying to government on bended knee."

Few judicial writers have mixed spirited writing with a serious tone better than Justice Scalia. And he's well remembered for accomplishing this feat in a single line—many times. The following examples are just a few of his best lines that persuade with power.

Words no longer have meaning if an Exchange that is not established by a State is "established by the State."[31]

The Court's next bit of interpretive jiggery-pokery involves other parts of the Act that purportedly presuppose the availability of tax credits on both federal and state Exchanges.[32]

The somersaults of statutory interpretation they have performed ("penalty" means tax, "further [Medicaid] payments to the State" means only incremental Medicaid payments to the State, "established by the State" means not established by the State) will be cited by litigants endlessly, to the confusion of honest jurisprudence.[33]

A candidate who says "If elected, I will vote to uphold the legislature's power to prohibit same-sex marriages" will positively be breaking his word if he does not do so (although one would be naive not to recognize that campaign promises are—by long democratic tradition—the least binding form of human commitment).[34]

The sheer applesauce of this statutory interpretation should be obvious.[35]

---

30. *Patel v. Texas Dep't of Licensing & Regulation*, 469 S.W.3d 69, 92-93 (Tex. 2015) (Willett, J., concurring) (citations omitted).

31. *King v. Burwell*, 135 S. Ct. 2480, 2496 (2015) (Scalia, J. dissenting).

32. *Id.* at 2500.

33. *Id.* at 2507.

34. *Republican Party of Minn. v. White*, 536 U.S. 765, 780 (2002).

35. *Zuni Pub. Sch. Dist. No. 89 v. Dep't of Educ.*, 550 U.S. 81, 113 (2007) (Scalia, J. dissenting).

**WRITING TIP:**
Justice Ruth Bader Ginsburg says that the "law should be a literary profession, and the best legal practitioners do regard law as an art as well as a craft."[36]

It takes confidence to inject words like "jiggery-pokery" and "applesauce" into an opinion, and it takes skill to successfully pull it off. But that's what judicial writing is all about. Judges take care in choosing their words and in telling the stories behind the cases they're deciding. This chapter shows how to be a storyteller and write like a judge—beautifully and authoritatively—in a way that leaves no doubt that your position is correct and makes your own mark in the world of judicial writing.

---

36. Interview by Bryan A. Garner with Justice Ruth Bader Ginsburg, 13 Scribes J. Legal Writing 133 (2010).

CHAPTER

# GRAMMAR, PUNCTUATION, AND WRITING STYLE CHECKUP

Judges know there's an art to putting together a good sentence. Many excel at showing us how to present complicated legal doctrine in simple language. That can be especially challenging when the starting point is a motion, brief, or case law with muddled explanations and legalese. This chapter shows you how to wade through legal jargon, refine your writing, and check that it is free of errors in grammar, punctuation, and style.

In legal writing, these errors can have disastrous consequences. A clumsily worded opinion could set unintended precedent—just as a poorly worded statute can lead to confusion over sentencing criminal defendants.[1] Comma mistakes and misplaced modifiers in legal writing have cost millions of dollars and caused years of litigation.[2] So judicial writing demands writing that is exact and infallible.

To help make your writing flawless, this chapter reviews basic grammar rules first—with tips on when to break those rules by injecting a zinger or two. Then, it shares more advanced writing tricks—like how to create parallelism and use em dashes. These tips will help make your writing impeccable—and with style like that of the best judges.

---

1. *See, e.g., Lockhart v. United States*, 136 S. Ct. 958 (2016) (affirming 6-2 a conviction and sentence based on the last antecedent rule).

2. *See, e.g., Payless Shoesource, Inc. v. Travelers Cos.*, 585 F.3d 1366, 1367 (10th Cir. 2009) ("This is a dispute over the meaning of a misplaced modifier.").

> ### Basic Grammar, Punctuation, and Style Checkup
>
> 1. Sentences
> 2. Commas
> 3. Semicolons
> 4. Colons
> 5. Modifiers
> 6. Pronouns
> 7. Apostrophes
> 8. Hyphens

## A. BASIC GRAMMAR, PUNCTUATION, AND STYLE CHECKUP

### 1. Sentences—Fragments, Subject-Verb Agreement, and Run-Ons

#### a. Fragments

First, a note about fragments.[3] Writers use sentence fragments to change their cadence, artfully turn a phrase, or emphasize a point. A majority of U.S. Supreme Court justices today regularly drop them into their opinions to do just that. Fragments can take a few different forms. They might lack the required subject or verb or both, like this one from U.S. Supreme Court Justice Sonia Sotomayor:

> But regulated entities are not without recourse in such situations. Quite the opposite.[4]

Or sentence fragments might be a subordinate clause, such as the following from U.S. Supreme Court Justice Elena Kagan:

> Truth be told, if forced to decide that issue, we would not know where or how to start. Which is one good reason why that is not our job.[5]

They also can contain an incomplete thought, like an answer to a question, as in these two zingers from U.S. Supreme Court Justice Antonin Scalia:

> It is bad enough for a court to cross out "by the State" once. But seven times?

> Would anybody reason that the bulletin implicitly presupposes that every professor has "graduate students," so that "graduate students" must really mean "graduate or undergraduate students"? Surely not.[6]

---

3. This is a sentence fragment because it has no verb. A complete sentence has both a main subject and a verb.

4. *Perez v. Mortgage Bankers Ass'n*, 135 S. Ct. 1199, 2010 (2015).

5. *Kimble v. Marvel Entm't*, 135 S. Ct. 2401, 2414 (2015).

6. *King v. Burwell*, 135 S. Ct. 2480, 2499, 2501 (2015) (Scalia, J. dissenting).

Too often in writing, fragments denote a mistake, rather than a literary choice. But good legal writers know how to distinguish a complete sentence from a deliberately incomplete one. They recognize that fragments can inject a little flair and are not just, as Justice Scalia once noted, "Pure applesauce." Since he introduced that provocative fragment in 2015, at least seven admiring lower court judges have quoted the phrase.[7]

Still, sentence fragments are rare in judicial opinions. U.S. Supreme Court Justices Samuel Alito, Stephen Breyer, Anthony Kennedy, and Clarence Thomas chose not to use fragments in any of their opinions or dissents over the 2015 and 2014 terms. U.S. Circuit Judge Richard Posner cautions that short sentences and fragments can "lower" the writing's tone, making it more conversational.[8] But even he calls for a balance and writes that eliminating all brevity could impart a tone that's too rigid. His colleague on the Seventh Circuit, Judge Frank Easterbrook, recently began an opinion with three memorable fragments bookending one short complete sentence:

> Rats. This case is about rats. Giant, inflatable rats, which unions use to demonstrate their unhappiness with employers that do not pay union-scale wages. Cats too—inflatable fat cats, wearing business suits and pinkie rings, strangling workers.[9]

Sentence fragments draw attention. So before using one, be sure the fragment has a purpose—that it is intentional and not a grammar mistake. Dropping a subject or a verb from a sentence to make a pithy point takes writing ability and confidence. Fragments can provoke and persuade with just a few words. Just like all judicial opinions should.

### b. Subject-Verb Agreement

Sentences can get convoluted when they describe the law—so much so that subjects and verbs can lose track of each other. Clauses might interrupt a sentence and the flow between a subject and verb. A proper sentence has a subject and a verb that match—and ideally, that are close together. Consider the successful staccato rhythm that Justice Kagan employs in this sentence, in which she keeps the subjects and verbs next to each other:

> Imagine a friend told you that she hoped to meet "an actor, director, or producer involved with the new Star Wars movie." You would know

---

7. *See, e.g., Anton Realty, LLC v. Fifth Third Bank*, No. 115CV00199RLYTAB, 2015 WL 8675188, at *6 (S.D. Ind. Dec. 11, 2015).

8. Richard A. Posner, *Judges' Writing Styles (And Do They Matter?)*, 62 U. Chi. L. Rev. 1420, 1427 (1995).

9. *Constr. & Gen. Laborers' Local Union No. 330 v. Town of Grand Chute, Wis.*, No. 15-1932, 2016 WL 4410073, at *1 (7th Cir. Aug. 19, 2016).

immediately that she wanted to meet an actor from the Star Wars cast—not an actor in, for example, the latest Zoolander.[10]

Even if a long phrase separates the main subject and verb, the subject and verb must match. Singular subjects take a singular verb. Plural subjects take a plural verb. Some singular subjects that can confuse writers include "each," "neither," "everyone," "corporation," and "defendant." All of those subjects take a singular verb (and a singular pronoun, but there's more on that later this chapter).

In the next example, the singular subject of "jury" takes a singular verb. The writer might incorrectly think that a plural verb fits, though, because the intervening clause has a plural subject. The second example shows the opposite—with a plural subject matching a plural verb—but with a potentially misleading singular clause between the two.

The singular "jury" matches the singular verb. — The jury, which is made up of four women and two men, plus two men who were alternates, announces the verdict after lunch.

The plural subject "jurors" takes the plural verb " announce." — The jurors, one of whom lived in the same neighborhood as the victim, announce the verdict after lunch

Check for subject-verb disagreement in longer sentences, where long phrases or clauses separate the main subject and verb. Identify the main subject and verb, and see that they match. Keep in mind that one principle of good writing is to keep subjects and verbs close together, so consider breaking up longer sentences and moving intervening phrases and clauses. U.S. Supreme Court Justice Ruth Bader Ginsburg keeps the action clear in the following passage by putting each of the sentence subjects next to the verbs, even with additional clauses and longer sentences in the mix.

> Judicial abstention left pervasive malapportionment unchecked. In the opening half of the 20th century, there was a massive population shift away from rural areas and toward suburban and urban communities. Nevertheless, many States ran elections into the early 1960's based on maps drawn to equalize each district's population as it was composed around 1900. Other States used maps allocating a certain number of legislators to each county regardless of its population. These schemes left many rural districts significantly underpopulated in comparison with urban and suburban districts.[11]

## c. Run-Ons

Legal writers create run-ons when they try to cram too much material before a single period. Fusing two or more complete clauses together without

---

10. *Lockhart*, 136 S. Ct. at 969 (Kagan, J., dissenting).
11. *Evenwel v. Abbott*, 136 S. Ct. 1120, 1123 (2016) (citations omitted).

the proper punctuation creates a run-on, not to mention that it makes the reader lose track of what you are trying to say.

Writers can combine complete sentences—those with both a main subject and verb—correctly to make compound sentences. But when they do so incorrectly, run-on sentences result. A common run-on occurs when a writer merges two or more complete sentences together with just a comma, or no punctuation at all. Here are two examples of common run-ons and five ways to fix them—using the wide variety of punctuation and conjunctions at the legal writer's disposal.

> **Run-on:** The inflatable rats and cats are staked to the ground to prevent the wind from blowing them away, those stakes led to this litigation.

—Separating two clauses that can operate independently as sentences makes a run-on.

> **Run-on:** The inflatable rats and cats are staked to the ground to prevent the wind from blowing them away and those stakes led to this litigation, Grand Chute forbids private signs on the public way.

—This run-on combines three sentences improperly. It's best to break them up.

### Fix no. 1: Use a Semicolon

The inflatable rats and cats are staked to the ground to prevent the wind from blowing them away; those stakes led to this litigation

—If two clauses are closely related, a semicolon can separate them.

### Fix no. 2: Use a Coordinating Conjunction—and, but, for, or, so, yet

The inflatable rats and cats are staked to the ground to prevent the wind from blowing them away, and those stakes led to this litigation.

—A short conjunction with a comma works too.

### Fix no. 3: Use a Conjunctive Adverb,[12] Semicolon, and Comma

The inflatable rats and cats are staked to the ground to prevent the wind from blowing them away; accordingly, those stakes led to this litigation.

—A long conjunction preceded by a semicolon and followed by a comma works.

### Fix no. 4: Make Two (or More) Sentences

The inflatable rats and cats are staked to the ground to prevent the wind from blowing them away. Those stakes led to this litigation.

—Short sentences prevail and require only an extra period.

The inflatable rats and cats are staked to the ground to prevent the wind from blowing them away. Those stakes led to this litigation. Grand Chute forbids private signs on the public way.

### Fix no. 5: Make One Clause Subordinate

Because Grand Chute forbids private signs on the public way, those stakes led to this litigation.

—One clause becomes subordinate with a conjunction—like "after," "because," and "since." The comma follows the introductory clause.

---

12. Conjunctive adverbs combine clauses and show their relation. Common conjunctive adverbs include the following: accordingly, consequently, furthermore, hence, however, instead, moreover, nevertheless, nonetheless, similarly, still, therefore, and thus.

Each of these fixes alters the emphasis within the sentence. The revisions also vary the sentence length, which can add interest and variety to writing. A page with sentences of similar length can seem monotonous. A page with too many long sentences can seem unwieldy. Sentences should average about 20 words each,[13] and paragraphs should contain a mix of short, average, and long sentences. Varying short sentences with longer ones can help you speed up the pace of your writing and keep the reader's attention.

## 2. Commas

Commas create confusion and frustration among legal writers. That's because a misplaced comma in legal writing can drastically change the meaning of a sentence and have costly results. Back in 1872, a misplaced comma in a tariff law cost the equivalent of $40 million in today's dollars.[14] The law listed import items exempt from taxation and included the following:

> fruit, plants tropical and semi-tropical for the purpose of propagation or cultivation.[15]

The comma between "fruit" and "plants," caused by a clerk's error, allowed importers to claim that the comma meant free imports of all tropical or semitropical fruits and plants. But drafters meant for only plants and seeds used to cultivate fruit to be exempt. Instead of a comma, they meant to use a dash and put the comma after "plants" to read like this:

> fruit—plants, tropical and semi-tropical for the purpose of propagation or cultivation

This reading would mean that under the category of fruit, only plants used for growing fruit are exempt. Congress fixed the mistake two years later but only after several pricey court battles.[16] Use the following five tips to fix comma mistakes before they get so costly.

---

13. Bryan A. Garner, *LawProse Lesson #269: Average Sentence Length,* http://www.lawprose.org/lawprose-lesson-269-average-sentence-length/ (last visited Mar. 1, 2017).

14. *See, e.g.,* Christina Sterbenz, *This Comma Cost America About $40 million*, Business Insider, Jan. 9, 2015, http://www.businessinsider.com/this-typo-cost-america-about-40-million-2015-1.

15. Benjamin A. Levett, *Oddities of Our Tariff Law Often Confuse the Shipper*, N.Y. Times, Oct. 7, 1934, at 12.

16. *Refunding Duties on Green Fruits*, 1614 Congressional Series of U.S. Public Documents 3-17 (1873).

### a. Comma Rule No. 1: Use Commas to Set Off Nonrestrictive Clauses

Nonrestrictive clauses add nonessential information to a sentence. These clauses do not restrict the meaning of a sentence—the sentence could still stand without them. They typically begin with "when," "where," "which," and "who." And they always require commas. Justice Ginsburg wrote an example of each of these nonrestrictive clauses in an opinion that held that states may draw their legislative districts based on total population.

---

### Comma Checkup

1. Use commas to set off nonrestrictive clauses.
2. Use the serial comma.
3. Use commas after the day and year in dates.
4. Use commas to separate elements in locations.
5. Use commas around clauses, phrases, and conjunctive adverbs for clarity.

---

Appellants, who live in Texas Senate districts with particularly large eligible- and registered-voter populations, filed suit against the Texas Governor and Secretary of State.

— These clauses add helpful information, but removing them would not cause the sentence to lose its basic meaning.

Just two years after *Baker*, in *Wesberry v. Sanders*, the Court invalidated Georgia's malapportioned congressional map, under which the population of one congressional district was "two to three times" larger than the population of the others.

Decisions of this Court, the District Court concluded, permit jurisdictions to use any neutral, nondiscriminatory population baseline, including total population, when drawing state and local legislative districts.

— These sentences work with or without the clauses separated by commas.

To support this assertion, appellants cite only a District Court decision, which found no significant deviation in the distribution of voter and total population in "densely populated areas of New York State."

The "quote" comes from the controversy over Senate apportionment, where the debate turned on whether to apportion by population at all.[17]

---

17. *Evenwel*, 136 S. Ct. at 1121, 1123, 1126, 1131, 1146 (emphasis and citations omitted).

### b. Comma Rule No. 2: Use the Serial Comma

Legal writing requires a lot of lists: lists of elements in a rule, lists of precedents, lists of reasons for a particular outcome. The serial comma—also known as the Oxford comma—clearly identifies each item in a list. Without it, you could have a potential misreading like in the next sentence, which incorrectly categorizes people as rats.

*Without the serial comma, the first sentence insults union bosses and employers as rats.*

— This case affects rats, union bosses and employers.

This case affects rats, union bosses, and employers.

Misreadings in legal writing can cost millions. A dairy company in Maine is set to lose about $10 million because a state law listing overtime exemptions left out a serial comma. The law stated that companies were not required to pay overtime for the following activities:

*The serial comma belongs before "or" in this clause.*

— The canning, processing, preserving, freezing, drying, marketing, storing, packing for shipment or distribution of:

> (1) Agricultural produce;
> (2) Meat and fish products; and
> (3) Perishable foods.

Without the serial comma before "or," an appeals court found that the phrase, "packing for shipment or distribution," refers only to the single activity of "packing."[18] But the drivers don't do the packing—they do the distributing. That means all the overtime hours the drivers spend distributing don't fall within the exemption, so the company must pay.

For clarity's sake, legal writers should always use the serial comma, like Justice Kagan illustrates here:

> Suppose a real estate agent promised to find a client "a house, condo, or apartment in New York." Wouldn't the potential buyer be annoyed if the agent sent him information about condos in Maryland or California? And consider a law imposing a penalty for the "violation of any statute, rule, or regulation relating to insider trading."[19]

### c. Comma Rule No. 3: Use Commas After the Day and Year in Dates

This rule is simple yet often not followed. Stick a comma after the day and year. Use the following examples as a guide.

---

18. *O'Connor v. Oakhurst Dairy*, No. 16-1901, 2017 WL 957195, at *2 (1st Cir. Mar. 13, 2017).

19. *Lockhart*, 136 S. Ct. at 969 (Kagan, J., dissenting).

The Court announced on June 26, 2015, the landmark decision in *Obergefell v. Hodges*. — A comma goes after the day and year.

On November 8, 2016, the Court of Appeals affirmed the conviction.

The Court decided the case in June 2015. — Use no comma when using only the month and year.

### d. Comma Rule No. 4: Use Commas to Separate Elements in Locations

This rule is another one to commit to memory: Put commas after both elements in a location, whether you are listing a city and state or a city and country.

A police officer spotted the defendant driving the streets of Bowman, North Dakota, in the fall of 2013.

The extradition treaty applied in Falluja, Iraq, but not in Kabul, Afghanistan, or Pyongyang, North Korea.

### e. Comma Rule No. 5: Use Commas Around Clauses, Phrases, and Conjunctive Adverbs for Clarity

Consider how often you pause when speaking. Commas can create that same pause in writing—but only when clarity requires it. Use a comma for clarity at the beginning, middle, or end of a sentence when you have a clause, phrase, or conjunctive adverb (a longer conjunction like "however" and "nevertheless"). At the beginning of a sentence, always use a comma to offset an introductory word or words. In the middle, use commas around conjunctive adverbs and other interrupting phrases and clauses. And at the end, use a comma to set off dependent clauses.

#### Beginning of a Sentence

But properly read, the modifier applies to each of the terms—just as in the examples above.

When the nouns in a list are so disparate that the modifying clause does not make sense when applied to them all, then the last-antecedent rule takes over.[20] — Use a comma no matter how long or short the introductory clauses.

Further, ICRA makes habeas review in federal court available to persons incarcerated pursuant to a tribal-court judgment.[21]

---

20. *Id.* at 969, 970.
21. *United States v. Bryant*, 136 S. Ct. 1954, 1966 (2016).

### Middle of a Sentence

Facts, by contrast, are mere real-world things— extraneous to the crime's legal requirements.

Commas belong on both sides of clauses that interrupt sentences.

And ACCA, as we have always understood it, cares not a whit about them.[22]

That ordinary understanding of how English works, in speech and writing alike, should decide this case.[23]

### End of a Sentence

That analysis holds equally for § 2252(b)(2), the sentencing provision at issue here.[24]

A comma sets off nonrestrictive clauses at the end of a sentence.

That approach is required only by the Court's statutory precedents, which Congress remains free to overturn.[25]

## 3. Semicolons

Semicolons can combine two sentences into one (as shown in two examples on page 151). Semicolons also can help keep items in a complex list clear. An item in a list is complex if it requires commas. In the next sentence, the list has six examples and three of the examples have commas. Using a comma to separate the items would be confusing, so use a semicolon instead:

### a. Semicolon Rule: Use a Semicolon to Separate Complex Items in a List

The first, third, and fifth items in this complex list have commas within them, so a semicolon separates each item for clarity.

The law defines such a victim's losses to include "medical services relating to physical, psychiatric, or psychological care; physical and occupational therapy or rehabilitation; necessary transportation, temporary housing, and child care expenses; lost income; attorneys' fees, as well as other costs incurred; and any other losses suffered by the victim as a proximate result of the offense."[26]

## 4. Colons

Colons help set off lists, quotations, and explanations. They also can combine two closely related sentences. But writers often overuse colons. When

---

22. *Mathis v. United States*, 136 S. Ct. 2243, 2248 (2016).
23. *Lockhart*, 136 S. Ct. at 969 (Kagan, J., dissenting).
24. *Id.* at 971.
25. *Mathis*, 136 S. Ct. at 2258 (Kennedy, J., concurring).
26. *Lockhart*, 136 S. Ct. at 970-71 (Kagan, J., dissenting).

introducing information, colons belong after only a complete clause—one with a subject and verb that can stand alone as a complete sentence:

### a. Colon Rule: Place a Colon Only After a Complete Clause

Incorrect: Colon Following Incomplete Clause

The elements of a contract include: offer, acceptance, and consideration.

Correct: No Colon

The elements of a contract include offer, acceptance, and consideration.

Also Correct: Make the Clause Preceding the Comma Complete—Like a Full Sentence

The elements of a contract include the following: offer, acceptance, and consideration.

The next examples from Justice Breyer show how to use a colon to properly set off information, including facts, a quote, and a list of factors

> Some but not all of the facts are undisputed: Michael Kingsley, the petitioner, was arrested on a drug charge and detained in a Wisconsin county jail prior to trial.

—The colon follows a complete clause and introduces facts, which may or may not be stated in a complete sentence.

> At the conclusion of the trial, the District Court instructed the jury as follows:

—The colon here introduces a long quotation.

>> Excessive force means force applied recklessly that is unreasonable in light of the facts and circumstances of the time. Thus, to succeed on his claim of excessive use of force, plaintiff must prove each of the following factors by a preponderance of the evidence:

—The quotation also has a colon, following a complete clause and introducing a list of four factors.

>> (1) Defendants used force on plaintiff; (2) Defendants' use of force was unreasonable in light of the facts and circumstances at the time; (3) Defendants knew that using force presented a risk of harm to plaintiff, but they recklessly disregarded plaintiff's safety by failing to take reasonable measures to minimize the risk of harm to plaintiff; and (4) Defendants' conduct caused some harm to plaintiff.[27]

## 5. Modifiers

Modifying the wrong word or clause can make a sentence confusing or wrong. Just like subjects and verbs should be placed close together, modifiers should be placed next to the word or clause they modify. Modifiers

---

27. *Kingsley v. Hendrickson*, 135 S. Ct. 2466, 2470 (2015) (emphasis omitted).

create problems in writing for two reasons: Their placement makes the sentence's meaning unclear or they are dangling. In the next examples, the meaning changes depending on where the modifier is placed.

### a. Modifier Rule No. 1: Avoid Unclear Placement of Modifiers

#### Incorrect: Unclear Placement

Maybe the suspect would only talk or maybe talk only to police — the meaning is vague.

— The suspect only wanted to talk to police.

#### Correct: "Only" Modifies the Subject Here

This placement means that the suspect—and not the victim or anyone else— wanted to talk to police.

— Only the suspect wanted to talk to police.

#### Correct: "Only" Modifies the Action Here

The suspect wanted to talk and nothing else — not to also give a written or video-taped statement or provide any other evidence.

— The suspect wanted only to talk to police.

#### Correct: "Only" Modifies the Object Here

The suspect wanted to talk to police and no one else.

— The suspect wanted to talk only to police.

The lesson here is to place words like "only," "primarily," "predominantly," "nearly," and "mainly" next to the word or phrase they modify. Placing modifiers gets a bit trickier when a longer clause is involved. The next examples illustrate how to fix misplaced modifying clauses.

#### Incorrect: The Modifier Placement Makes the Sentence Unclear

This placement means that the drugs were registered to the girlfriend.

— The jury weighed the evidence about the defendant and the car containing a large bag of marijuana, which was registered to the defendant's girlfriend.

#### Correct: The Clause Modifies the Correct Noun

This placement conveys the facts correctly.

— The jury weighed the evidence about the defendant and the car, which was registered to the defendant's girlfriend and contained a large bag of marijuana.

### b. Modifier Rule No. 2: Avoid Dangling Modifiers

Another problem with modifiers occurs when they are "dangling," or modifying a noun that is either unclear or doesn't exist in the sentence. Here are two examples of dangling modifiers and how to fix them—by making the actor in the sentence clear.

#### Dangling Modifier—Missing Antecedent

The court or judge reversing the conviction is missing.

— Finding the evidence mishandled, the conviction was reversed.

Fix by Adding the Main Subject

Finding the evidence mishandled, the judge reversed the conviction. — Switch the passive voice to active, and add the subject to fix.

Dangling Modifier—Missing Antecedent

Having filed the brief a day late, a motion for extension of time was required. — Passive voice allows the actor to be missing.

Fix by adding the main subject

Having filed the brief a day late, the attorney was required to file a motion for extension of time. — Adding the actor back into the sentence fixes the dangling modifier.

## 6. Pronouns

Pronoun errors create ambiguity and imprecision in writing. The following four rules will help keep the pronouns in your prose clear so that the reader always knows who the "he," "she," "it," and "they" are in a document.

### a. Pronoun Rule No. 1: Make Pronouns and Antecedents Match

Pronouns that represent a singular noun or a collective noun should be singular. Some common collective nouns that should be represented by "it" include court, jury, board, company, majority, committee, family, or team. Using "they" for collective nouns is incorrect—there is no "singular they" in legal writing. Reserve the use of "they" for plural nouns. Jurors and corporations pair with "they." And use "who"—not "that"—when clauses refer to people.

Incorrect

The appellate panel erred when they affirmed the defendant's conviction. — An appellate panel is a collective noun and should be paired with "it."

Correct

The appellate panel erred when it affirmed the defendant's conviction. — If using "it" to refer to a panel of three judges seems awkward, rewrite the sentence.

Also Correct

The appellate judges erred when they affirmed the defendant's conviction.

Incorrect

The appellate judges that affirmed the defendant's conviction agreed to rehear the case en banc.

Correct

The appellate judges who affirmed the defendant's conviction agreed to rehear the case en banc. — Use "who," not "that" when a clause refers to people.

> ### Pronoun Checkup
> 1. Make pronouns and antecedents match.
> 2. "It's" is a contraction, not a possessive.
> 3. Pronouns should refer to an existing antecedent.
> 4. "Who" is for subjects; "whom" is for objects.

## b. Pronoun Rule No. 2: "It's" Is a Contraction, Not a Possessive

The word "it's" means "it is" and should be used only when you want to use an informal contraction, a rarity in judicial writing. The word "its" is the possessive of "it" and may be used when paired with a singular or collective noun.

### Incorrect

The Supreme Court issued it's decision.

### Correct

"Its" denotes the possessive — The Supreme Court issued its decision.
correctly here.

## c. Pronoun Rule No. 3: Pronouns Should Refer to an Existing Antecedent

Avoid using a pronoun when it refers to an ambiguous idea or a nonexisting noun. Pronouns that often are ambiguous when used in legal writing include "it," "this," "that," "such," and "which." A pronoun should always refer clearly to its antecedent. In the previous sentence, the only possible antecedent for "its" is "pronoun."

### Incorrect

"Them" could refer to errors — Judges become annoyed with attorneys who make pronoun errors, so
or judges. carefully proofread your document to eliminate them.

### Correct

Judges become annoyed with attorneys who make pronoun errors, so carefully proofread your document to eliminate all errors.

### Incorrect

Even if the writer thinks that — This means that you should vacate the conviction.
the reasons for vacating
the conviction were clearly
spelled out in the document,      ### Correct
"this" is unclear here.
"This" and other ambiguous        This lack of evidence means that you should vacate the defendant's
pronouns should always be         conviction.
followed with an explicit
noun.

### d. Pronoun Rule No. 4: "Who" Is for Subjects; "Whom" Is for Objects

Confusing "who" and "whom" is among the most common of grammar mistakes. Use the pronoun "who" when referring to the subject of a sentence or the subject of a clause, just as you would use "she" or "he." When referring to the object of a sentence, use "whom," "her," or "him."

Here is a trick to figure out whether to use "who" or "whom": Rework the clause to use either "he" or "him" instead. If the clause would use "he," the pronoun is a subject and "who" is the correct pronoun. If the clause would use "him," the pronoun is an object and "whom" is the correct choice. See how this tip works in the examples below.

Incorrect

The judge sealed the records relating to the juvenile, whom was identified only as "TM" in publicly released documents.

— Try the trick: If you rework the clause to use "he" or "him," it reads: "He was identified only as TM in court documents." So you can conclude that "who" is the correct pronoun because "he" refers back to a subject, not an object.

Correct

The judge sealed the records relating to the juvenile, who was identified only as "TM" in publicly released documents.

Incorrect

The newspaper contained allegedly defamatory statements about Terri J. Spencer, who the union hopes to elect to the vacant County Commission seat.

— Use the tip and rework the clause to use "he" or "him" (even though Terri is female). It reads: "The union hopes to elect 'him.'" Thus, "whom" is required because it refers to the object of the union's efforts.

Correct

The newspaper contained allegedly defamatory statements about Terri J. Spencer, whom the union hopes to elect to the vacant County Commission seat.

## 7. Apostrophes

Apostrophes form possessives. To use an apostrophe correctly, add an apostrophe and an "s" to singular nouns to form the possessive. For plural nouns, add just the apostrophe. Apostrophes also form contractions. Many legal writers avoid contractions because they are too informal, but some judges will use them sparingly.

### a. Apostrophe Rule No. 1: For Singular Nouns, Add an Apostrophe and an "s"

Incorrect

The defendants testimony led to the court's decision to dismiss the contract dispute case.

— This sentence is missing the apostrophe to form the possessive.

Correct

In this sentence, only one defendant testified.

— The defendant's testimony led to the court's decision to dismiss the contract dispute case.

---

### Apostrophe Checkup

1. For singular nouns, add an apostrophe and an "s."

2. For plural nouns, add just the apostrophe.
3. For singular nouns ending in "s," follow rule 1 or 2 consistently.
4. Use contractions conversationally and sparingly.

---

### b. Apostrophe Rule No. 2: For Plural Nouns, Add Just the Apostrophe

Also Correct

Here, two defendants testified.

— The defendants' testimony led to the court's decision to dismiss the contract dispute case.

### c. Apostrophe Rule No. 3: For Singular Nouns Ending in "s," Follow Rule 1 or 2 Consistently

When a singular noun ends in "s," you may follow either option. To form the possessive, add an apostrophe or add an apostrophe and an "s." For example, both Congress' and Congress's are grammatically correct—U.S. Supreme Court justices write the possessive both ways. Just make sure that you are consistent in applying one rule throughout your document.

Justice Kagan demonstrates how to follow rule no. 1 for singular nouns ending in "s" in the next example. She adds an extra "s" to the possessive of "process," a singular noun. She leaves it off the possessive of "plants" because the word is plural.

Writing either process' or process's is grammatically correct. Just pick one rule and follow it consistently.

— At the outset, EPA determined that regulating plants' emissions of hazardous air pollutants is "appropriate and necessary" given the harm they cause, and explained that it would take costs into account in developing suitable emissions standards.... Indeed, EPA could not have measured costs at the process's initial stage with any accuracy.[28]

---

28. *Michigan v. EPA*, 135 S. Ct. 2699, 2709-10, 2714-15 (2015) (Kagan, J., dissenting).

### d. Apostrophe Rule No. 4: Use Contractions Conversationally and Sparingly

Many writers consider contractions too informal for the serious nature of judicial writing. Justice Scalia called them "intellectually abominable, but commercially reasonable."[29] While he never used one, plenty of judges who are respected for their writing prowess inject contractions in their writing, particularly when they are the lone author of an opinion. Justice Kagan explains, "I use contractions in dissents. Only in dissents.... Even in dissents I don't always use them. But sometimes I just get started, and it seems like I'm writing in a kind of an informal way and I use them."[30]

Justice Kagan avoids contractions in majority opinions "in part because some of my colleagues don't like it, and in part just because when you're writing a majority, you're writing more for the Court. And I try to write it a little bit more formally—still in a way that I hope everybody can understand."[31]

With their questionable acceptability, use contractions sparingly. And only use those you would use in normal conversation. Avoid uncommon contractions, like shan't (shall + not), double contractions she'd've (she + would + have), and archaic constructions, like 'twas (it + was). The following lines show how to use contractions successfully in judicial writing. All are from a single Justice Kagan dissent.

> The concurring opinion similarly, if more vaguely, contends that "tangible object" should refer to "something similar to records or documents"—and shouldn't include colonial farmhouses, crocodiles, or fish.

> To my knowledge, no court has ever read any such provision to exclude things that don't record or preserve data; rather, all courts have adhered to the statutory language's ordinary (i.e., expansive) meaning.

> By contrast, § 1519 wouldn't ordinarily operate in that context because a federal court isn't a "department or agency."

> The plurality doesn't—really, can't—explain why it instead interprets the same words used in two provisions of the same Act addressing the same basic problem to mean fundamentally different things.[32]

---

29. Alex Carp, *Writing with Antonin Scalia, Grammar Nerd*, New Yorker, July 16, 2012, http://www.newyorker.com/news/news-desk/writing-with-antonin-scalia-grammar-nerd.

30. Interview by Bryan A. Garner with Justice Elena Kagan, United States Supreme Court Building, West Conference Room, in Washington, D.C. (July 16, 2015).

31. *Id.*

32. *Yates v. United States*, 135 S. Ct. 1074, 1091-92, 1095-96, 1097 (2015) (Kagan, J., dissenting).

## 8. Hyphens

A hyphen combines compound adjectives when they precede a noun. When you can write hyphenated adjectives or nouns as a single word, use the simpler, non-hyphenated version. For instance, "re-written" should be "rewritten," "semi-colon" should be "semicolon," "by-laws" should be "bylaws," and so on.

Plenty of compound adjectives, though, cannot be combined into a single word. So "dueprocess analysis" should be "due-process analysis." Add a hyphen to compound adjectives like "due process" when needed to avoid ambiguity—and when they precede the noun. One exception is to not hyphenate words ending in "-ly" because typically, their modifying purpose is clear. Use the following three guidelines to choose when and how to hyphenate.

---

### Hyphen Checkup

1. Hyphenate phrases with multiple adjectives.
2. Hyphenate when ambiguity could result.
3. No hyphen follows words ending in "-ly"

---

### a. Hyphen Rule No. 1: Hyphenate Phrases with Multiple Adjectives

Hyphens show that this long phrase describes "factor." — Finally, in *Johnson v. Glick*, a malicious-and-sadistic-purpose-to-cause-harm factor was not suggested as a *necessary* condition for liability, but as a factor, among others, that might help show that the use of force was excessive.

Hyphens show the compound adjective for "questions." — We consider a legally requisite state of mind. In a case like this one, there are, in a sense, two separate state-of-mind questions.

### b. Hyphen Rule No. 2: Hyphenate When Ambiguity Could Result

With no hyphen, this phrase would mean that "second judgments" are split. — Officers facing disturbances "are often forced to make split-second judgments—in circumstances that are tense, uncertain, and rapidly evolving."

"Legally requisite" and "negligently inflicted" do not require a hyphen for clarity. — That heuristic makes good sense for considered decisions by the detaining authority, but is much weaker in the context of excessive-force claims.[33]

---

33. *Kingsley*, 135 S. Ct. at 2469, 2472, 2474, 2478.

### c. Hyphen Rule No. 3: No Hyphen Follows Words Ending in "-ly"

We consider a legally requisite state of mind. That is because, as we have stated, "liability for negligently inflicted harm is categorically beneath the threshold of constitutional due process."[34]

— "Legally requisite" and "negligently inflicted" do not require a hyphen for clarity.

## B. ADVANCED GRAMMAR PRINCIPLES

> ### Advanced Grammar Principles
> 1. Active and Passive Voice
> 2. Parallelism
> 3. Quotations
> 4. Em Dashes and Parentheses

### 1. Active and Passive Voice

Legal writers prefer active sentences to passive ones. The active voice is more direct, and it keeps the actor and action in a sentence clear and concise. In rare instances, a writer may use passive voice to alter the emphasis in a sentence or deflect attention away from the actor. In the next sentences, the emphasis shifts from the jury to the verdict, depending on whether the verb is active or passive.

**Active Voice**

The jury announced the verdict.

— This statement is direct with the actor and action clear.

**Passive Voice**

The verdict was announced by the jury.

— The actor—the jury—here is in a wordy prepositional phrase.

**Passive Voice**

The verdict was announced.

— This construction is vague because the actor is unknown.

Learn to identify passive voice by its wordy verb phrase that has two or more words, typically beginning with "was," "were," "has," "has been," "have," or "have been." Then, make the sentence active by adding the subject back to the sentence or swapping the object in the prepositional phrase for the subject. The active voice sentence is likely better.

---

34. *Id.* at 2472 (emphasis omitted).

Although writers generally prefer active voice, some legal writers may choose to use passive voice when they need to shift the emphasis in a sentence. For instance, consider why the defense team for JK Corp. would prefer the third example, where the actor is unnamed.

### Active Voice

This sentence emphasizes the actor, JK Corp.

— JK Corp. allegedly spilled billions of gallons of oil into the Gulf of Mexico.

### Passive Voice

This construction emphasizes the oil and identifies the actor.

— Billions of gallons of oil were spilled into the Gulf of Mexico allegedly by JK Corp.

### Passive Voice

This construction avoids referencing the actor.

— Billions of gallons of oil were spilled into the Gulf of Mexico.

## 2. Parallelism

Parallel phrasing adds elegance and clarity to writing. Consider the symmetry in the following famous lines from Abraham Lincoln's Gettysburg Address:

These three phrases match exactly.

— But, in a larger sense, we cannot dedicate—we cannot consecrate—we cannot hallow—this ground. The brave men, living and dead, who struggled here, have consecrated it, far above our poor power to add

These first two phrases are parallel and match the wording in the second clause.

— or detract. The world will little note, nor long remember what we say here, but it can never forget what they did here.

Parallelism means using a similar grammatical form for elements in a pair or series. Use parallel phrasing each time you list two or more elements, which are typically joined by a conjunction, including "and," "but," "either," neither," "nor," "not," "or," and "yet." Lincoln's address uses em dashes to combine three matching clauses: "we cannot dedicate," "we cannot consecrate," and "we cannot hallow." Each has a subject and a present tense verb, which makes the series parallel. The fact that each phrase begins with "we cannot" makes the match even more striking.

---

### Parallelism Checkup

1. Identify a list, series, or pair of elements, which are typically joined by a conjunction, like "and," "nor," or "either."
2. Make sure all elements match—as all nouns, all adjectives, all independent clauses, all verbs, etc.
3. Verb tenses must match exactly.

---

Once you identify a pair, list, or series that should be parallel, check that the elements match. When the elements begin with a verb, each element must begin with a verb in the same tense. When the elements begin with a noun, each element must begin with a noun, although the nouns can be singular or plural or include an adjective. When the elements include an independent clause with a subject and verb, each element must have a subject and a verb with tenses that match the other verbs in the series.

Try to identify the pair or series that needs to be parallel in the next sentences. Note how the corrected sentences aren't just grammatically correct—they sound better when you read them too.

#### Incorrect: Mismatched Noun and Verb

By the time the lawsuit concludes, the election will be over and the litigants in most cases will have neither the incentive nor, perhaps, gather the resources to carry on, even if they could establish that the case is not moot because the issue is "capable of repetition, yet evading review." — The elements following "neither" do not match because one is a noun and one is a verb.

#### Correct: Parallel Nouns

By the time the lawsuit concludes, the election will be over and the litigants in most cases will have neither the incentive nor, perhaps, the resources to carry on, even if they could establish that the case is not moot because the issue is "capable of repetition, yet evading review."[35] — The nouns following "neither" match, even though one is singular and the other plural.

#### Correct: Parallel Pair of Verbs

By the time the lawsuit concludes, the election will be over and the litigants in most cases will neither have the incentive nor, perhaps, have the resources to carry on, even if they could establish that the case is not moot because the issue is "capable of repetition, yet evading review." — Verbs with matching verb tenses also create parallelism. The verbs following "neither" also match, though this edit makes the sentence wordier.

---

35. *Citizens United v. Fed. Election Comm'n*, 558 U.S. 310, 334 (2010).

### Incorrect: Mismatched Verb Tenses

The elements following "when" do not match.

— Under the Illinois burglary statute, is a vacant lot curtilage when it surrounds an abandoned shed, the former owner had abandoned the shed, enclosed by a few bushes, and has been used by neighborhood kids for Chicago-style softball games?

### Correct: Parallel List of Complete Clauses with Matching Verbs

The elements match because each is a complete clause with a present-tense verb. The second element in the incorrect example was removed because it was repetitive.

— Under the Illinois burglary statute, is a vacant lot curtilage when the lot surrounds an abandoned shed, a few bushes enclose the lot, and neighborhood kids use the lot for Chicago-style softball games?

### Correct: Parallel List of Dependent Clauses with Matching Verbs

This phrasing is parallel because it contains three clauses with matching verbs—each of which could start the sentence on its own.

— If elected officials succumb to improper influences from independent expenditures; if they surrender their best judgment; and if they put expediency before principle, then surely there is cause for concern.[36]

## 3. Quotations

Careful legal writers ensure that each quotation they use is exact. When legal writers change a quote, they use brackets, ellipses, or both to mark the change. A legal writer's credibility depends on quoting sources accurately. And when writers alter a quote without proper punctuation, they could mislead readers. The following four rules illustrate how to use quotations and punctuate them correctly.

---

### Quotations

1. Use double quotation marks for quotes and single quotation marks for quotes within quotes.
2. Commas and periods always go inside quotation marks.
3. Use brackets, an ellipsis, or both to show a change to a quote.
4. For essential, longer quotes, indent the quote as a text block.

---

36. *Id.* at 361.

### a. Quotations Rule No. 1: Use Double Quotation Marks for Quotes

Quotations should be surrounded by double quotation marks. Single quotation marks denote a quote within a quote.

#### Incorrect

Chief Justice Roberts wrote, 'Our cases make clear that students do not "shed their constitutional rights to freedom of speech or expression at the schoolhouse gate."[37]

—All three quotation marks are incorrect here.

#### Correct

Chief Justice Roberts wrote, "Our cases make clear that students do not 'shed their constitutional rights to freedom of speech or expression at the schoolhouse gate.'"

—The quote is surrounded by double quotation marks. Chief Justice Roberts' quote from *Tinker* is surrounded by single quotation marks, so the closing quote includes the single and double quotation marks.

### b. Quotations Rule No. 2: Commas and Periods Always Go Inside Quotation Marks

Commas and periods always belong inside quotations, no matter their placement in the original quote. Place larger punctuation marks—colons, semicolons, exclamation points, and question marks—inside quotation marks only when they are part of the original quote.

#### Incorrect

The court noted that "[t]he way Frederick was going to fulfill his ambition of appearing on television was by unfurling a pro-drug banner at a school event;" however, Frederick's motive was unclear.

—The semicolon is not part of the original text and belongs after the quotation mark.

#### Correct

The court noted that "[t]he way Frederick was going to fulfill his ambition of appearing on television was by unfurling a pro-drug banner at a school event"; however, Frederick's motive was unclear.[38]

#### Incorrect

"But that is a description of Frederick's motive for displaying the banner"; however, Frederick did not provide any interpretation of the text.

#### Correct

"But that is a description of Frederick's motive for displaying the banner;" however, Frederick did not provide any interpretation of the text.[39]

—The semicolon is in the original quote, so it is placed inside the quotation marks.

---

37. *Morse v. Frederick*, 551 U.S. 393, 396 (2007) (quoting *Tinker v. Des Moines Indep. Cmty. Sch.*, 393 U.S. 503 (1969)).

38. *Morse*, 551 U.S. at 402 (emphasis omitted).

39. *Id.* (emphasis omitted).

### c. Quotations Rule No. 3: Use Brackets, an Ellipsis, or Both to Show a Change to a Quote

Legal writers denote any alteration of a quote with brackets, ellipses, or both. The following examples show how to alter the beginning, middle, and end of a quote. Note that an ellipsis never starts a quotation. Instead, a bracket indicates a change in capitalization, which shows an alteration to the start of a quoted sentence.

#### Original Quote

"Our cases make clear that students do not 'shed their constitutional rights to freedom of speech or expression at the schoolhouse gate.'"

#### Brackets Mark a Change at the Quote's Beginning

A bracket — not an ellipsis — marks the change in capitalization at the beginning of a quote.

— As Chief Justice Roberts wrote, "[o]ur cases make clear that students do not 'shed their constitutional rights to freedom of speech or expression at the schoolhouse gate.'"

#### Brackets Mark a Change to a Word

A bracket shows that the writer changed the verb tense to "made."

— Chief Justice Roberts wrote that previous cases "ma[de] clear that students do not 'shed their constitutional rights to freedom of speech or expression at the schoolhouse gate.'"

An ellipsis — consisting of three spaced periods — marks an omission in the middle of a quote.

— **An Ellipsis Marks an Omission in the Middle**

As Chief Justice Roberts wrote, "[o]ur cases make clear that students do not 'shed their constitutional rights . . . at the schoolhouse gate.'"

Here, the ellipsis consists of three spaced periods, plus the period to end the sentence. It marks an omission of the end of a quote.

— **An Ellipsis Marks an Omission at the End**

As Chief Justice Roberts wrote, "[o]ur cases make clear that students do not 'shed their constitutional rights to freedom of speech or expression. . . ."

### d. Quotations Rule No. 4: For Essential, Longer Quotes, Indent the Quote as a Text Block

Legal writers should use quotes sparingly. Quotes with multiple brackets and ellipses can appear unreadable, so rewrite these clunky quotations whenever possible. Pages with more quotations than original text appear uninspired. When a page strings together quotations, try rewriting and paraphrasing the lines to make your point more directly. On the rare occasion that you need to use a quote of 50 or more words, set it off without quotation marks, indent it on the right and left, and use single-spacing.[40]

---

40. *See The Bluebook: A Uniform System of Citation* Rules B5.2 and 5.1(a) (Columbia Law Review Ass'n et al. eds., 20th ed. 2015).

### 4. Em Dashes and Parentheses

Em dashes have had a starring role in legal writing since before the time of Abraham Lincoln, who skillfully weaved seven em dashes within two sentences in the Gettysburg Address.

> But, in a larger sense, we cannot dedicate—we cannot consecrate—we cannot hallow—this ground. . . .
>
> It is rather for us to be here dedicated to the great task remaining before us—that from these honored dead we take increased devotion to that cause for which they here gave the last full measure of devotion—that we here highly resolve that these dead shall not have died in vain—that this nation, under God, shall have a new birth of freedom—and that government of the people, by the people, for the people, shall not perish from the earth.

The em dash calls attention to information—pointing to it with a double-hyphen devoid of spaces. Legal writers also can set off information in a sentence with commas and parentheses—and each demands a varying degree of notice. Em dashes provide the most emphasis to the information contained within, while parentheses provide the least. All of these forms of punctuation should be used in moderation.

#### Two Em Dashes

The fact that the Air Force chooses to secure a portion of the Base more closely—be it with a fence, a checkpoint, or a painted green line—does not alter the boundaries of the Base or diminish the jurisdiction of the military commander.[41]

—Two em dashes call attention to the information in the middle of the sentence.

The Base commander has also publicly stated that persons who are barred from Vandenberg—for whatever reason—may not come onto the Base to protest.[42]

#### One Em Dash

In a single stroke, the United States gained 365 million acres of land—an area more than twice the size of Texas.[43]

—One em dash sets off information at the beginning or end of the sentence.

#### Multiple Em Dashes

The first step of *Seagate*—objective recklessness—is reviewed *de novo*; the second—subjective knowledge—for substantial evidence; and the ultimate decision—whether to award enhanced damages—for abuse of discretion.[44]

—Multiple em dashes can set off a series.

---

41. *United States v. Apel*, 134 S. Ct. 1144, 1152 (2014).
42. *Id.*
43. *Sturgeon v. Frost*, 136 S. Ct. 1061, 1064 (2016).
44. *Halo Elecs., Inc. v. Pulse Elecs., Inc.*, 136 S. Ct. 1923, 1930 (2016).

## Parentheses: Secondary Information

The *Seagate* test aggravates the problem by making dispositive the ability of the infringer to muster a reasonable (even though unsuccessful) defense at the infringement trial.[45]

*Parentheses show the information contained within is of secondary importance.*

Will a jury find that the company behaved "recklessly," simply for failing to spend considerable time, effort, and money obtaining expert views about whether some or all of the patents described in the letter apply to its activities (and whether those patents are even valid)?[46]

## Parentheses: Secondary Source Information

According to Elonis, every definition of "threat" or "threaten" conveys the notion of an intent to inflict harm. E.g., 11 Oxford English Dictionary 353 (1933) ("to declare (usually conditionally) one's intention of inflicting injury upon"); Webster's New International Dictionary 2633 (2d ed. 1954) ("*Law*, specif., an expression of an intention to inflict loss or harm on another by illegal means"); Black's Law Dictionary 1519 (8th ed. 2004) ("A communicated intent to inflict harm or loss on another").[47]

*The parentheticals here offer three different definitions from three dictionaries.*

As a result, the Act does not reflect the type of care and deliberation that one might expect of such significant legislation. *Cf.* Frankfurter, *Some Reflections on the Reading of Statutes*, 47 Colum. L. Rev. 527, 545 (1947) (describing a cartoon "in which a senator tells his colleagues 'I admit this new bill is too complicated to understand. We'll just have to pass it to find out what it means.'").[48]

*A parenthetical about a source may include a clause, often beginning in -ing, or a full sentence.*

It did not escape the attention of the Framers that the Treaty Power was drafted without explicitly enumerated limits on what sorts of treaties are permissible. *See, e.g., Hamilton*, The Defence No. XXXVI, in 20 Papers of Alexander Hamilton 6 (H. Syrett ed. 1974) ("A power 'to make treaties,' granted in these indefinite terms, extends to all kinds of treaties and with all the latitude which such a power under any form of Government can possess.").[49]

*Note the period inside and outside the parenthetical. One ends the parenthetical sentence and the other ends the citation.*

---

45. *Id.* at 1933.
46. *Id.* at 1937 (Breyer, J., concurring).
47. *Elonis v. United States*, 135 S. Ct. 2001, 2008 (2015) (some citations omitted).
48. *King*, 135 S. Ct. at 2492.
49. *Bond v. United States*, 134 S. Ct. 2077, 2106 (2014).

## C. GOOD BOOKS ON GOOD WRITING

Good writing takes practice. Crafting a clear and effective judicial document requires a command of style, sound analytical thinking, solid organization, and extensive rewriting and revision. To keep improving your writing skills, practice writing a range of documents and practice editing your writing and the writing of others. Read examples of good writing—from law or literature. And read about good writing. The following list includes some favorite books on good writing, legal and otherwise.

> **WRITING TIP:**
> Chief Justice John G. Roberts says "the only good way to learn about writing is to read good writing." Outside of the law, he likes crime fiction and historical biographies.[50]

- Bryan A. Garner, *Garner's Dictionary of Legal Usage* (3d ed., Oxford Univ. Press 2011).
- Bryan A. Garner, *The Elements of Legal Style* (2d ed., Oxford Univ. Press 2002).
- Anne Lamott, *Bird by Bird* (Anchor 1995).
- William Strunk, Jr. & E.B. White, *The Elements of Style* (4th ed., Pearson 1999).
- John R. Trimble, *Writing with Style* (Prentice Hall 1975).
- Lynn Truss, *Eats, Shoots & Leaves* (Avery 2006).

---

50. Interview by Bryan A. Garner with Chief Justice John G. Roberts, 13 Scribes J. Legal Writing 39-40 (2010).

CHAPTER

# 10

❧━━◆◆◆━━❧

# RESEARCH AND
# CITATION CHECKUP

Researching a legal question in judicial writing is like unraveling a mystery. All the clues from one side point to "yes," all the clues from the other side point to "no," and many of the clues you discover on your own point to "it depends." Your task will be to break down the mystery and make sense of it all. Your answer could end a legal dispute for good.

All researchers have felt intimidated by the task ahead, about where to start, where to end, or what to do at some point in between. The good news is that research in judicial writing does not start from scratch. Judicial interns, clerks, and judges can use the parties' filings—and the many citations contained within them—as a starting point for research. This chapter explains step by step how you can best use these documents to jumpstart your research, while also conducting your own independent searches to verify, update, and add to the authorities that the parties cited.

Every research project in judicial writing begins with the basic question of jurisdiction. So to begin, this chapter reviews the levels of state and federal courts, or hierarchy of authority, and the doctrine of following precedent known as "stare decisis."

Then, the chapter describes how to create a research plan for your specific question and how to first use secondary sources—those sources that explain and comment on the law. Judicial clerks and interns often need to master a dizzying array of substantive areas of law quickly. One day, a judge might decide a motion for summary judgment in an employment discrimination suit; the next day might bring oral arguments in a contract dispute; and on the next day, a complex appeal could arrive in a products liability case. While some trial judges specialize in a specific area of law, like criminal, family, juvenile, or probate, many courts have a diverse caseload. Appellate judges especially hear a wide array of cases from both civil and criminal law. Secondary sources will be your link to understanding all of these legal topics. They also will point you to primary sources—the constitutions, statutes, and cases making up the law—that you need to unravel your legal mystery.

Finally, this chapter will explain how to recognize when you're ready to stop researching. And then, to ensure your citations are perfect, this chapter will show you how to check every comma, font, parenthesis, period, quotation mark, and space in your citations so that they are consistent and conform to citation rules.

## A. JURISDICTION: THE REACH AND STRUCTURE OF AMERICAN COURTS

Precedent is the backbone of the American judicial system. Each case could make a difference for the next. George Washington noted this weighty responsibility when he remarked, "In our progress towards political happiness,... I walk on untrodden ground. There is scarcely any part of my conduct [which] may not hereafter be drawn into precedent."[1]

But just like every new president doesn't lead exactly like George Washington, legal precedents present thorny questions for courts as well. American courts follow the precedents established by earlier cases—the practice known as "standing by things decided" or "stare decisis" in Latin. Yet the reach of those precedents can be limited. In general, *stare decisis* means that once a court decides a matter, the ruling applies to that court and lower courts that are bound to follow its rulings.

Figuring out your jurisdiction and what precedents are binding for your legal question can be tricky. First, consider that American courts are divided into two main systems: federal courts and state courts. The nation has one federal court system—with the U.S. Supreme Court at the pinnacle—and every state has its own court system. All court systems have a tiered structure—with a trial court at the lowest level and a high court of last resort at the top. Most also have an intermediate appellate court of appeals.[2]

---

1. Letter from George Washington to Catherine Macaulay Graham (Jan. 9, 1790), in 30 *The Writings of George Washington from the Original Manuscript Sources 1745-1799*, at 496 (John C. Fitzpatrick ed., 1939).

2. Montana, for example, does not have an intermediate appellate court. *See, e.g.*, Montana Courts, http://courts.mt.gov/courts.

The names of these courts, though, vary among the federal and state court systems, which creates confusion when you try to figure out the level of court and whether its precedent is binding authority. For instance, trial courts in the federal system are called district courts, but they have several different names in the states: California superior courts, Florida circuit courts, the Massachusetts Trial Court, Pennsylvania courts of common pleas, and Texas district courts are all state trial court systems.

The highest courts in the states also have different names, for example, the New York Court of Appeals and the Texas Supreme Court. (Check the state courts' websites or Table 1 in *The Bluebook*[3] to learn the specific names for the courts in your state.) The next chart shows the structure of federal and state courts and the conflicting names among a few jurisdictions.

Figuring out the court structure is the first step in determining jurisdiction and deciding whether a court's precedent is binding. That's because courts are bound to follow the decisions of higher courts in their jurisdiction. So California trial courts, for instance, must follow the rulings of the state's courts of appeal and supreme court.[4] And the federal district

**Figure 10.1**[5]

| FEDERAL | STATE |
|---|---|
| | |

| | | |
|---|---|---|
| 3 | U.S. Supreme Court | highest court, e.g., Florida Supreme Court; New York Court of Appeals |
| | *discretionary appeal* | |
| 2 | U.S. Courts of Appeals organized by 12 regional circuits with one specialized court with nationwide jurisdiction, e.g., Eleventh Circuit Court of Appeals | intermediate appellate courts, e.g., Florida Third District Court of Appeal; New York State Supreme Court Appellate Division First Department |
| | *appeal as a right* | |
| 1 | U.S. District Courts organized by federal districts with at least one in each state, e.g., District Court for the Southern District of Florida | trial courts, e.g., Eleventh Judicial Circuit of Florida; New York State Supreme Court |

---

3. *The Bluebook: A Uniform System of Citation* 233-306 (Columbia Law Review Ass'n et al. eds., 20th ed. 2015).

4. *See, e.g., Auto Equity Sales, Inc. v. Superior Court of Santa Clara Cty.*, 369 P.2d 937, 939 (Cal. 1962); *but see Commercial Disc. Corp. v. King*, 515 F. Supp. 988, 990 (N.D. Ill. 1981) ("Under Illinois law a trial court is bound by the decisions of all Appellate Courts, but is bound by the Appellate Court in its own district when the Appellate Courts differ.").

5. Jill Barton & Rachel H. Smith, *The Handbook for the New Legal Writer* 20 (2014).

courts and U.S. Circuit Courts of Appeals must follow U.S. Supreme Court decisions. This concept of following higher courts is known as "vertical *stare decisis*."

Going in the other direction—a concept known as "horizontal *stare decisis*"—gets a little trickier. In general, horizontal *stare decisis* means that a court is bound by its previous decisions when a case involves the same law and similar facts. So the U.S. Supreme Court should follow its prior decisions in similar cases, and the North Dakota Court of Appeals should follow its prior decisions. *Stare decisis* then promotes the law's stability, reliability, and efficiency because courts aren't forced to reexamine established precedents.

U.S. Supreme Court Justice Antonin Scalia wrote in a 2015 opinion that *stare decisis* "matters because it 'promotes the evenhanded, predictable, and consistent development of legal principles.'"[6] But he then went on—in the same opinion—to overrule two prior U.S. Supreme Court cases.[7] The ability of a court to overrule itself makes horizontal *stare decisis* especially interesting: Exceptions to the doctrine mean that the law can change. Courts may overrule their prior decisions when those decisions become untenable, intolerable, or unworkable,[8] as the Court found in overruling the 1896 decision of *Plessy v. Ferguson* with *Brown v. Board of Education* in 1954.

**WRITING TIP:**
The *Plessy* decision shows "you that sometimes you write beyond the present," explains Justice Clarence Thomas. "[W]hat you put in [your opinion], you put in it with care. Not with erudition, but with care, so that people in the future can access some interpretation of their Constitution."[9]

When considering whether *stare decisis* applies, the best answer is one commonly heard in law school: "It depends." While courts view vertical *stare decisis* as an obligation, some view horizontal *stare decisis* merely as sound policy.[10] Courts have reasoned that horizontal *stare decisis* "is not an inexorable command" but "instead, a recognition of the principle that our system of justice works best when the law does not change erratically, but rather develops in a principled, intelligible fashion."[11]

If you've heard of a circuit split, you're already familiar with the messy concept of horizontal *stare decisis*. A decision by

---

6. *Johnson v. United States*, 135 S. Ct. 2551, 2563 (2015) (quoting *Payne v. Tennessee*, 501 U.S. 808, 827 (1991)).

7. *Id.* (overruling *James v. United States*, 550 U.S. 192 (2007) and *Sykes v. United States*, 564 U.S. 1 (2011)).

8. *See, e.g., Planned Parenthood of Se. Pa. v. Casey*, 505 U.S. 833, 854 (1992) ("Rather, when this Court reexamines a prior holding, its judgment is customarily informed by a series of prudential and pragmatic considerations designed to test the consistency of overruling a prior decision with the ideal of the rule of law, and to gauge the respective costs of reaffirming and overruling a prior case. Thus, for example, we may ask whether the rule has proven to be intolerable simply in defying practical workability.").

9. Interview by Bryan A. Garner with Justice Clarence Thomas, 13 Scribes J. Legal Writing 128 (2010).

10. *O'Casek v. Children's Home & Aid Soc'y*, 892 N.E.2d 994, 1014 n.4 (Ill. 2008).

11. *Id.*

one federal circuit court of appeals is not binding on another federal circuit.[12] The circuits may disagree, and only a decision by the U.S. Supreme Court can settle the matter for all the circuits.[13] For instance, while the Sixth, Seventh, and D.C. Circuits have defined the term "law enforcement officer" narrowly under a U.S. code provision, the Second, Fifth, Eighth, Ninth, Tenth, Eleventh, and Federal Circuits have construed the term broadly.[14] The U.S. Supreme Court would have to weigh in to force the circuits to adopt a uniform approach to interpreting the term.

> **RESEARCH TIP:**
> To find what decisions apply in your court, search state cases in your jurisdiction using key terms like "horizontal *stare decisis*" and phrases like "previous decisions as controlling or as precedents."

Despite the caveats to horizontal *stare decisis*, the doctrine does have some teeth to its reach. Take appellate courts, which typically decide matters in panels of three judges. Once one panel has established a precedent, another panel—even if it is composed of three different judges—cannot overrule the prior decision.[15] To set a new precedent, the appeals court must hear the case "en banc," meaning that all the judges on the court consider the matter.[16] The next charts give examples of how *stare decisis* works at the trial court and appeals court levels for a state and federal case.

---

12. *See, e.g., Hart v. Massanari*, 266 F.3d 1155, 1172-73 (9th Cir. 2001) ("Circuit law . . . binds all courts within a particular circuit, including the court of appeals itself.").

13. U.S. Supreme Court decisions may also bind state courts in certain matters. *See, e.g., Presley v. State*, 204 So. 3d 84, 87 (Fla. Dist. Ct. App. 2016) ("This Court is bound, on search and seizure issues, to follow the opinions of the United States Supreme Court regardless of whether the claim of an illegal arrest or search is predicated upon the provisions of the Florida or United States Constitutions.").

14. *See, e.g., Ortloff v. United States*, 335 F.3d 652, 660 (7th Cir. 2003); *Bramwell v. U.S. Bureau of Prisons*, 348 F.3d 804, 807 (5th Cir. 2003) (both interpreting 28 U.S.C. § 2680(c)).

15. *Sykes v. Anderson*, 625 F.3d 294, 319 (6th Cir. 2010).

16. *Salmi v. Sec'y of Health & Human Servs.*, 774 F.2d 685, 689 (6th Cir. 1985) ("A panel of this Court cannot overrule the decision of another panel. The prior decision remains controlling authority unless an inconsistent decision of the United States Supreme Court requires modification of the decision or this Court sitting en banc overrules the prior decision.").

Figure 10.2  Example of binding authority in state law case[17]

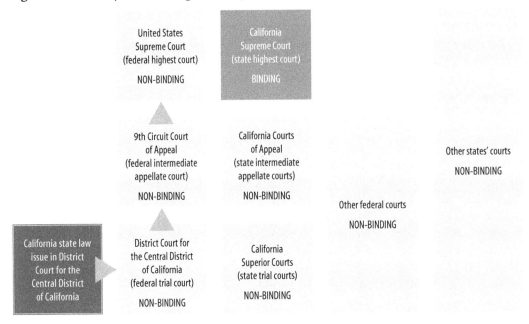

Figure 10.3  Example of binding authority in federal law case[18]

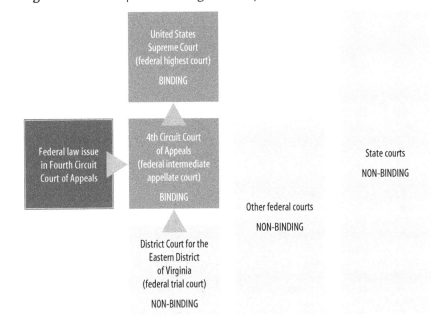

---

17. Barton & Smith, *supra* note 5, at 26.
18. *Id.* at 25.

## B. CREATING A RESEARCH PLAN

### 1. Develop and Refine Your Research Questions

Figuring out the jurisdiction in your case is like setting the scene for your legal mystery. The jurisdiction defines which cases provide binding precedent, so it gives you the framework for picking the best clues to solve the mystery. Once you've deciphered your jurisdiction, you will know where you should research and what types of cases are binding. Then, you can figure out a set of research questions.

Different courts use different wording to describe the same legal actions and issues. Good researchers identify all the variations in terminology to develop a set of related research questions. In this way, they cast a wide research net and capture all relevant sources.

Each research question will revolve around a single legal issue. Defining the legal issue for any judicial writing project is nearly always straightforward. At the trial and appellate levels, the parties do most of the work for you, by stating the legal issues in their motions and briefs. The following example shows how the opposing sides and the court stated the issue in a Fourth Amendment case.

#### Issue in Appellant's Brief

Officer Lobello did not have the necessary reasonable suspicion that Mr. Cole was armed to justify the frisk. She likewise lacked probable cause to arrest him. Because all of the evidence in this case was the fruit of these unlawful searches and seizures, the lower court erred in denying the motion to suppress.[19]

#### Issue in Appellee's Brief

The trial court properly denied Appellant's Motion to Suppress since the officer had reasonable suspicion to conduct an investigatory stop and subsequent pat down which led to probable cause for an arrest.[20]

#### Issue in Appellate Opinion

Cole concedes the initial traffic stop was lawful. Thus, the first issue we must address is whether Officer Lobello had reasonable suspicion to conduct the subsequent patdown search of Cole.[21]

Although the two sides use some different wording—frisk versus pat down, for example—the legal issue is exactly the same: Did the officer have

---

19. Initial Brief of Appellant at i, *Cole v. State*, 190 So. 3d 185 (Fla. Dist. Ct. App. 2016) (No. 3D14-2574) (on file with author).

20. Answer Brief of Appellee at i, *Cole*, 190 So. 3d at 185 (on file with author).

21. *Cole*, 190 So. 3d at 188

the required reasonable suspicion? The judge's issue statement states that question, using some of the appellant's wording and some of the appellee's.

In nearly all cases, the legal issue will be right in front of you, just like these examples illustrate. That's because the parties cannot raise any legal issues outside of what they originally submitted to the court. But a few exceptions exist. For example, judges can raise a new issue "on their own motion" or "sua sponte" in Latin.

One of the rare instances where judges can raise a new issue would be if a court does not have jurisdiction over the subject matter.[22] A Mississippi state trial court, for example, doesn't have jurisdiction over a celebrity's claim against an impersonator under California's right of publicity law. And a patent court does not have jurisdiction to hear a tort case about negligent infliction of emotional distress.

Another potential new issue would be recusal, which is why bench memos require clerks to identify the parties and their attorneys correctly at the top of the first page. Judges then can quickly check the names to see if they have a personal conflict and need to recuse themselves. If your research reveals a new issue or a jurisdiction question, talk with your co-clerks or judge to decide if the issue calls for more digging.

The procedural rules that generally forbid courts from raising new legal issues also forbid them from finding new facts. In the same way that a juror should not visit the crime scene to gather new evidence or ideas, judges, judicial clerks, and interns cannot conduct independent fact-finding missions. They cannot reimagine or re-investigate the case for new facts. That prohibition extends to virtual investigations too—so using Google's Street View and other outside sources isn't allowed either.

---

### Creating a Research Plan

1. Develop and Refine Your Research Questions
2. Start with Secondary Sources
3. Know How to Start: Primary Authorities
4. Know When to Stop: Primary Authorities

---

Because you will begin your research with the legal issues in hand, your task is to figure out the various ways you can state the legal issue and key related terms. That means broadening, narrowing, and rewording important words and phrases to develop a set of research questions.

---

22. *See, e.g., Doe v. Blair*, 819 F.3d 64, 66 (4th Cir. 2016).

The parties might describe the issue differently in their motions and briefs. The appellant in the previous example uses the terms "reasonable suspicion," "frisk," "probable cause," and "fruit of unlawful searches and seizures." The appellee repeats some of those terms but also uses "investigatory stop" and "pat down." From these terms, a set of related research questions emerges:

- When does an officer have probable cause?
- When does an officer have reasonable suspicion?
  - For a stop?
  - For an investigatory stop?
  - For a frisk?
  - For a pat down?
- When is a frisk or pat down an unlawful search?

This set of research questions addresses the same legal issue in different ways. A researcher who searches only for "pat downs" could miss a case that addresses only "frisks." Developing a list of synonyms and alternate terms allows researchers to canvass all potential sources and collect every source that can help. With that collection, you will be one step closer to resolving your legal mystery.

## 2. Start with Secondary Sources

For any research project, the best place to start is with secondary sources. Secondary sources are not law. But they explain and analyze the law in an accessible way, often with examples and always with annotations to primary authorities—the constitutions, statutes, and cases that do make up the law. Even if you feel confident that you understand an area of law, checking secondary sources for summaries of the law is helpful. At the least, the review will remind you of basic terminology, so you can continue to develop your research questions. It also will help you collect relevant primary, binding authorities. The following list describes some common secondary sources.

### Secondary Sources

- **Legal encyclopedias:** Use these alphabetical volumes to find a brief summary of a legal topic and primary authority citations. Many states have their own legal encyclopedias. These include *Florida Jurisprudence*, *New York Jurisprudence*, and *Pennsylvania Law Encyclopedia*. Two national legal encyclopedias are *American Jurisprudence* ("Am. Jur.") and *Corpus Juris Secundum* ("C.J.S.").
- **American Law Reports ("ALR"):** These reports offer more in-depth articles, called annotations, that summarize and analyze specific legal

issues. The annotations cite numerous primary authorities, with case citations organized by jurisdiction.

- **Restatements of the Law:** Restatements synthesize the common law from various jurisdictions, summarizing the consensus on a variety of legal topics, including contracts, torts, agency, and property. When a state court addresses a legal issue for the first time, it may cite the Restatement and make it law. Restatements include an appendix listing the cases that have cited the Restatement.

- **Treatises:** Written by experts, a treatise is a book that explains broader legal subjects in depth. Treatises cite primary authorities and may be organized in a single volume or multiple volumes. Examples of well-known treatises include *Fundamentals of Antitrust Law* by Phillip E. Areeda & Herbert Hovenkamp; *Nimmer on Copyright* by David Nimmer; and *Substantive Criminal Law* by Wayne LaFave & Austin Scott.

- **Practice guides:** A type of treatise, practice guides are useful for researching for procedural questions. Practice guides offer pragmatic advice, often with helpful forms and checklists. They cite primary authorities. Commonly used practice guides include *Moore's Federal Practice*; Wright & Miller, *Federal Practice & Procedure*; *Florida Practice & Procedure*; and The Rutter Group, *Federal Civil Procedure Before Trial*.

- **Law review and journal articles:** Law review and journal articles are scholarly publications written by law school professors, judges, lawyers, and law students that usually discuss emerging or cutting-edge legal issues. These articles typically cite numerous primary and secondary sources.[23]

### 3. Know How to Start: Primary Authorities

In a perfect world, the parties' motions and briefs would cite every authority you need to answer your legal question. And they would describe the law in relevant constitutions, statutes, and cases thoroughly and fairly. But it works differently in many cases. U.S. Circuit Judge Ruggero J. Aldisert explained that the parties' filings rarely do your research for you: "Often, the cases cited in the briefs are inapplicable (as when the attorneys unreasonably 'stretch' a case's holding), and the law clerks must conduct significant research to understand the relevant law."[24]

That research is easier when you start with secondary sources. Not only will you find a primer on your legal issue, but you also will find citations and thus, a list of relevant primary sources. Use these primary sources as a

---

23. *See* Barton & Smith, *supra* note 5, at 273.
24. Ruggero J. Aldisert, *Opinion Writing* 169 (3d ed. 2012).

starting point. Compare them to what the parties have cited. Then, expand your list of relevant primary sources by searching legal databases, like LexisNexis and Westlaw.

Use your set of research questions, and continue to expand your list of key words from each new source you find. Look for terms that describe claims, legal relationships, and legally significant actions.[25] Then, consider synonyms. The law has many, especially when you consider outdated language. "Chattel," for instance, is synonymous with personal property; "demurrer" is synonymous for failure to state a claim. Defamation includes both libel (the written form) and slander (the spoken form), but some courts use all three terms interchangeably.

Once you have a list of key terms and synonyms, work on making your search broader and deeper.[26] If no binding precedent exists, broaden your search to persuasive authorities in other jurisdictions. Look for cases in sister courts with similar fact patterns.

When binding precedent exists, you can still broaden your search by looking at more general points of law. The table of contents in a secondary source is one helpful place to check. Some entries even begin with a heading called "in general" or "overview." For example, a table of contents that includes an entry for the specific claim of libel shows a broader heading for defamation, and above that, a heading for the broader area of privacy law.[27] By searching for cases related to a broader area of law, you can make sure you're finding all relevant sources.

You also can deepen your search by making it more specific. One easy way to do this is to scan a secondary source's table of contents again, this time for even more specific entries. Suppose, for example, the plaintiff in your defamation case is a celebrity or politician. Under the general defamation heading in your secondary source, the table of contents lists specific elements and numerous variations of the claim. One variation concerns the degree of negligence required for defaming a public figure.[28] The entry cites more than a dozen on-point cases, and each can lead you to many more. Right there, you've discovered the best clue to answer your legal mystery.

## 4. Know When to Stop: Primary Authorities

Armed with key terms, synonyms, and ideas for deepening and broadening your search, your list of primary, binding authorities will take shape. As you read through cases, you'll recognize common themes, issues, and facts.

---

25. Barton & Smith, *supra* note 5, at 271.
26. *Id.*
27. *See, e.g.,* 19 Fla. Jur. 2d Defamation & Privacy § 1 (2017).
28. *Id.* § 6.

Take notes and organize your sources along the way. That's easily done using the convenient organizing, highlighting, and note-taking tools that LexisNexis and Westlaw offer.

As you continue to read and research—and read and research some more—create a comprehensive list of relevant primary sources. Just like you used secondary sources to find primary sources early in your research, you can now use your primary sources to find more. All cases cite other cases, and LexisNexis and Westlaw offer additional tools, like headnotes, key numbers, and topic indexes that will lead you to additional cases that address the specific areas you are researching. You should also use citators, tools like KeyCite in Westlaw and Shepard's in LexisNexis, that help you confirm that a source is still good law. Citators update and validate your research, but they also show what newer cases have cited the cases you already have found.

As you repeat your searches, using different terms, methods, and sources, you will know it's time to stop when you start researching in circles. In other words, you keep doing searches in different ways but end up in the same place with the same sources. It takes confidence to say that you've found everything available to answer your legal question. Every case is different, and once you've reached the researching-in-circles phase, it's time to stop. A perfect source isn't hiding just beyond your reach with the perfect answer. Instead, that perfect answer is within your pile of research— and the analysis you'll complete with your mind. As soon as you digest and synthesize your sources, you'll be ready to untangle your legal mystery and answer your question.

## Research Checklist
➤◄

- ☐ Identify your jurisdiction and what precedents are binding.
- ☐ Identify the legal issue for your research questions, using the parties' filings as a starting point.
- ☐ Develop and refine your set of research questions, considering narrower and broader statements of the legal issue.
- ☐ Consult secondary sources.
- ☐ Begin to develop a comprehensive list of relevant primary authorities and key terms.
- ☐ Expand your list of key words and phrases by considering (1) synonyms, (2) words that describe claims, legal relationships, and legally significant actions, and (3) related terms that are broader and more specific.
- ☐ Expand your list of relevant primary authorities by broadening and deepening your search.
- ☐ If no binding precedent exists, consider persuasive authorities from other jurisdictions with similar facts.

☐ Keep track of your research, taking notes on common themes, issues, and facts; consider using the organizing, highlighting, and note-taking tools in LexisNexis and Westlaw.

☐ Use citators—KeyCite and Shepard's—to continue to expand your list of relevant primary authorities.

☐ Know when to stop and recognize that you have compiled a comprehensive set of relevant primary authorities.

☐ Use citators to update your research throughout the research process and later to confirm that your sources are still good law.

## C. CITATION CHECKUP

In 1819, U.S. Supreme Court Chief Justice John Marshall read these spirited words in attorney Daniel Webster's brief: "An unlimited power to tax involves, necessarily, a power to destroy." The line made an impression, so much so that Chief Justice Marshall used it verbatim in his opinion in *M'Culloch v. State.*[29] The problem, though, was that the chief justice used no citation. The mishap gave rise to one of the more famous cases of plagiarism in judicial writing.[30]

Lawyers and judges use citations constantly and consistently throughout their legal writing. Judicial clerks and interns should follow suit. As U.S. Supreme Court Chief Justice John G. Roberts explains, "[w]hen I see a reference to a case, I expect to see a citation."[31]

In judicial writing, it's not the credibility of the judge or law clerk who wrote an opinion that's at stake, but the credibility of the entire court. Legal writers must cite every source they use—every statute, every case, every law review article, every filing by the parties. And pincites that pinpoint specific page numbers are not just helpful but essential to finding the original source material.

Chief Justice Marshall's borrowed line was not just missing the citation and pincite; it also was missing quotation marks. As a general rule, use quotation marks when you copy five or more words exactly as they appear in a source, or when you copy any word or phrase that seems original.

Paying attention to every detail in a citation matters, right down to every comma, font, parenthesis, period, quotation mark, and space. This section provides a brief rundown of how to double and triple check the

---

29. 17 U.S. 316, 327 (1819).
30. Gerald Lebovits, *Ethical Judicial Writing—Part III*, 79 N.Y. St. B.J. 64 (2007).
31. Interview by Bryan A. Garner with Chief Justice John G. Roberts, 13 Scribes J. Legal Writing 38-39 (2010).

citations in any judicial document so that your final document is polished and reliable.

## 1. Consistency Is Key

The first rule in citing is to be consistent. That's not easy considering how many different citation formats are out there. Much of the legal writing world follows *The Bluebook*[32] and will expect citations to follow the exhaustive list of formats that the manual details. Another acceptable and well-known citation system,[33] developed by the Association of Legal Writing Directors, is the *ALWD Guide to Legal Citation*.[34] Other citation manuals add additional colors to the mix and include the online *Indigo Book*[35] and *The Maroonbook*.[36]

Different judges and courts will have different preferences and practices. U.S. Circuit Judge Richard Posner is among the most vocal critics of a uniform citation system.[37] Other judges have created their own practices. Texas Supreme Court Justice Don Willett, for instance, finds citations clunky, so he puts them in footnotes, rather than in the text.

To figure out what kind of citation format to follow, check local court rules, which may specify preferred citation formats. Montana federal court rules, for example, allow either the *Bluebook* or *ALWD* citation formats.[38] California state courts dictate that citations should follow *The Bluebook* or the *California Style Manual*.[39] Other sources also may provide citation guidance. Cornell University Law School has compiled a helpful chart of the citation practices and rules for all 50 states, with examples from each.[40]

In addition to checking court rules, review previous opinions by your judge and other judges at your court to figure out common practices. Then, stick with a single citation format and style consistently throughout every document that you write.

---

32. *The Bluebook*, *supra* note 3.
33. *See, e.g.*, D. Mont. Rule 1.5(c) (2016).
34. *ALWD Guide to Legal Citation* (Coleen M. Barger ed., 6th ed. 2017).
35. Christopher J. Sprigman et al., *The Indigo Book: A Manual of Legal Citation*, Public Resource (2016).
36. *The Maroonbook: The University of Chicago Manual of Legal Citation* (Reeves Jordan et al. eds., 2017).
37. *See, e.g.*, Richard A. Posner, *The Bluebook Blues*, 120 Yale L.J. 850, 853 (2011).
38. D. Mont. R. 1.5(c).
39. Cal. Ct. R. 1.200 (2017); Edward W. Jessen, *California Style Manual: A Handbook of Legal Style for California Courts and Lawyers* (4th ed. 2001).
40. Legal Information Institute, § 7-500. Table of State-Specific Citation Norms and Practices (2016), https://www.law.cornell.edu/citation/7-500.

## 2. Perfecting Citation Practices

The following list describes the various ways that courts cite common documents and explains how the citations might differ from the *Bluebook* format. The list provides examples of citation formats from state and federal courts for constitutions, statutes, cases, secondary sources, and record documents. The annotations list relevant *Bluebook* rules for each source and citation type. All examples come from the courts' slip opinions.

### U.S. Supreme Court

- **Constitution (with reference within text):**
  - No person, the Double Jeopardy Clause states, shall be "subject for the same offense to be twice put in jeopardy of life or limb." Amdt. 5.[41]  —This version is shorter than *Bluebook* Rule B11 format: U.S. Const. amend. V.
- **Statutes with the signal "see" to indicate an inference:**[42]
  - This case addresses the question of the proper remedy when there is a violation of the False Claims Act (FCA) requirement that certain complaints must be sealed for a limited time period. See 31 U.S.C. § 3730(b)(2).[43]  —"See" is underlined or italicized under *Bluebook* Rule B1.2.
- **Cases:** While the reporters add longer, parallel citations, U.S. Supreme Court justices follow a simplified *Bluebook* format and use pincites to specific page numbers consistently.
  - **Long form citation:** This Court has answered yes, in those circumstances, the acquittal has preclusive force. *Yeager v. United States*, 557 U.S. 110, 121–122 (2009).[44]  —This citation follows *Bluebook* Rule B10.1, except for the pincite that would read "121-22."
  - **Short form citation:** One cannot know from the jury's report why it returned no verdict. "A host of reasons" could account for a jury's failure to decide—"sharp disagreement, confusion about the issues, exhaustion after a long trial, to name but a few." *Yeager*, 557 U.S., at 121.[45]  —This citation follows *Bluebook* Rule 10.9, except for the added comma after U.S.
  - **String citation form with explanatory parentheticals:** The theory underlying both the honest services fraud and Hobbs Act extortion charges was that Governor McDonnell had accepted bribes from Williams. *See Skilling v. United States*, 561 U.S. 358, 404 (2010) (construing honest services fraud to forbid "fraudulent schemes to deprive another of honest services through bribes or kickbacks"); *Evans v. United States*, 504 U.S.  —These case cites follow *Bluebook* Rule B10.1.5.

---

41. *Bravo-Fernandez v. United States*, 137 S. Ct. 352, 357 (2016).
42. *Bluebook* Rule 1.2(a).
43. *State Farm Fire & Cas. Co. v. United States ex rel. Rigsby*, 137 S. Ct. 436, 439 (2016).
44. *Bravo-Fernandez*, 137 S. Ct. at 357.
45. *Id.*

255, 260, 269 (1992) (construing Hobbs Act extortion to include "'taking a bribe'").[46]

- **Secondary sources:** Dictionaries consistently define the noun "use" to mean the "act of employing" something. Webster's New International Dictionary 2806 (2d ed. 1954) ("[a]ct of employing anything"); Random House Dictionary of the English Language 2097 (2d ed. 1987) ("act of employing, using, or putting into service"); Black's Law Dictionary 1541 (6th ed. 1990) ("[a]ct of employing," "application").

- **Record documents:** As Governor, McDonnell spoke about economic development in Virginia "on a daily basis" and attended numerous "events, ribbon cuttings," and "plant facility openings." App. 4093, 5241.[47]

*Note the quote within a quote for the three-word phrase in the last parenthetical here.*

*These book citations follow Bluebook Rule B15.1.*

*The cite abbreviates appendix according to Bluebook table BT1.*

## U.S. Court of Appeals for the Fourth Circuit

- State statutes, long and short form:
  - The FSA provides that a person may neither "transport an assault weapon into the State" nor "possess, sell, offer to sell, transfer, purchase, or receive an assault weapon." See Md. Code Ann., Crim. Law § 4- 303(a). The banned assault weapons include "assault long gun[s]" and "copycat weapon[s]." Id. § 4-301(d).[48]

*The cite follows Bluebook Rules B12.1.2 (for state statutes) and B12.2 (for short forms), using underlining instead of italics.*

**WRITING TIP:**
Pick a font and stick to it. Both underlining and italicizing words in citations work—just pick one style and use it consistently. Check *Bluebook* Rule B2 for more.

- Record documents:
  - The AR-15, semiautomatic AK-47, and other assault weapons banned by the FSA have a number of features designed to achieve their principal purpose—"killing or disabling the enemy" on the battlefield. See J.A. 735.[49]

*The cite abbreviates joint appendix per Bluebook table BT1.*

## Arizona Supreme Court

- Federal and state constitutions:
  - Where the national and state constitutions conflict irreconcilably, however, the latter must yield under the Supremacy Clause. U.S. Const. art. VI, cl. 2; *see also* Ariz. Const. art. 2, § 3.[50]

*The cite follows Bluebook Rules B1.2 and B11.*

---

46. *McDonnell v. United States*, 136 S. Ct. 2355, 2365 (2016).
47. *Id.* at 2361.
48. *Kolbe v. Hogan*, 849 F.3d 114, 121 (4th Cir. 2017).
49. *Id.* at 125.
50. *Simpson v. Miller*, 387 P.3d 1270, 1274 (Ariz. 2017).

- Online materials:
  - All ballot arguments supporting Proposition 103 focused on protecting public safety by preventing additional crimes. *See* Ariz. Sec'y of State, 2002 Publicity Pamphlet 16-17 (2002), *available at* http://apps.azsos.gov/election/2002/Info/pubpamphlet/english/prop103.pdf.[51]

> —This cite, though recent, follows an older version of what is now *Bluebook* Rule 18 and B18.1. The phrase "available at" is no longer required as an explanatory phrase.

## D. RESEARCHING FROM BEGINNING TO END

Research happens behind the scenes, so it can lack the glamour of the writing process. Judges are remembered not for their researching prowess but for penning witty phrases like "pure applesauce" and authoring opinions that protect constitutional rights. Yet behind every great opinion and every great line is impeccable research.

Author Zora Neale Hurston wrote, "Research is formalized curiosity. It is poking and prying with a purpose."[52] Your purpose in researching any legal question and writing any judicial document is also to poke and pry. You will poke and pry your way through legal authorities, untangling them for clues. You will poke and pry your way through examples of judicial documents, shaping your own. You will poke and pry your way through the writing process, questioning, rewriting, and revising your own work. And finally, you will poke and pry each word and each citation in your document, making sure every character is perfect. Along the way, you will uncover every piece of research, all the substance you need to explain the law and justify your decision. And once you wrap your words around that research, your purpose is complete.

---

51. *Id.* at 1276.
52. Zora Neale Hurston, *Dust Tracks on a Road* 143 (HarperCollins 1996).

# INDEX